Microsoft®
Windows® XP
fast&easy™

Diane Koers

Premier
Press

Premier Press, Inc. is a registered trademark of Premier Press, Inc.

Publisher: Stacy L. Hiquet
Associate Marketing Manager: Heather Buzzingham
Managing Editor: Sandy Doell
Project Editor: Estelle Manticas
Technical Reviewer: Keith Davenport
Copy Editor: Elizabeth Agostinelli
Interior Layout: Marian Hartsough
Cover Design: Mike Tanamachi
Indexer: Kelly Talbot

Microsoft and Windows are registered trademarks of Microsoft Corporation in the United States and/or other countries.

All other trademarks are the property of their respective owners.

Important: Premier Press cannot provide software support. Please contact the appropriate software manufacturer's technical support line or Web site for assistance.

Premier Press and the author have attempted throughout this book to distinguish proprietary trademarks from descriptive terms by following the capitalization style used by the manufacturer.

Information contained in this book has been obtained by Premier Press from sources believed to be reliable. However, because of the possibility of human or mechanical error by our sources, Premier Press, or others, the Publisher does not guarantee the accuracy, adequacy, or completeness of any information and is not responsible for any errors or omissions or the results obtained from use of such information. Readers should be particularly aware of the fact that the Internet is an ever-changing entity. Some facts may have changed since this book went to press.

ISBN: 1-931841-41-1
Library of Congress Catalog Card Number: 2001096479
Printed in the United States of America

01 02 03 04 RI 10 9 8 7 6 5 4 3 2 1

In loving memory of my father

James Lowe 1928–1979

Acknowledgments

I am deeply thankful to the many people at Premier Publishing who worked on this book. Thank you for all the time you gave and for your assistance.

To Debbie Abshier and Lynette Quinn for the opportunity to write this book and their confidence in me. A very special thank you to Estelle Manticas for her assistance (and patience) in the book development; to Elizabeth Agostinelli for her help making this book grammatically correct and to Keith Davenport for checking all the technical angles. Also, a BIG thank you to all those behind the scenes at Premier who helped this book become a reality. It's been an interesting transition.

Lastly, to my husband. Thank you again Vern, for all your support and never-ending faith in me. For thirty-three years you've believed in me and as I come to this big over-the-hill hump in my life, I'm sure glad you're here!

About the Author

DIANE KOERS owns and operates All Business Service, a software training and consulting business, formed in 1988, that services the central Indiana area. Her area of expertise has long been in the PC-based world of DOS, Windows, word-processing, spreadsheet and graphics areas of computing as well as providing training and support for Peachtree Accounting Software. Diane's authoring experience includes sixteen other books on topics such as Microsoft Windows 98, Window Me, Office, Word, Works, Lotus SmartSuite, Corel WordPerfect, Paint Shop Pro, and Peachtree Accounting. She has also developed and written software training manuals for her clients.

Active in her church and civic activities, Diane enjoys spending her free time traveling and playing with her three grandsons and her three Yorkshire Terriers.

Contents at a Glance

Introduction xix

PART I
UNDERSTANDING BASIC
WINDOWS OPERATIONS 1

Chapter 1   Discovering the Windows Desktop 3
Chapter 2   Using Windows Programs 17
Chapter 3   Asking for Help with Windows 45

PART II
WORKING WITH THE ACCESSORIES 57

Chapter 4   Using the Calculator 59
Chapter 5   Writing with WordPad 65
Chapter 6   Painting with the Paint Program 77
Chapter 7   Playing Around with the Games 85
Chapter 8   Discovering Multimedia 93

PART III
MANAGING FILES 107

Chapter 9   Organizing Files and Folders
Chapter 10   Managing the Recycle Bin 129
Chapter 11   Searching for Items 135

PART IV
CUSTOMIZING WINDOWS 145

Chapter 12 Customizing the Desktop 147
Chapter 13 Tinkering with the Control Panel 159
Chapter 14 Having Fun with the Control Panel 179
Chapter 15 Setting Accessibility Options 189

PART V
PREPARING FOR AN EMERGENCY 201

Chapter 16 Working with Printers 203
Chapter 17 Preparing for Disasters—Backing up Your Data 225
Chapter 18 Troubleshooting Problems 237
Chapter 19 Improving System Performance 249

PART VI
CONNECTING TO OTHER COMPUTERS 259

Chapter 20 Using a Network 261
Chapter 21 Connecting to the Internet 277
Chapter 22 Surfing with Internet Explorer 287
Chapter 23 Working with Outlook Express 303
Chapter 24 Using the Windows Address Book 325
Chapter 25 Using Windows Messenger 337

Appendix A Upgrading to Windows XP 355

Index 363

Contents

Introduction xix

PART I
UNDERSTANDING BASIC
WINDOWS OPERATIONS 1

Chapter 1 **Discovering the Windows Desktop** 3

Logging On from the Welcome Screen 4

Understanding the Windows Desktop 4

Opening Icons 5

Looking at Other Desktop Items 6

Working with the Taskbar 7

Operating the Start Button 7

Using the Quick Launch Bar 10

Investigating the System/Notification Tray 10

Logging On and Off 12

Discovering Fast User Switching—
Logging On a Different User 12

Logging Off a User 13

Shutting Down Windows 14

Shutting Down Windows the Right Way 14

Restarting Windows 15

Shutting Down Windows When Your Computer Locks Up . . . 16

Chapter 2   **Using Windows Programs** **17**

Opening a Windows Program. 18

Switching between Programs 19

Identifying Window Elements. 20

    Using Scroll Bars 21

    Managing Window Size 22

        Minimizing a Window. 22

        Maximizing a Window 23

        Manually Resizing Windows 24

Using Windows Menus and Dialog Boxes 25

    Making Menu Choices 26

        Selecting with a Mouse 26

        Selecting with the Keyboard 27

    Working in a Dialog Box. 29

Creating Documents 31

    Saving a Document. 32

    Printing a Document. 33

    Closing an Application 35

    Opening a Document 35

Learning Common Windows Commands 36

Handling a Locked Up Application 38

Working with Compatibility Mode 39

Chapter 3   **Asking for Help with Windows** **45**

Taking the Windows Tour 46

Exploring the Help and Support Window. 47

    Using the Help Topics. 48

    Getting Assisted Support. 49

        About Microsoft Assistance 50

        About Remote Assistance 52

    Using the Help Index 53

    Searching for Help 55

Part I Review Questions 56

PART II
WORKING WITH THE ACCESSORIES 57

Chapter 4 **Using the Calculator** 59

Starting the Calculator 60

Identifying Calculator Buttons 60

Using the Calculator 61

Copying Values from the Calculator 62

Changing the Style of the Calculator 63

    Viewing the Scientific Calculator 64

    Returning to the Standard Calculator. 64

Chapter 5 **Writing with WordPad** 65

Starting WordPad 66

Creating a Document 67

Editing a Document. 68

    Adding Text. 68

    Deleting Text. 68

Inserting the Current Date and Time 69

Selecting Text 70

Cutting and Pasting Text. 72

Formatting Text. 73

    Changing the Font 73

    Modifying the Alignment 74

    Adding Bullets. 75

Chapter 6 **Painting with the Paint Program** 77

Starting the Paint Program 78

Discovering the Paint Tools. 78

    Drawing with the Paintbrush 80

    Drawing a Rectangle or Circle 81

    Filling in the Background Color 82

    Selecting and Moving an Object 83

Chapter 7   **Playing Around with the Games** **85**
    Starting Single-User Games 86
    Connecting to an Internet Game 88

Chapter 8   **Discovering Multimedia** **93**
    Using Media Player 94
        Playing a Music CD 94
            Starting a Music CD 94
            Discovering Visualizations 95
            Choosing from the Playlist 96
        Working with the Media Player 97
        Listening to Web Radio 98
            Selecting a Preset Radio Station 98
            Searching for Radio Stations 99
        Applying Skins 100
    Using the Windows Volume Control 102
    Adding a Media Clip to a Document 104
    Part II Review Questions 106

PART III
MANAGING FILES **107**

Chapter 9   **Organizing Files and Folders** **109**
    Looking at My Computer 110
        Exploring My Computer 110
        Viewing Disk Drive Contents 112
        Browsing the Task Pane 113
    Peeking in the Explorer Window 114
        Identifying Explorer Components 115
        Expanding Folder Levels 116
    Selecting Files and Folders 117
    Moving and Copying Files and Folders 118
    Creating New Folders 120
    Renaming Files and Folders 121

Modifying the Explorer Display 123
Displaying Toolbars. 123
Moving Toolbars 123
Changing the Way Files Are Displayed 125
Sorting Files 127
Modifying Folder Options 127

Chapter 10 Managing the Recycle Bin 129
Deleting Files and Folders 130
Deleting Items from a Window. 130
Deleting Items from an Application 131
Deleting an Item from the Desktop 132
Recovering an Item from the Recycle Bin. 132
Emptying the Recycle Bin 134

Chapter 11 Searching for Items 135
Finding a File or Folder. 136
Looking for a File by Date. 138
Searching for People in the Address Book. 141
Part III Review Questions 144

PART IV
CUSTOMIZING WINDOWS. 145

Chapter 12 Customizing the Desktop 147
Displaying Desktop Items 148
Creating Desktop Folders. 149
Creating a Shortcut 150
Modifying Icons. 151
Moving an Icon 152
Deleting an Icon 152
Changing an Icon 153
Renaming an Icon 154

Customizing the Taskbar 155

　　Unlocking the Taskbar 155

　　Moving the Taskbar 156

　　Changing Taskbar Options 157

Chapter 13 **Tinkering with the Control Panel 159**

Opening the Control Panel 160

Changing the Current Date and Time 160

Changing Mouse Response 162

　　Changing Basic Mouse Responses 163

　　Changing Mouse Pointers 163

　　Changing Mouse Visibility 165

Adding and Removing Programs 166

　　Installing a New Program 166

　　Uninstalling a Program 168

　　Adding Windows Program Components 169

Managing Users 172

　　Adding Users 172

　　Changing User Options 174

　　　Changing the User Name 174

　　　Creating a Password 175

　　　Changing the User Picture 176

　　　Deleting Users 177

Chapter 14 **Having Fun with the Control Panel 179**

Changing Sounds 180

Enhancing Your Display 182

　　Changing Backgrounds and Colors 182

　　Selecting a Screen Saver 183

　　Changing the Colors of Your Windows 185

　　Changing Screen Resolution 186

　　Lowering Resolution with Compatibility Mode 188

Chapter 15 **Setting Accessibility Options**. **189**

Working with the Magnifier. 190

Using Microsoft Narrator 192

Displaying the On-Screen Keyboard. 193

Activating the SoundSentry 195

Part IV Review Questions 200

PART V
PREPARING FOR AN EMERGENCY **201**

Chapter 16 **Working with Printers** **203**

Installing a Local Printer 204

Discovering Printer Options 208

Sharing a Printer 209

Connecting to a Network Printer 211

Making a Printer the Default. 213

Creating a Desktop Shortcut to the Printer 214

Controlling Print Jobs 215

Pausing a Print Job 216

Deleting a Print Job 217

Faxing from the Computer 218

Installing the Fax Component 218

Faxing a Document. 219

Configuring the Fax 220

Using the Send Fax Wizard 221

Chapter 17 **Preparing for Disasters—**
Backing Up Your Data **225**

Installing the Backup Program 226

Backing Up Files 229

Restoring Files. 233

Chapter 18 **Troubleshooting Problems** **237**

Scanning for Hard Disk Errors 238

Using System Restore 240

Creating a Restore Point 240

Restoring Your System 242

Getting Windows Updates 244

Getting an Windows Update Manually 244

Setting Automatic Updates 247

Chapter 19 **Improving System Performance** **249**

Defragmenting Your Hard Drive 250

Using Disk Cleanup 252

Automatically Scheduling Tasks 254

Part V Review Questions 258

PART VI
CONNECTING TO OTHER COMPUTERS 259

Chapter 20 **Using a Network** **261**

Preparing to Network 262

Working with My Network Places 262

Browsing Other Computers 263

Browsing the Entire Workgroup 264

Creating a Network Place 265

Choosing a Network Drive in an Application 269

Mapping a Network Drive 270

Disconnecting from a Network Drive 274

Sharing Your Computer with Others 275

Chapter 21 **Connecting to the Internet** **277**

Setting Up an Internet Connection 278

Starting the New Connection Wizard 278

Signing Up for a New Internet Account 279

Setting Up an Existing Internet Account 282

Dialing Your Connection 284

Starting Your Web Browser 285

Chapter 22   Surfing with Internet Explorer 287

Browsing the Web with Internet Explorer 288

Starting Internet Explorer 288

Exploring the Internet Explorer Window 289

Following Hyperlinks 290

Moving Backward and Forward 291

Returning to Your Home Page 291

Entering a Specific Web Address 292

Playing Favorites 293

Adding Favorites 293

Accessing Your Favorite Sites 294

Searching for Information Online 295

Viewing Your Surfing History 296

Setting Content Restrictions 297

Chapter 23   Working with Outlook Express 303

Starting Outlook Express 304

Setting Up an E-mail Account 304

Creating an E-mail Message 308

Formatting an E-mail Message 310

Attaching Files to E-mail 312

Retrieving Incoming E-mail 314

Replying to a Message 315

Forwarding a Message 316

Receiving E-mail with Attachments 317

Managing E-mail 318

Creating an E-mail Folder 318

Moving an E-mail Message 320

Deleting an E-mail Message 320

E-mailing a File from Windows 322

Minding Your-e-Manners 323

Chapter 24   Using the Windows Address Book **325**

Managing Address Book Contacts 326

Adding Contacts 326

Editing Contacts 330

Deleting Contacts 331

Sorting Address Book Contacts 331

Printing a Phone List 332

Closing the Address Book 333

Sending E-mail to a Contact 334

Chapter 25   Using Windows Messenger **337**

Staring Windows Messenger 338

Signing Up for a Passport 338

Signing On to Messenger 341

Adding Contacts 341

Being Added to a Contact List 342

Sending Instant Messages 343

Inviting Others to Join a Conversation 344

Changing the Message Font 345

Adding Emoticons 345

Typing Emoticons 346

Displaying a List of Emoticons 346

Sending a File 347

Answering an Invitation 348

Changing Your Status 349

Modifying Your Personal Settings 349

Checking E-mail 351

Signing Out 351

Part VI Review Questions 353

Appendix A **Upgrading to Windows XP** **355**

Understanding the Upgrade Process 356

System Requirements 356

Installing the Windows XP Upgrade 357

Activating and Registering Windows 361

Index **363**

Introduction

This new *Fast & Easy* guide from Premier Publishing helps you unleash the power of Windows XP—the newest release of the world's most popular operating system. Microsoft has long had a reputation for delivering the type of products its users ask for; this means that each time a new version of MS software comes out, it contains new features. Windows XP is no exception. This version has everything most people want in an operating system, including better support for devices such as scanners and digital cameras, and a number of tasks wizards for simpler setup. With the new multiple user support, Windows helps you get the maximum use out of one desktop by allowing each system user to retain their own settings and preferences.

Windows XP is available in two flavors, Professional and Home. This book is based on the Home version, which is really a subset of the Professional version. Note that current users of Windows 2000 and Windows NT cannot upgrade to Windows XP Home Edition; they must use Windows XP Professional Edition.

Microsoft Windows XP Fast & Easy shows you how to accomplish the most common Windows tasks—from playing games to connecting to your favorite Web site. *Fast & Easy* guides use a step-by-step approach and are written in easy-to-understand informal language. Each step is accompanied by a visual representation of your screen, so that you can follow along and make sure you're on the right track.

The book is broken into six different parts, each focusing on a different area of Windows XP. Review questions are provided at the end of each part to assist you in assessing your understanding of the covered subjects, and you'll find an appendix to assist with the upgrading process.

This book cannot teach you everything you can do with Windows XP, nor will it give you all the different ways to accomplish a task. What I *have* tried to do is give you the fastest and easiest way to get everyday tasks done so that you can get on with your life.

Who Should Read This Book?

This book can be used as a learning tool or as a step-by-step task reference. The easy-to-follow, highly visual nature of this book makes it the perfect learning tool for a beginning computer user as well as those seasoned computer users who are new to this version of Windows. By using this *Microsoft Windows XP Fast & Easy* guide, any level of user can quickly look up steps for a task without having to plow through pages of descriptions.

Added Advice to Make You a Pro

You'll notice that this book focuses on the steps necessary for a task and keeps explanations to a minimum. Included in the book are elements that provide some additional information to help you master the program without slowing your progress through the steps:

- **Tips** offer shortcuts when performing an action, and they describe a feature that can make your work in Windows quicker and easier.

- **Notes** give you a bit of background or additional information about a feature; they also give advice about how to use the feature in your day-to-day activities.

This book truly is the *fastest and easiest* way to learn Windows. Enjoy!1

PART I

Understanding Basic Windows Operations

Chapter 1
Discovering the Windows Desktop **3**

Chapter 2
Using Windows Programs **17**

Chapter 3
Asking for Help with Windows **45**

1

Discovering the Windows Desktop

You've got to start somewhere, so why not at the beginning:
What happens when you first turn on your computer? What are all
those things that show up on your screen? In this chapter you'll
learn how to:

- Log on to Windows
- Look at and maneuver around the Windows desktop
- Log off and shut down your computer

Logging On from the Welcome Screen

When you first turn on your computer, Windows XP will automatically load and a screen will appear asking you to Log On. Logging on is the process of telling Windows who you are. Windows can store preferences for each person who uses your computer, so by telling it who you are, Windows knows which preferences to load.

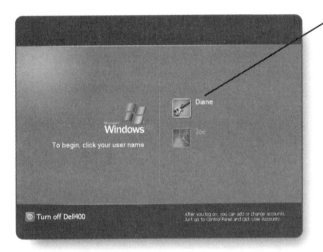

1. Click on your **user name**. You may be prompted for a password. If you are not prompted for a password skip steps 2 and 3. Your user preferences will load and the Windows desktop will appear.

NOTE

You'll learn how to modify your user name and settings in Chapter 13, "Tinkering with the Control Panel."

---

2. If prompted, **type** your **password**. The password will appear as a series of dots.

3. Press the **Enter key**. The user preferences will load and the Windows desktop will appear.

Understanding the Windows Desktop

The *desktop* is the main workspace in Windows XP. Everything you do starts from the desktop, so it's a good idea to become acquainted with it.

Several pictures or icons may display on your computer desktop. You need to recognize these icons in order to operate many of the Windows XP features. Depending on the configuration of your computer and the type of Windows XP installation, you may not have all of these choices or you might have several others.

Opening Icons

Most icons on the desktop will either open a window from which you can make selections or open a program for you to use. For example, the My Computer icon can be opened into a different window so that you can quickly and easily see everything on your computer.

1. Double-click on the **My Computer icon**. The My Computer window will appear.

> ### NOTE
> This figure shows the contents of My Computer on my machine. Your My Computer window may display different items.

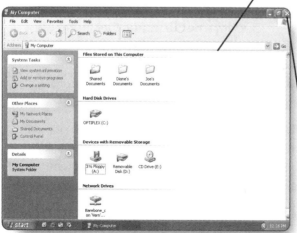

You will learn about the different parts of a window in the next chapter, and you'll learn about working with My Computer in Chapter 9, "Organizing Files and Folders."

When you are finished looking at the window, you need to close it.

2. Click on the **Close button ([X])** located in the upper-right corner of the window. The Windows desktop will reappear.

Looking at Other Desktop Items

A couple of other icons on the desktop should be mentioned at this point. You'll learn more about most of these icons in later chapters.

- **My Documents.** Windows created the My Documents folder as a convenient place to store documents or files that you may need to access quickly and easily. Managing items in different folders is covered in Chapter 9, "Organizing Files and Folders."

- **Windows Media Player.** Use Windows Media Player to play CD's, video, and listen to Web Radio. Chapter 8, "Discovering Multimedia," shows you all about the Windows Media Player.

- **My Network Places**. The My Network Places icon allows you to browse other computers that may be connected to yours. Chapter 20, "Using a Network," shows you how to work with other computer from My Network Place.

- **Recycle Bin.** This icon represents the place where your files go after they are deleted. Discover the Recycle Bin in Chapter 10, "Managing the Recycle Bin."

- **Internet Explorer.** One of the Web browsers supplied with Windows. A Web browser is necessary if you want to access the Internet. Learn to use Internet Explorer in Chapter 22, "Surfing with Internet Explorer."

- **Outlook Express.** This icon provides access to a popular Microsoft e-mail program. If you have Internet access, Outlook Express can help you manage incoming and outgoing e-mail. You'll learn about Outlook Express in Chapter 23, "Working with Outlook Express."

Working with the Taskbar

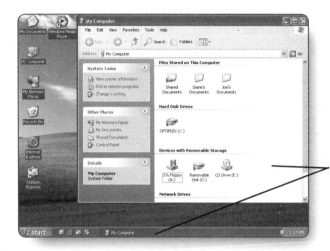

Windows calls the bar located across the bottom of your screen the *Taskbar*. The Taskbar represents several different components. It displays the button representing the main Start menu and buttons for each application you have open and running on your computer.

When a window is open, a button appears in the Taskbar.

TIP

Pause your mouse pointer across any of the buttons on the Taskbar to see a small box, called a ToolTip, indicating the name of each button.

Operating the Start Button

You generally use the Start button to access your programs and documents. You'll find the Start button located on the lower-left side of your screen.

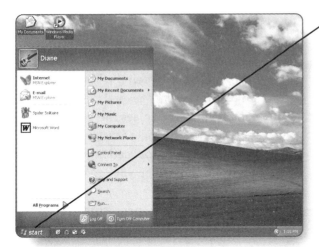

1. Click on the **Start button**. The Start menu will appear.

TIP

If you have one of the newer keyboards, you probably have a key between the Ctrl key and the Alt key that has the Windows logo (a flying window) on it. This is the Windows key. You can also open the Start menu by pressing this key.

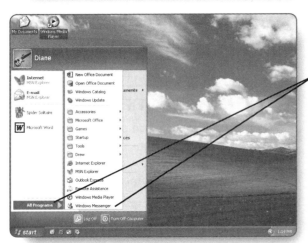

2. Click on the **desired option**. One of several things will happen next:

- If you click on All Programs, a submenu allowing you to make another selection will appear. Notice that this item has a small right-facing arrow next to the option. The arrow indicates that a cascading submenu menu will appear.

TIP

Windows lists recently used applications above the All Programs menu. Click on a recently used application to launch it.

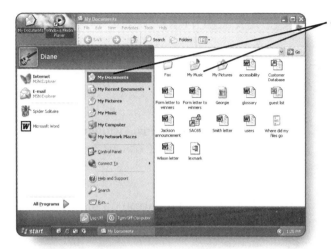

● If you click on options like Control Panel, My Documents, or My Network Places, a window will appear just as with the My Computer window you opened earlier in this chapter.

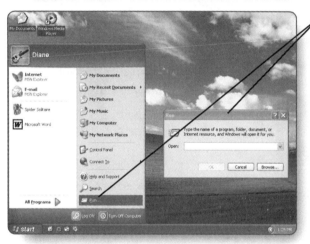

● If you select Run, a dialog box will appear asking you for more information. Dialog boxes are discussed in Chapter 2, "Using Windows Programs." Notice that Run has three dots displayed after the menu choice. The dots are called an *ellipsis* and indicate that a dialog box will appear.

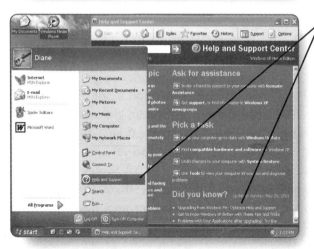

● If you select Help and Support, the Help and Support system opens. You'll learn about Help in Chapter 3, "Asking for Help with Windows."

Using the Quick Launch Bar

Windows provides several ready-made toolbars that can display on the Taskbar. One of these toolbars, the Quick Launch toolbar, provides shortcuts to several often-used programs, including Internet Explorer, Outlook Express, or Windows Media Player.

1. Click on any **button** on the Quick Launch bar. The selected program will launch.

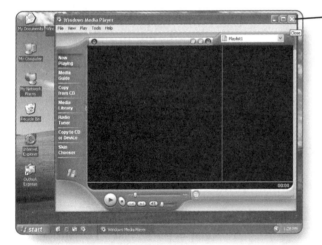

2. Click on the **Close button** ([X]). The activated program will close.

Investigating the System/Notification Tray

Applications sometimes put icons in the System/Notification tray to indicate the status of an operation or to notify you about an event. For example, an application might put a printer icon in the status area to show that a print job is under way, or a small yellow window may pop up indicating that an update is available for one of your applications. Items such as the current time, anti-virus programs, and volume control also appear in the System/Notification Tray. The System/Notification Tray can also manage power options that you'll find particularly helpful if you are using a laptop computer.

In order to save space on the Taskbar, Windows will hide the inactive icons in the System/Notification tray until you ask to see them.

1. **Click** on the **left-facing arrow**. The System/Notification tray will expand to display available icons.

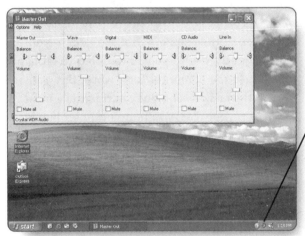

As with the Quick Launch bar, you can position your mouse pointer on top of a choice in the System Tray to see a Tool Tip with a description of that feature.

1. **Double-click** on a **System tray feature**. A dialog box will open pertaining to the selected feature.

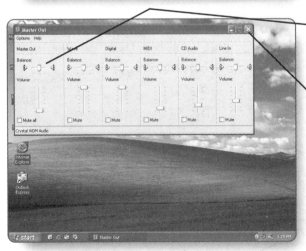

2. **Make** any desired **changes** in the dialog box. In the example shown, I am changing the volume settings.

3. **Click** on the **Close button.** The dialog box will close.

Logging On and Off

Logging on and off is a process each user must complete to begin or end a session on the computer. You learned at the beginning of this chapter that you have to log on as a user when you first start up your computer. You can have many different users, each with their own preferences. (Setting up users is discussed in Chapter 13, "Tinkering with the Control Panel.")

Discovering Fast User Switching—Logging On a Different User

So you're working away and in comes little Joey, who wants to play his new computer game. What the heck—you need a break, so you're going to let him use the computer for a while. But, rather than risk letting Joey accidentally mess up your files, you're going to let him log on as a different user.

1. Click on **Start**. The Start menu will appear.

2. Click on **Log Off**. The Log Off Windows dialog box will open.

3. Click on **Switch User**. The Windows Log On screen will appear.

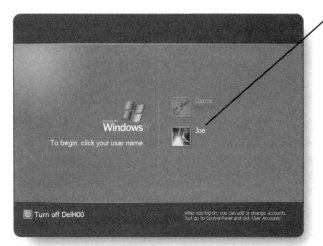

4. Click on the **user name** you want to use. The settings for that user will appear.

Each user can have his or her own desktop settings.

The current user name is displayed at the top of the Start menu.

TIP
Press the Windows key and the letter L to quickly switch back and forth between users.

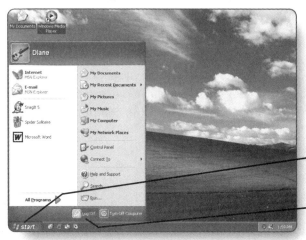

Logging Off a User

If you've finished working on the system but want to leave it up and running for another user, you can simply log off. Logging off keeps your settings and documents safe from the hands of other users.

1. Click on **Start**. The Start menu will appear.

2. Click on **Log Off**. The Log Off Windows dialog box will open.

3. Click on **Log Off**. The Log On screen will reappear.

Shutting Down Windows

Shutting down the computer involves a series of steps. One thing you should *not* do (if at all possible) is just turn off the power. This can cause errors on the hard drive of the computer.

Shutting Down Windows the Right Way

It's best to let Windows "do its thing" and shut down using normal procedures.

1. Close any **open programs**, saving any documents, if necessary.

2. Click on the **Start button**. The Start menu will appear.

3. Click on **Turn Off Computer**. The Turn Off Computer dialog box will open.

4. Click on **Turn Off.** The computer will begin its shutdown procedure and turn itself off or display a message that you can safely turn off the computer.

NOTE

Windows shutdown also includes a hibernation feature wherein your computer saves your current Windows settings, writes any information stored in memory to the hard drive, and turns off the computer. Unlike with the shutdown procedure, when the computer is restarted your desktop appears exactly as it was before you chose hibernation. Not all computers can support hibernation.

Restarting Windows

Sometimes your computer just acts a little flaky. Perhaps it doesn't want to open a window that normally works fine, or a program takes a longer than normal time to load, or a particular screen doesn't display correctly. It may be time to refresh your Windows session by restarting your system. It's sort of like those days we all have when we just need to go back to bed and start the day over.

1. Close any **open programs**, saving any documents, if necessary.

2. Click on the **Start button**. The Start menu will appear.

3. Click on **Turn Off Computer**. The Turn Off Computer dialog box will open.

4. Click on **Restart.** The computer will begin its shut down procedure and restart itself, ending up at the Windows log on screen.

Shutting Down Windows When Your Computer Locks Up

When the computer gremlin gets into your machine (and it will!) and the Windows program crashes, you can try closing the individual programs. If that doesn't help, or the computer is totally unresponsive to your selections, there's nothing else you can do but turn your machine off and let it restart.

1. Turn off the **power** to the computer.

2. Count slowly to **10**. This gives the fans and internal components time to stop.

3. Turn on the **computer**. The rebooting process will begin. Your computer will automatically run ScanDisk, a Windows utility used to repair errors on a hard drive.

After the utility has completed its job, Windows will continue to load and the Log On Screen will appear.

NOTE

You'll learn more about ScanDisk (also known as Check Disk) in Chapter 18, "Troubleshooting Problems."

2

Using Windows Programs

One of the nice features of Windows is that all applications, in order to call themselves a Windows application, must follow certain guidelines. These guidelines provide a common interface between all programs. Therefore, once you've learned the basics of any Windows application, you can spend your time learning the real capabilities of another application instead of relearning the basics. Appreciate this—it didn't used to be this way! In this chapter you'll learn how to:

- Open a Windows application
- Identify the elements of a Window
- Manage a window size and position
- Create, save, print, close, and reopen a document
- Handle a locked-up application
- Explore Compatibility mode

Opening a Windows Program

Programs can be accessed from the Start button.

> ## NOTE
> Your selections may differ from the following illustration. For most of the exercises in this chapter, we'll be working with the WordPad application. (You'll learn more about WordPad in Chapter 5, "Writing with WordPad.")

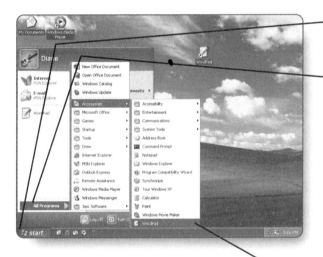

1. **Click** on the **Start button**. The Start menu will appear.

2. **Click** on **All Programs**. The All Programs menu will appear.

> ## NOTE
> As in the illustration, your program may be buried in one or more additional levels. Continue clicking on the cascading menus until you reach the item for which you are looking.

3. **Click** on the **program** you want to use. The program will open.

> ## TIP
> If you have an icon on your desktop for the desired program, simply double-click on the icon to launch the application.

Switching between Programs

Windows allows you to have multiple programs operating at the same time in your computer. A button will appear on the Taskbar for every program you have open. When you have multiple programs open, it is easy to switch back and forth between them.

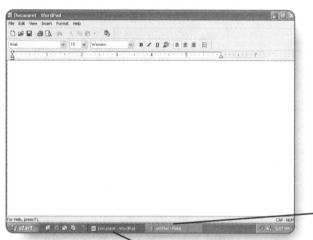

NOTE
Follow the steps in the previous section to open a second application.

A button on the taskbar appears for each open application.

1. **Click** on the **Taskbar button** for the program you want to make active. The window for that program will return to the front of the screen.

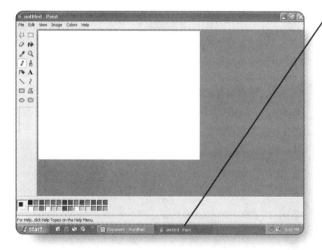

2. **Click** on a **different Taskbar button**. The newly selected program will appear in front.

TIP
You can also press Alt+Tab to switch between open programs.

TIP
If the WordPad application is not already opened, click on Start, All Programs, Accessories, WordPad.

Identifying Window Elements

Most of the features listed in this section appear whether the window displays from a program or from a folder. The WordPad window is an example of a typical window and its components.

- **Title Bar.** The title bar displays the name of the open window or program.

- **Minimize.** The Minimize button temporarily hides a window.

- **Maximize.** The Maximize button enlarges a window to its largest size.

- **Close.** The Close button closes a window.

- **Toolbars.** Most program windows have a Toolbar. In fact, a window may have several different toolbars. Toolbars are shortcuts to menu selections. As you position the mouse pointer over many of the buttons, a *ToolTip*—a small yellow box reflecting the name of the button—displays.

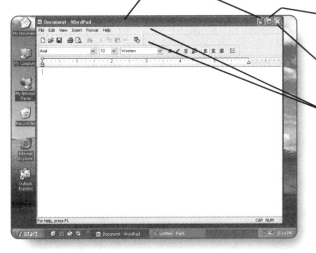

- **Vertical Scroll Bar.** The vertical scroll bar allows you to view a window from top to bottom.

- **Horizontal Scroll Bar.** The horizontal scroll bar allows you to view a window from left to right.

- **Window Borders.** Window borders frame the perimeter of a window and are used to resize a window.

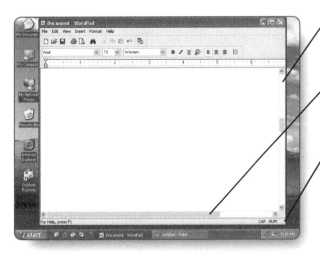

Using Scroll Bars

Scroll bars appear on a window when there is more to see than can be displayed in the window. Depending on the window, you may see one or two scroll bars. The horizontal scroll bar will appear at the bottom of the window and the vertical scroll bar will appear on the right side of the window.

Although you will look primarily at the vertical scroll bar, all the options listed in this section apply to the horizontal scroll bar as well.

Each scroll bar has two arrows and a small box called the *scroll box*. Picture the scroll box as an elevator. If the scroll box is at the top of the bar, this is like being on the top floor. The only direction you can go is down—so use the down arrow to scroll down through the window.

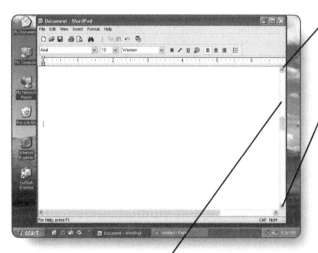

1. **Click** on the **up arrow** of the vertical scroll bar. The next row of text or objects located farther up in the window will appear.

2. **Click** on the **down arrow** of the vertical scroll bar. The next row of text or objects located farther down in the window will appear.

3. **Click** on the **scroll bar** just above the scroll box. The screen moves up one page at a time. You can also click on the scroll bar just below the scroll box to moves the screen down one page at a time.

Another method of moving with the scroll bar is drag the scroll box up or down the bar to quickly move through a window. (Sort of like an express elevator.)

4. **Press and hold** the **mouse button** and **drag** the **scroll box** to the top or bottom of the scroll bar. The screen text moves in the direction you are dragging the scroll box.

5. **Release** the **mouse button**. The text or objects located at the top or bottom of the window appear.

TIP

You can also drag the scroll box to any point in the scroll bar. The scroll bar is relative to the length of the document or window. For example, if you have a 10-page report and you drag the scroll box about half way down the scroll bar, the screen stops at approximately page five.

Managing Window Size

Each window is available in three sizes, *maximized* (taking up the full screen), *minimized* (taking up no screen), or restored to a *manual size* (you decide how much screen).

Minimizing a Window

Occasionally a window may be on top of something you need to see on your desktop. You can move a window, as covered in the next section, or you can minimize it. Minimizing a window does not close it, but simply sets it aside for later use.

Windows calls the first of the three buttons located in the upper-right corner of the window the Minimize button.

1. Click on the **Minimize button**. The window will temporarily disappear from your screen.

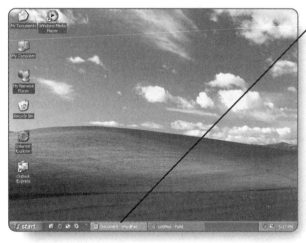

2. Click on the **program application button** on the Taskbar. The window will be restored to its previous size.

Maximizing a Window

Maximizing the window is a favorite choice for many users. To maximize is to make it as large as possible—as large as your screen allows. The Maximize button is the middle of the three buttons located in the upper-right corner of the window.

1. Click on the **Maximize button**. The window will enlarge to the size of your screen.

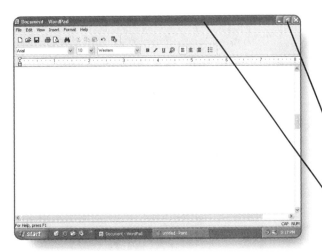

Notice that the appearance of the Maximize button has changed. When a window is already maximized, the button is called the Restore button.

2. Click on the **Restore button**. The window will return to the previous size.

TIP

You can also double-click on the title bar of a window to maximize it. Double-click on the title bar again to restore it.

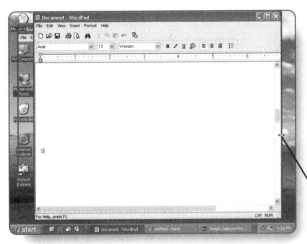

Manually Resizing Windows

If a window is too small or too large, you can resize it by using your mouse. However, you cannot resize a window when it's maximized.

1. Position the **mouse pointer** on an outside edge of a window. The mouse pointer will become a double-headed arrow.

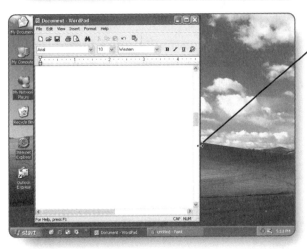

2. Press and hold the **mouse button** while moving the mouse. The window will resize in the direction you move the mouse.

3. Release the **mouse button** when the window is the desired size. The window will remain at the new size.

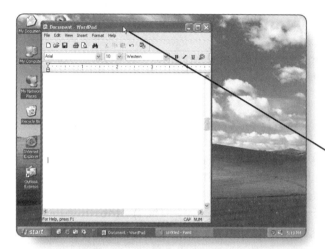

Moving a Window

Besides resizing a window, you can also move a window to a different location on the desktop. A window cannot be moved if maximized.

1. Position the **mouse pointer** on the title bar of the window to be moved.

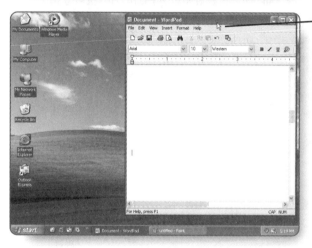

2. Press and hold the **mouse button** on the title bar while moving the mouse. The window will move to the new position.

3. Release the **mouse button**. The window will remain in the new location.

Using Windows Menus and Dialog Boxes

We make choices every day—what we'll wear, what we'll eat, who we'll talk with, and so forth. Why should working with Windows be any different? In Windows applications you'll find lots of choices.

Making Menu Choices

When you go into a restaurant, you make selections from a menu. So it is with a Windows program.

Selecting with a Mouse

When you open an application, the main menus containing program options appear at the top of the window in the area called the *Menu Bar*. Selecting an option from the main menu with your left mouse button leads you to another menu selection. Occasionally that second menu leads to a third menu. Windows calls this a *cascading menu or submenu*.

Most Windows applications have several menu selections in common. The first one is usually File, the second is Edit, the third is View, and the last one is usually Help. The menu selections in between View and Help vary from application to application.

1. Click on the **desired menu**. The menu selections will appear.

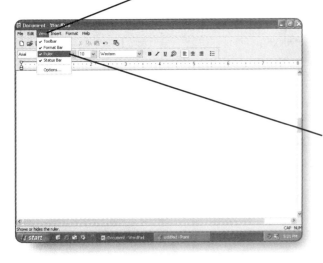

> **TIP**
>
> If you click on a menu in error, click outside of the menu to close it.

2. Choose a **selection** from the displayed menu. One of several things will happen: Windows will take the action you requested, a cascading menu will appear, or a dialog box will open.

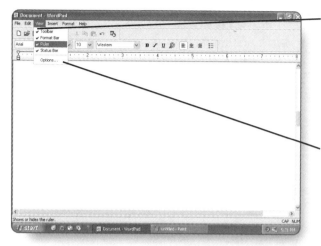

If you choose an item with a check mark beside it, Windows turns off the feature. Check marked items are like toggle switches—a check means the item is active, and no check mark means the item is not active.

If you choose a menu item with an ellipsis (. . .) following the menu selection, a dialog box will open, prompting you for further information. If you choose a menu item with a cascading menu, you will need to select another choice from that menu.

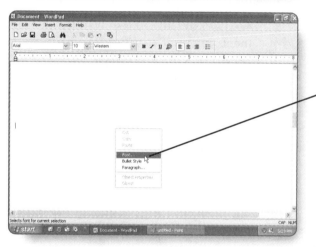

TIP

Many programs offer a selection when you click the right mouse button. Windows calls this a *shortcut menu*—a variable collection of frequently used choices that are relative to your mouse pointer position.

Selecting with the Keyboard

You do not need to use the mouse to make a selection from the menu. You can use the keyboard to access all menu selections. Notice that each menu selection has an underlined letter. Using the Alt key and the underlined letter gives you control of the menu from your keyboard. Again, remember the magic key: the Alt key.

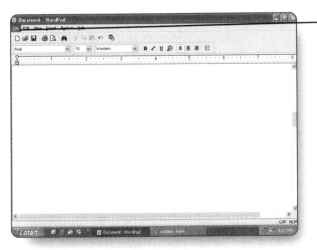

1. Press and release the **Alt key**. The first menu (File) will be selected with a three-dimensional box around it.

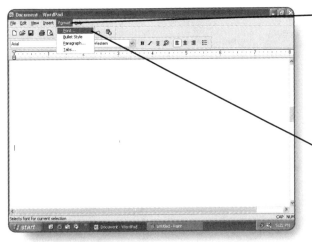

2. Type the **underlined letter** for the menu you want to select. The menu will appear and the first item in the menu will be highlighted. (In the figure shown, I pressed the letter "o" for the Format menu.)

3. Type the **underlined letter** for the item you want to select from the menu. You do not need to press the Alt key again because you are already using the menu.

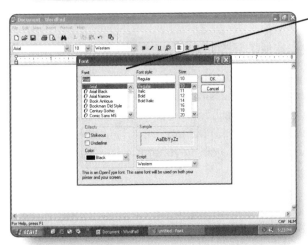

4. Make any necessary **selections** if a dialog box appears. In this figure, we're seeing the Format, Font dialog box.

Working in a Dialog Box

Menu selections that have three dots after it, called ellipses (. . .), indicate that a dialog box will open if you choose that menu item. A *dialog box* prompts you for additional information. Although dialog boxes differ in purpose, common types of selections can be made from most dialog boxes.

1. **Click** on the **desired choice** in a list box. The item you selected displays in the box at the top of the list. *List boxes* enable you to select an item from a displayed list. If the list is too large to be displayed, a scroll bar becomes available.

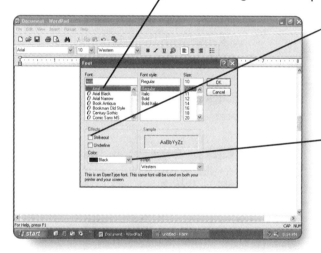

2. **Click** on the **check boxes** next to your desired choices. *Check boxes* allow you to choose multiple selections. When you select a check box, a check mark (✔) will appear in the box.

3. **Click** on the **down arrow** (▼) next to a drop-down list box. A list of possible selections will appear. *Drop-down list boxes* allow you to select an item from a list that will appear.

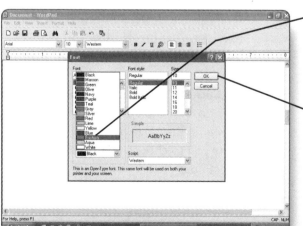

4. **Click** on the **desired choice**. The list of possible selections will close and the selected choice will appear in the drop-down list box.

5a. **Click** on the **OK button**. The dialog box will close and your selections will be accepted.

OR

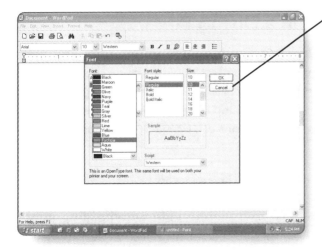

5b. Click on the **Cancel button**. The dialog box will close and your selections will be ignored.

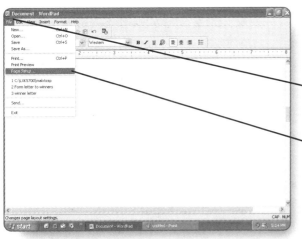

An illustration of another type of dialog box is seen with the WordPad Page Setup dialog box.

6. Click on **File**. The File menu will appear.

7. Click on **Page Setup**. The Page Setup dialog box will open.

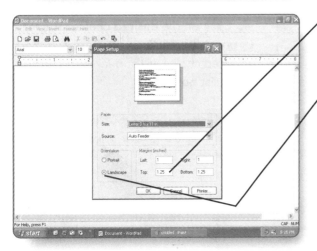

8. Type the **desired information** in a text box. *Text boxes* allow you to type specified information in a box.

9. Click on the **option button** next to your desired choice. A small dot will appear in the circle. *Option buttons* allow you to choose one of several selections.

NOTE

If you want to use your keyboard to select from a dialog box, use the Tab key to move from section to section within the dialog box. You can then use your down arrow key to select from a list box, drop-down list box, or option buttons; or you can use the spacebar to select/ deselect choices with check boxes. When presented with an OK button, press the Enter key to accept the choices or the Esc key to cancel your selections.

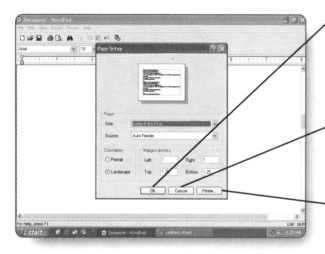

10a. **Click** on the **OK button**. The dialog box will close and your selections will be accepted.

OR

10b. **Click** on the **Cancel button**. The dialog box will close and your selections will be ignored.

The Printer button has an ellipsis after it. Clicking on this button will open another dialog box.

Creating Documents

Most programs that allow you to create something, such as a memo or a spreadsheet or a drawing, automatically begin with a blank sheet ready for you to create away. After you create the document you'll need to process it a little further. You may want to save it, print it, or close it to work on something else. You may even want to reopen it at a later time.

Saving a Document

In most applications, when you work on a document, the changes you make are stored only in the computer memory. That memory is erased when you turn off the computer, if the power fails, or if the computer locks up. To avoid losing a document, you should save it to a file.

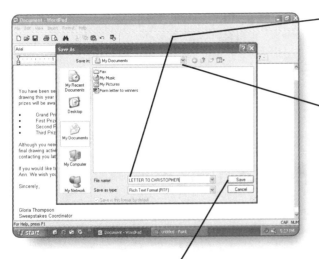

1. Click on **File**. The File menu will appear.

2. Click on **Save**. The Save As dialog box will open.

3. Type a **descriptive name** for the file in the File name: text box.

NOTE

The default folder for saving many documents is the My Documents folder stored on the desktop. You can save the file in any other location by clicking on the down arrow next to the Save in: list box and selecting a different folder.

---

4. Click on **Save**. The file will be saved.

The name of the file will appear in the title bar of the application window and on the Windows Taskbar.

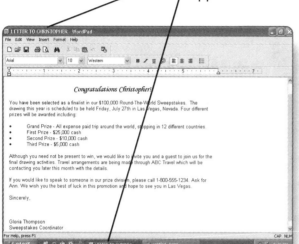

TIP

Don't wait to until you've finished a document to save it. You should save your work about every 10 minutes. After the document is saved for the first time, no questions will be asked. The saved file will simply and quickly be updated with the changes you've made since it was last saved.

Printing a Document

Many programs offer a print preview feature , so that you can review your document prior to printing it.

1. Click on the **Print Preview button**. The screen will change to a non-editable bird's eye view of your document.

TIP

Optionally, click on File and choose Print Preview.

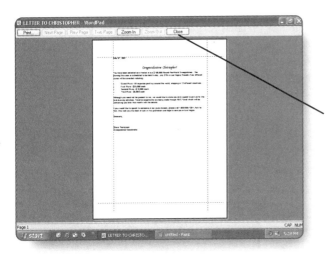

Don't worry if you can't read it very well. You're not supposed to! At this point you are checking out the overall appearance of the document, not the content.

2. Click on the **Close button**. The screen will return to the document-editing screen.

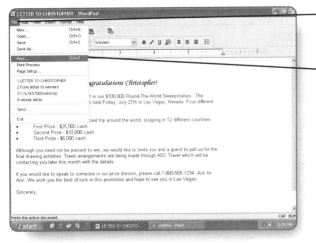

3. Click on **File**. The File menu will open.

4. Click on **Print**. The Print dialog box will open.

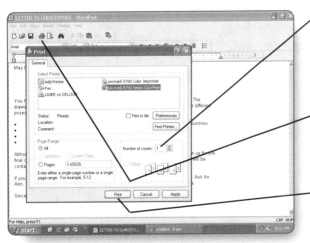

5. Make any desired **changes** in the Print dialog box.

TIP

Click on the **Print button** to bypass the Print dialog box and print the document with the default settings.

---

6. Click on **Print**. The document will print on paper.

Closing an Application

When you are finished using a program you should close it. Keeping a program or document open unnecessarily uses computer resources that you may need for other areas.

In many applications, you can have multiple documents open from the same program. In other applications (WordPad, for example), you can only have one file open at a time.

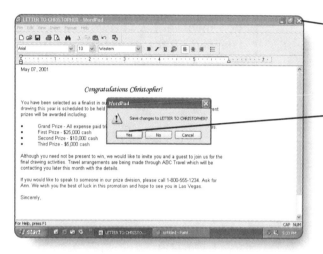

1. **Click** on the **Close box**. The current document will close. Windows will prompt you if your document needed saving before closing.

2. **Click** on **Yes** if you want to save your changes to the document. The document will close and changes will be saved.

NOTE

If you click on No, the document is not saved and all changes are lost.

If the document you close is the only document open for the application, the application may close as well.

Opening a Document

If you want to work on a previously created and saved document, you must open it. When you open a file, the computer places a copy of that file into the computer memory. You can then make any desired changes and save the file again.

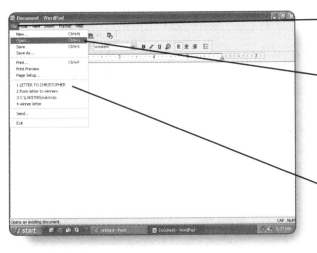

1. **Click** on **File**. The File menu will appear.

2. **Click** on **Open**. The Open dialog box will open and display the contents of the My Documents folder.

TIP

Many applications list recently used documents at the bottom of the File menu. If the document you want is listed, click on the desired document to open it.

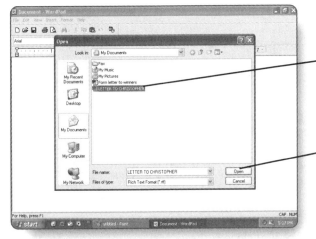

3. **Click** on the **name** of the file you want to open. The file name will be selected and will appear in the File name: text box.

4. **Click** on the **Open button**. The Open dialog box will close, and the document will appear onscreen, ready for you to edit.

Learning Common Windows Commands

Software developers conform to certain conditions in order to designate their products as Windows products. Part of these conditions are common commands that Windows programs can use, whether you're using your word processing program, spreadsheet, or Internet browser. The following table illustrates some of the common commands, along with their descriptions and common shortcut keys. Many (but not all) software programs use the same shortcut keys.

Feature	Shortcut	Description
Open	Ctrl+O	Opens an existing document or file. You are prompted for a file name.
Save	Ctrl+S	Saves the current document or file. If it is the first time the document or file has been saved, Windows prompts you for a file name.
Select All	Ctrl+A	Selects the entire text of a document or all files in a folder
Cut	Ctrl+X	Takes selected text or file and copies it to the Windows Clipboard, then removes the original text or file
Copy	Ctrl+C	Takes selected text or file and copies it to the Windows Clipboard. The original text or file remains in place.
Paste	Ctrl+V	Places the text or file from the Clipboard to the current location in the document or folder
Undo	Ctrl+Z	Reverses the last action you took in the current program
Print	Ctrl+P	Prints the current document
Close	Ctrl+W	Closes the current document, but leaves the program open
Exit	Alt+F4	Closes the current document and will close the program
Help	F1	Starts the Help program. The type of help varies according to the specific software you use.

TIP

When a shortcut key begins with Ctrl or Alt, you need to press and hold down the Ctrl or Alt key, and then tap the second required key.

Handling a Locked Up Application

As much as you try to avoid it, sometimes application programs simply crash and quit responding. The reasons are varied and far too numerous to mention. The real question is, "How do I get out of it?" If a program locks up and quits responding, you can try to "unfreeze" Windows.

NOTE

Sometimes an error message will appear with the words "Illegal Operation" or "Fatal Exception." Don't worry, you didn't do anything illegal or fatal. This is the way Windows lets you know that it doesn't want to play anymore. If you get one of these error messages, follow the instructions on the screen.

---

1. Press and hold the **Ctrl key** while **pressing** the **Alt** and **Delete keys**. The Windows Task Manager window will open.

2. Click on the **program name** giving you problems. The application name will be highlighted.

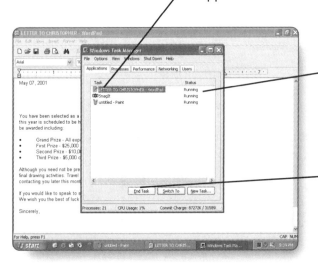

TIP

Although not seen in this figure, a frozen or locked up application will indicate the words "not responding" in the Status column.

---

3. Click on the **End Task button**. The selected program will shut down.

4. Click on the **Close box**. The Windows Task Manager window will close.

You can try restarting the application again. Occasionally, you need to restart your computer to get the application to launch again. Refer to Chapter 1, "Discovering the Windows Desktop" for instructions on restarting your computer.

Working with Compatibility Mode

While most programs will run just fine with Windows XP, occasionally you'll find one that was written specifically for earlier versions of Windows. If you happen to have one of these programs (usually a game), you can use the Windows Compatibility Wizard to set specific options for Windows XP to use when running the selected program.

1. Click on **Start**. The Start menu will appear.

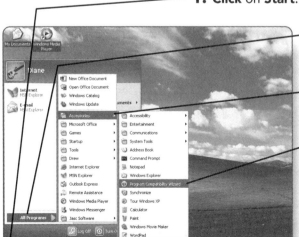

2. Click on **All Programs**. The All Programs menu will appear.

3. Click on **Accessories**. The Accessories submenu will appear.

4. Click on **Program Compatibility Wizard**. A Help and Support window will appear with the Program Compatibility Wizard.

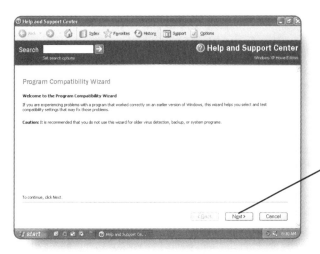

You'll learn about the Help and Support window in Chapter 3, "Asking for Help with Windows."

Microsoft suggests you do not use the Program Compatibility Wizard for setting up virus, system, or backup programs.

5. **Click** on **Next**. The next screen will appear.

You need to tell Windows where the conflicting program is located.

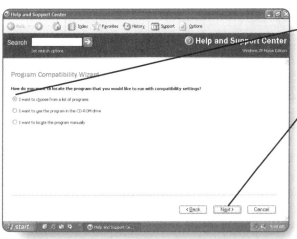

6. **Click** on **I want to choose from a list of programs**. The option will be selected.

7. **Click** on **Next**. Windows will search for a list of all installed applications.

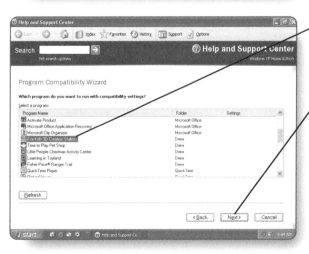

8. **Click** on the **program** giving you the difficulty. The application name will be highlighted.

9. **Click** on **Next**. The next screen will appear.

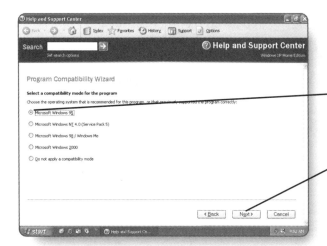

You now must advise Windows as to the preferences for the conflicting application.

10. Click on the **operating system** recommended for your application. The option will be selected.

11. Click on **Next**. The next screen will appear.

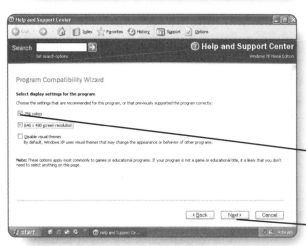

Some applications require special display options. This screen of the Wizard lets you specify those special options. You'll learn about other ways to work with the screen resolution in Chapter 14, "Having Fun with the Control Panel."

12. Click on any necessary **options**. Selected options will have a check mark next to them.

13. Click on **Next**. A verification screen will appear.

Next you should test the application. If the application requires that you run a CD, insert the CD now.

14. Click on **Next**. The application will start.

15. **Run** the **application** and see if it appears to run correctly.

16. **Close** the **application**. The Program Compatibility Wizard will redisplay.

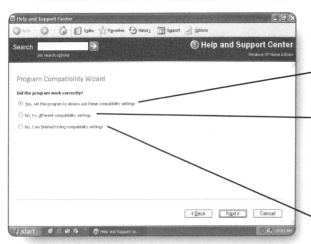

17. **Click** on an **option**. The option will be selected.

● Click here if the application functioned correctly.

● Click here if the application didn't function correctly. You will be redirected to try different compatibility settings and then retest the program.

● Click here if you just want to give up and forget about the Compatibility Wizard.

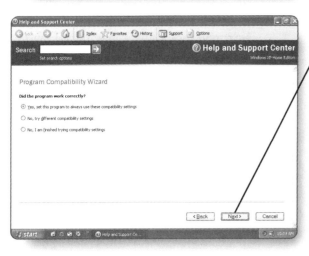

18. **Click** on **Next**. The next screen will appear.

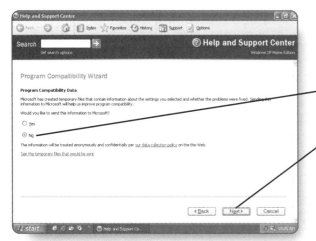

You can choose to send or not send the compatibility information to Microsoft Corporation.

19. **Click** on an **option**. The option will be selected.

20. **Click** on **Next**. The final screen of the Program Compatibility Wizard will appear.

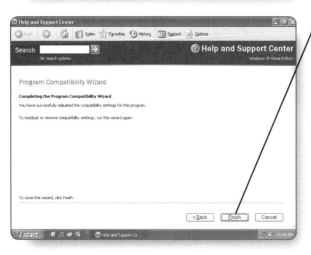

21. **Click** on **Finish**. The Program Compatibility Wizard screen will close.

NOTE

You can learn about other ways to work with the Compatibility feature and screen resolution in Chapter 14, "Having Fun with the Control Panel."

3

Asking for Help with Windows

Though you'll probably find most answers to your Windows XP questions in this book, sometimes you will need additional information. Windows XP includes a revamped, informative help center complete with tours, step-by-step instructions, troubleshooting techniques, product updates, and other helpful links to the Web. In this chapter, you'll learn how to:

- Take the Windows XP tour
- Explore the Help and Support window
- Get assisted support
- Use the Help index
- Search for help

Taking the Windows Tour

Windows XP comes with an informative multimedia tour of XP features. Turn up the volume, sit back, and watch the show!

1. Click on **Start**. The Start menu will appear.

2. Click on **All Programs**. The All Programs menu will appear.

3. Click on **Accessories**. The Accessories submenu will appear.

4. Click on **Tour Windows XP**. The presentation will begin.

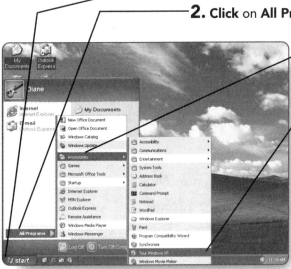

5. Click on **Next**. An introductory message will appear.

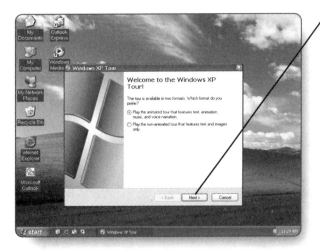

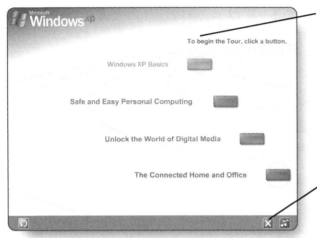

After the introduction plays, a list of tour subjects will appear.

6. Click on **any subject**. The tour will continue with information on the selected subject.

TIP

Click on the Close button at any time during the tour to change tour selections. You can also click on the Close button when you are finished with the Windows XP tour.

Exploring the Help and Support Window

Now take a look at some of the components in the Help and Support Center window. The beginning screen is called the Home screen.

1. Click on **Start**. The Start menu will appear.

2. Click on **Help and Support**. The Help and Support Center window will open.

The Help and Support Center window includes a Web-like toolbar containing several helpful buttons.

The Home button takes you back to the original Help and Support screen (the one you're presently viewing).

An Index button provides an alphabetical list of Windows keywords and terms from which you can choose.

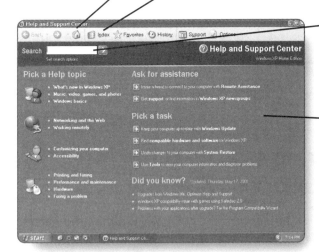

A Search box is provided into which you can type the topic you want. The Help and Support system will then find and display items related to that topic.

You can choose from several different topics of assistance from the category window.

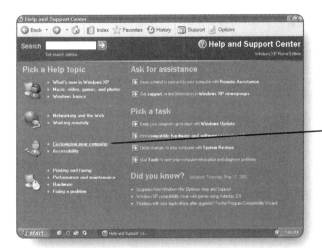

Using the Help Topics

If you need step-by-step instructions for accomplishing a task, use the Pick a Help topic to guide you.

1. From the Pick a Help topic section, **click** on the **task or feature** with which you need assistance. A list of applicable topics will appear.

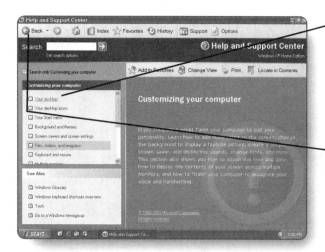

2. Click on the **topic** closest to your need. You may need to click through several screens until the final information is displayed.

TIP

Click on the Back button to return to the previous screen.

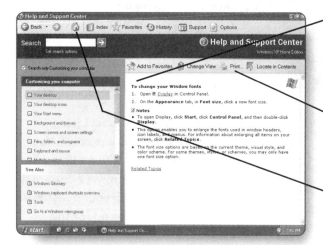

The steps for accomplishing your task will be displayed on the right frame of the screen.

TIP

Click on Print to print the information.

3. Click on the **Home button**. The opening Help and Support Center screen will appear.

Getting Assisted Support

Do you know someone who is knowledgeable with computers? You probably do. If you need assistance you can ask that person to connect to your computer and help you out. Or, you can contact Microsoft for assistance.

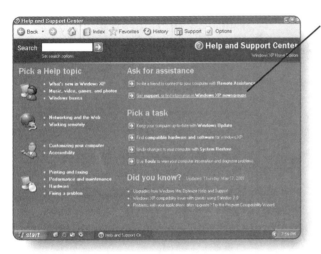

1. Click on an **option** under the Ask for Assistance heading. The Support screen will appear.

2. Click on the **type of assistance** you need. Instructions on available assistance will appear.

About Microsoft Assistance

You can obtain online support from Microsoft by submitting a request. Your question will be directed to a Microsoft support professional who, via e-mail, will attempt to help you with your question. There may be a fee involved for this service.

1. Click on **Get help from Microsoft**. The Microsoft Online Assisted Support screen will appear.

NOTE
If you are not already connected to the Internet, you will be prompted to connect now.

2. Click on **Ask a Microsoft Support Professional for help**.

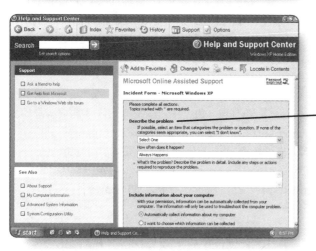

The Help and Support system will prompt you for information such as your operating system, name, e-mail address and other information.

3. Answer any required **information**. An incident report will be created for future reference.

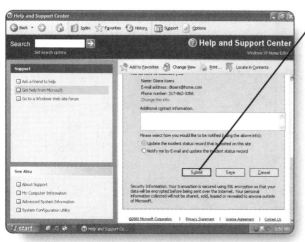

4. Click on **Submit**. The request will be sent to a Microsoft Support Professional.

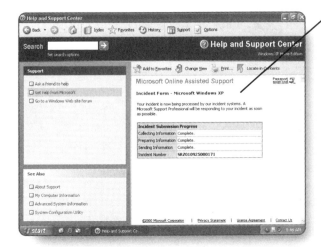

A confirmation screen will appear after the information is sent. Microsoft will assist you via e-mail or when you return to the Help and Support Center assistance window.

About Remote Assistance

If you choose Remote Assistance, Windows will first send an e-mail or other type of message to the helper. After your assistant is connected, he or she will be able to view your screen, chat online with you, or even use his or her mouse and keyboard to work with you on your computer. You will be prompted to give the assistant permission to access your computer remotely.

Both you and your assistant must be using either Windows Messenger, Microsoft Outlook, or Outlook Express. You'll learn about Microsoft Outlook Express in Chapter 23, "Working with Outlook Express," and about Windows Messenger in Chapter 25, "Discovering Windows Messenger."

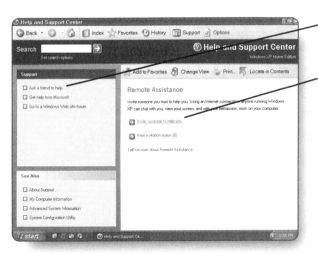

1. Click on **Ask a friend for help**. The Remote Assistance screen will appear.

2. Click on **Invite someone to help you**.

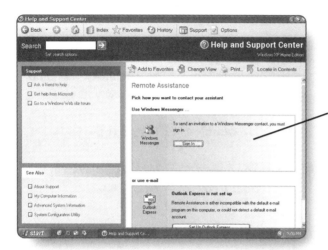

Windows will prompt you for a method with which to contact your helper—either with Microsoft Messenger or Outlook Express.

3. Select a contact **method**.

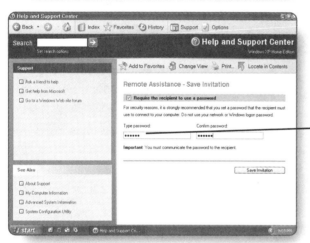

The Help and Support system will prompt you for information such as your helper's e-mail information and a password for him or her to use before accessing your computer.

4. Enter the **information** as requested by Remote Assistance. Your helper will be contacted and after his or her response, your screen will prompt you on what to do next.

Using the Help Index

The Windows Help Index is a list of every available topic covered in the Windows Help feature.

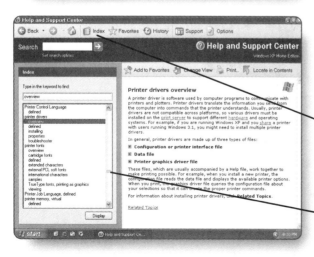

1. Click on the **Index button**. The topics are listed alphabetically in the left-hand frame. Some topics will display a list of subtopics.

2a. Scroll through the **list of topics** until you find the topic you are looking for.

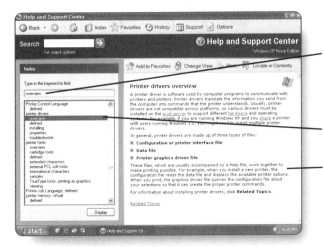

OR

2b. Type the **first word** of the topic you are looking for. The index will jump alphabetically to the word you typed.

3. Double-click on the **topic** you want.

The information will be displayed in the right frame on the screen.

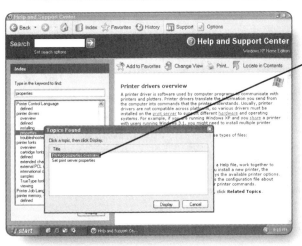

NOTE

Some topics have more than one article of information. Double-click on the article that is most appropriate for your search.

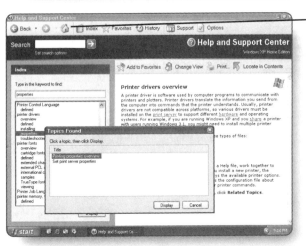

4. Click on the **Home button**. The main Help and Support Center window will reappear.

Searching for Help

Another help method is the Search Help and Support box. If you've used the Internet, you've probably used search engines to help you locate a Web page in which you're interested. The Help and Support search engine works much like an Internet search engine.

1. Click in the **Search Help and Support text box**. A blinking insertion point will appear.

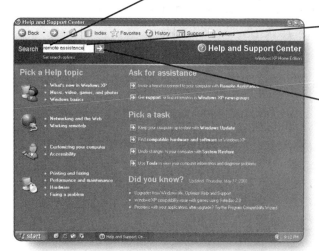

2. Type the **topic** you want to search. The search text can be one word or several.

3. Click on the **Start Searching arrow**. A Search Results window will appear, listing topics that respond to your query.

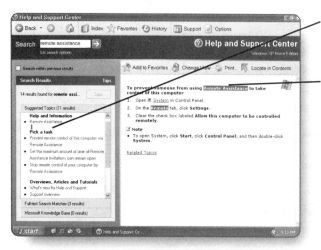

4. Click on the **topic** that most closely resembles your request.

Information on the selected topic will display on the right frame of the screen.

Part I Review Questions

1. What character is displayed when you type a password? *See "Logging on from the Welcome Screen" in Chapter 1*

2. What is another word for the little pictures that appear on your desktop? *See "Understanding the Windows Desktop" in Chapter 1*

3. What is the name of the bar located across the bottom of your screen? *See "Working with the Task Bar" in Chapter 1*

4. What two keys can you press as a quick way to switch back and forth between users? *See "Discovering Fast User Switching – Logging On a Different User" in Chapter 1*

5. What are the three sizes available for a window? *See "Managing Window Size" in Chapter 2*

6. What is usually the first menu choice in a Windows application? *See "Selecting with a Mouse" in Chapter 2*

7. How do you access a shortcut menu? *See "Selecting with a Mouse" in Chapter 2*

8. How many choices can be selected from a dialog box with option buttons? *See "Working in a Dialog Box" in Chapter 2*

9. What does pressing Ctrl+S usually do in a Windows application? *See "Learning Common Windows Commands" in Chapter 2*

10. What Windows feature assists you with issues such as personalizing your computer or connecting to a network? *See "Exploring the Help and Support Window " in Chapter 3*

PART II

Working with the Accessories

Chapter 4
Using the Calculator **59**

Chapter 5
Writing with WordPad. **65**

Chapter 6
Painting with the Paint Program. **77**

Chapter 7
Playing Around with the Games **85**

Chapter 8
Discovering Multimedia. **93**

4

Using the Calculator

Call me the absentminded professor, but I have trouble keeping track of my pocket calculator. Does that ever happen to you? Windows offers a calculator that's always available at your fingertips—it's much harder to lose. In this chapter, you'll learn how to:

- Start using the Calculator
- Identify Calculator buttons
- Copy values from the Calculator to another program
- Change the style of the Calculator program

Starting the Calculator

The Calculator program is located in the Accessories folder.

1. Click on the **Start button**. The Start menu will appear.

2. Click on **All Programs**. The Programs menu will appear.

3. Click on **Accessories**. The Accessories menu will appear.

4. Click on **Calculator**. The Calculator will appear.

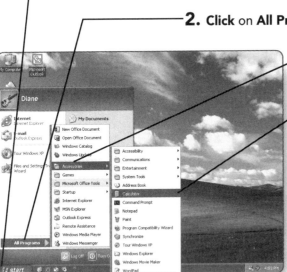

Identifying Calculator Buttons

By default, the Calculator program is a standard 10-key calculator used to perform basic mathematical functions. Besides the normal 0–9 numeric keys, you should know several other important keys.

Some commonly used Calculator keys (and their keyboard equivalents) are the following:

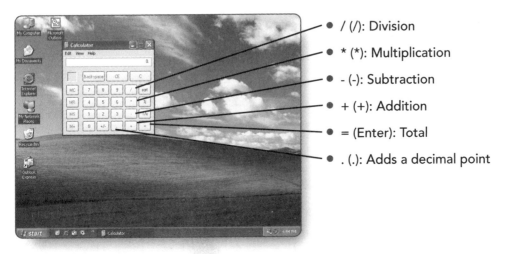

- / (/): Division
- * (*): Multiplication
- - (-): Subtraction
- + (+): Addition
- = (Enter): Total
- . (.): Adds a decimal point

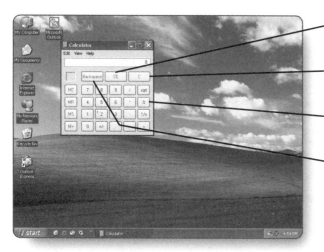

● Clear Entry (Delete): Clears the displayed number

● Clear All (Esc): Clears the current calculation

● % (%): Displays the result of multiplication as a percentage

● Backspace (Backspace): Deletes the last digit of the displayed number

Using the Calculator

You can use the keyboard or the mouse to enter values into the calculator. If you are already proficient with a 10-key calculator, you might prefer to use the numeric keypad on the right side of your keyboard. When entering values, be sure to use the decimal point if the value you are entering is not a whole number. For example, to enter the price of a new shirt, type **29.95** not **2995**.

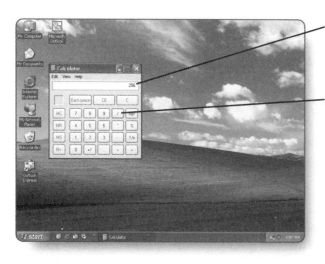

1. Type or **click** on the **first number** in the calculation. The number will appear in the display box of the Calculator.

2. Type or **click** on the **operator** needed.

3. Type or **click** on the **second number** in the calculation. The number will appear in the display box of the Calculator.

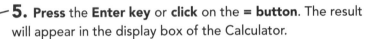

4. Type or **click** on another **operator** and **number**, if needed.

5. Press the **Enter key** or **click** on the **= button**. The result will appear in the display box of the Calculator.

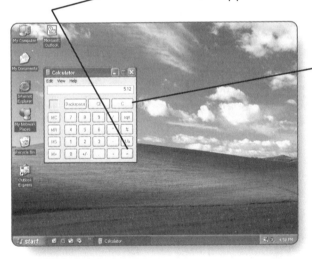

TIP

You can clear the totals on the Calculator by pressing the Esc key or by clicking on the Clear All button (C).

Copying Values from the Calculator

Windows includes a feature called the *Clipboard*. The Clipboard is a special holding area that assists you with transferring information from one document to another, or from one program to another. Transferring information can be accomplished by using two features of Windows called *copy* and *paste*.

The Windows copy and paste function also works with the Calculator. After you get the results of the calculation, you can then paste them into another document; for example, into a Microsoft Word document.

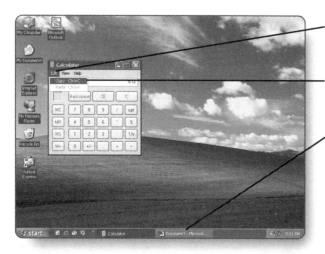

1. Click on **Edit**. The Edit menu will appear.

2. Click on **Copy**. The value on the calculator is to the Clipboard.

3. Start or **switch to** your **word processing** or other **program**. The Calculator may be temporarily hidden from view.

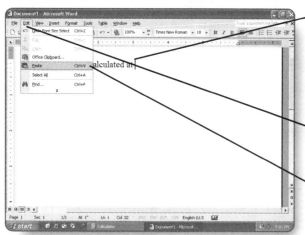

4. Click the **mouse pointer** at the location you want the data to appear.

A blinking insertion point will appear at the location you clicked.

5. Click on **Edit**. The Edit menu will appear.

6. Click on **Paste**. The Edit menu will close.

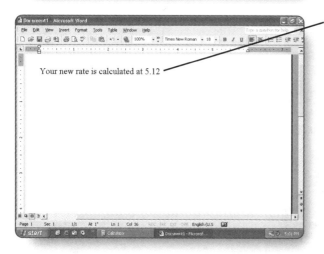

The value from the Clipboard is inserted into your document.

Changing the Style of the Calculator

Besides the standard 10-key calculator, Windows also gives you the option to use a scientific calculator.

Viewing the Scientific Calculator

This calculator will calculate most trigonometric and statistical functions. This calculator operates much the same as the standard calculator does when it comes to the basics.

1. Click on **View**. The View menu will appear.

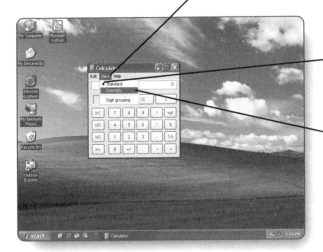

NOTE

The current view is indicated with a dot beside it.

2. Click on **Scientific**. The calculator will change to the scientific style.

Returning to the Standard Calculator

If you're not a person who'll have much need for the scientific calculator (like me!), viewing it can be a little overwhelming. Don't worry—you're just two clicks away from having your normal little calculator back.

1. Click on **View**. The View menu will appear.

2. Click on **Standard**. The calculator will change to the standard style.

TIP

Click on the Close button to close the Calculator.

5

Writing with WordPad

One of the basic uses of a computer is word processing. Windows includes a small word processing program called WordPad. It's a simple program that includes most of the basic features of many popular word processing programs. In this chapter, you'll learn how to:

- Start WordPad
- Enter and edit text
- Insert the current date
- Change the appearance of text
- Add bullet points to a list

Starting WordPad

WordPad is similar to Microsoft Word. You can use it to create letters, memos, and other such documents. The WordPad program is included with Windows as an accessory.

1. Click on the **Start button**. The Start menu will appear.

2. Click on **All Programs**. The Programs menu will appear.

3. Click on **Accessories**. The Accessories menu will appear.

4. Click on **WordPad**. The WordPad program will begin.

The WordPad opening screen has several important components.

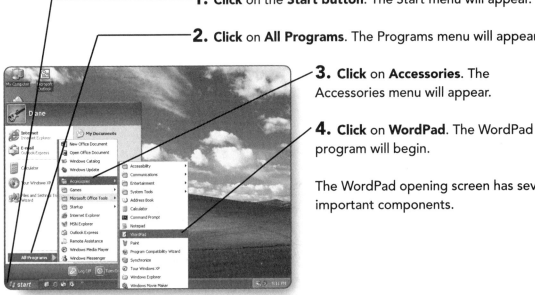

- Menu bar
- Toolbars
- Ruler
- Document typing area
- Insertion point

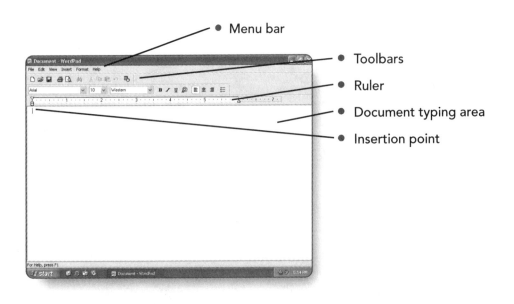

Creating a Document

When you type text into a document, WordPad monitors the lines within a paragraph. If the word you are typing does not fit entirely on the current line, WordPad goes to the next line. This feature is called *word wrap*. To end a paragraph, press the Enter key. You can press the Enter key twice if you want an extra blank line between paragraphs. A short line of text—a date or greeting, such as "Dear Mr. Jones"—counts as a paragraph all by itself.

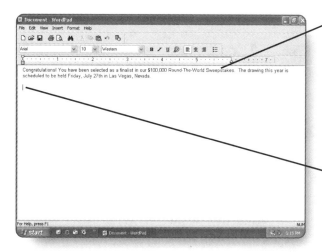

1. Type the desired **text**. The text appears at the location of the insertion point. Do not press the Enter key until you complete the entire paragraph.

2. Press the **Enter key**. The insertion point will move down one line.

3. Press the **Enter key again.** A blank line will appear between the paragraphs, and the insertion point will move down one line.

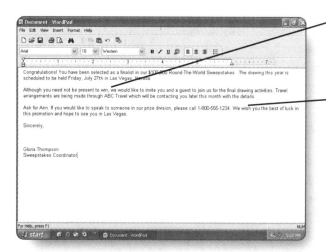

4. Type the **next paragraph** of the document. The text will appear on your screen.

5. Repeat steps 1 through **4** for each paragraph of the document.

Editing a Document

We all make mistakes, right? Errors are easy to correct with WordPad, whether you need to add something you forgot or delete something you didn't mean to type.

Adding Text

WordPad begins in *insert mode*. This means that when you want to add more text to your document, WordPad makes room for the new text by moving existing text to the right.

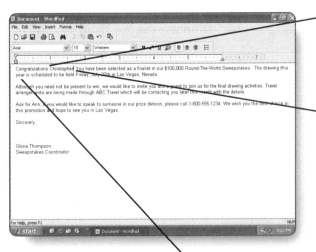

1. **Click directly in front** of the location where you want the new text to appear. The insertion point will move to that position.

2. **Type** any new **word** or **phrase**, adding a space before or after as necessary. WordPad will insert the additional words at the position of the insertion point.

Notice how the words previously at the end of the line on which you began typing no longer fit on the first line and have dropped down to the second line. This is WordPad's word wrap feature at work!

Deleting Text

Text can be deleted one character, one word, or even one paragraph at a time. You can use one of two keys to delete a single character: The Backspace key or the Delete key. The Backspace key deletes a character to the left of the insertion point, while the Delete key deletes a character to the right of the insertion point.

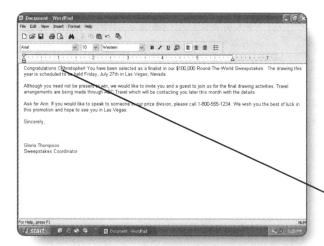

An easy way to remember the difference between the Backspace key and the Delete key is the Backspace key has an arrow on it pointing to the left.

1. Click directly in front of the character you want to delete. The insertion point will move to that position.

2. Press the **Delete key**. The empty space is filled by the existing text from the right.

Inserting the Current Date and Time

Instead of searching around the house or all over your desk for a calendar, let WordPad put today's date in your document for you. Today's date is determined by your computer's system date. Chapter 13, "Tinkering with the Control Panel," shows you how to change your system date.

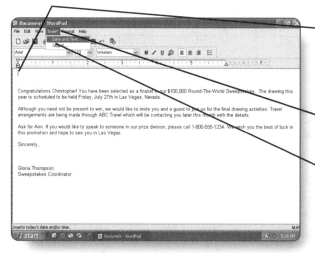

1. Position the **insertion point** at the location where you want the date or time to appear. The blinking insertion point will appear.

2. Click on **Insert**. The Insert menu will appear.

3. Click on **Date and Time**. The Date and Time dialog box will open.

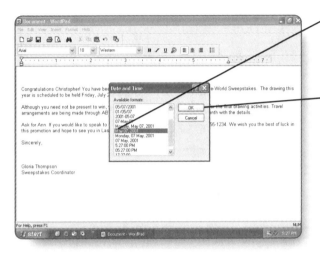

4. Click on the **date and time format** you want to use in your letter. The format is selected.

5. Click on **OK**. The Date and Time dialog box will close, and WordPad will insert the date into your document.

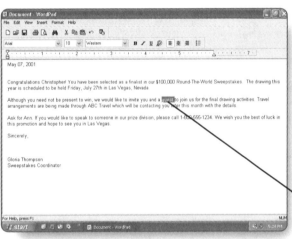

Selecting Text

Before you can change formatting and alignment, or delete an area of text, you need to select the text you want to modify. WordPad allows you to select a word, a paragraph, the entire document, or any portion of a document for these changes.

1. Double-click on a **word**. The word is highlighted.

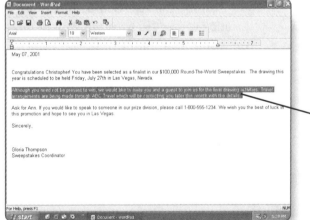

TIP
To deselect text, click anywhere outside of the highlighted area.

---

2. Triple-click anywhere in a paragraph. The entire paragraph is selected.

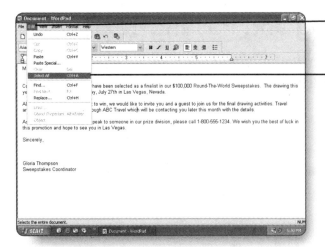

3. Click on **Edit**. The Edit menu will appear.

4. Click on **Select All**. The entire document is selected.

You also have the option of selecting any portion of a document. That might be three words, two paragraphs, or six pages of a document.

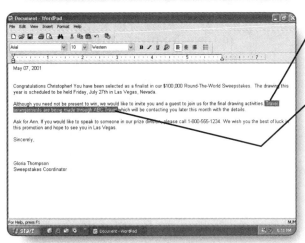

5. Position the **mouse pointer** at the beginning of the text you want to select. The blinking insertion point will appear.

6. Press and **hold** the **mouse button** and **drag** the **mouse pointer** to the end of the selection. The area is highlighted.

7. Release the **mouse button**. The text is selected.

NOTE

You can select to the right, to the left, up, or down in the document by moving the mouse pointer in those directions.

Cutting and Pasting Text

If you have mistakenly placed text in the wrong spot, don't delete it and retype it—use the Windows Clipboard feature to move it.

1. Select the **text** to be moved. The text will be selected.

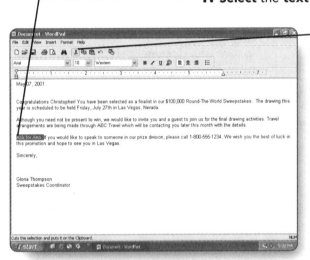

2. Click on the **Cut button**. WordPad will remove the selected text from the document.

TIP

You can also press Ctrl+X or click on the Edit menu and choose Cut.

The selected text looks like it has disappeared, but it hasn't! WordPad placed the text on the Windows Clipboard and is waiting for you to tell it where the text should be placed.

3. Position the **insertion point** where you want the text to be placed. The insertion point will move to the selected location.

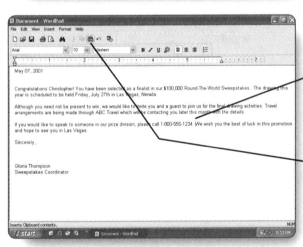

4. Click on the **Paste button**. The text will appear in the new location.

TIP

You can also press Ctrl+V or click on the Edit menu and choose Paste.

Formatting Text

Formatting is changing the appearance of text, such as the font, the color, or such attributes as bolding or underlining. Formatting can also include changing the alignment of text.

Changing the Font

The default font is a 10-point Arial font. Font selections can vary depending on the software installed on your computer.

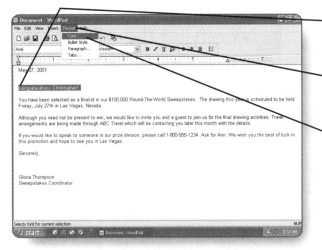

1. Select the **text** to be formatted. The text will be highlighted.

2. Click on **Format**. The Format menu will appear.

3. Click on **Font**. The Font dialog box will open.

From this dialog box you can select the font, the font style, the size, the color, and special effects.

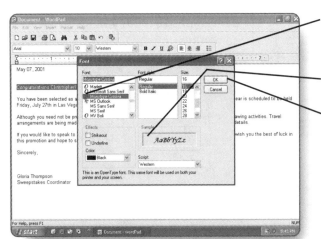

4. Make any desired **changes**. The options you choose will be selected.

The Sample box displays your choices.

5. Click on **OK**. The dialog box will close, and the font choice you selected will be applied to the highlighted text.

Font choices can also be made to selected text from the WordPad toolbar.

● Font name

● Font size

● Bold, Italic, or Underline

● Font color

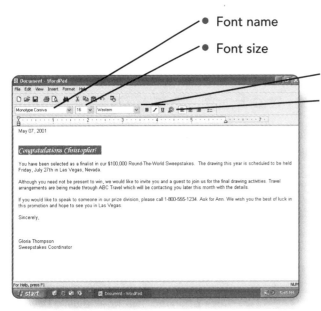

Modifying the Alignment

Alignment is the arrangement of text to the margins of a document. It can also be called *justification*. Alignment choices are applied to an entire paragraph and are made from the WordPad toolbar.

1. Select the **paragraph** you want to modify. The text will be highlighted.

TIP

Optionally, drag across multiple paragraphs to modify them at the same time.

---

2. Click on the desired **alignment button**. The selected button appears "pushed in" to show the current selection, and the current paragraph is modified.

- Left-aligned text is even with the left margin and uneven on the right margin.

- Center-aligned text is centered between the left and right margins.

- Right-aligned text is even with the right margin and uneven on the left margin.

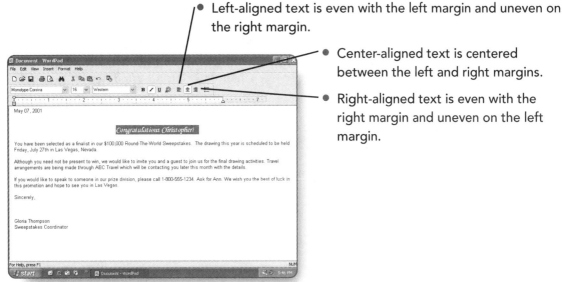

Adding Bullets

Bullets call attention to specific points in a document. WordPad indicates bulleted items with a small black circle in the front and the text indented to the right of it.

1. Click on or **select** the **paragraphs** you want to bullet.

2. Click on the **Bullets button**. The button appears "pushed in" and bullets are applied to the selected paragraphs.

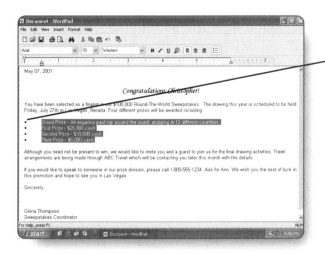

TIP

To remove a bullet, repeat steps 1 and 2.

Remember, you can save and close your WordPad document as you learned in Chapter 2, "Using Windows Programs."

6

Painting with the Paint Program

Those (like me) who have little artistic skill will be glad to know that the Microsoft Paint program is included with Windows XP. This program is designed to assist you with making drawings. In this chapter, you'll learn how to:

- Identify the paint tools
- Draw with the paintbrush
- Draw a rectangle or circle
- Fill in the background color
- Select and move an object

Starting the Paint Program

The Paint program is one of the accessories supplied with Windows.

1. Click on the **Start button**. The Start menu will appear.

2. Click on **All Programs**. The Programs menu will appear.

3. Click on **Accessories**. The Accessories menu will appear.

4. Click on **Paint**. The Paint program will open with a clean, blank screen.

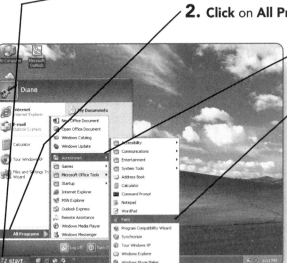

Discovering the Paint Tools

Many tools are available to assist you with your drawing. The Tool box appears on the left side of your screen. You will use the 16 tools in the Tool box to create or edit the objects you need for drawing.

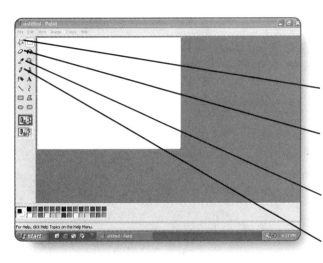

The first two tools on the top row are selection tools. Some of the drawing tools include the following:

- **Free-Form Select.** Selects an irregular shaped area to edit.

- **Erase/Color Eraser.** Erases a portion of the picture or replaces a color with another color.

- **Pick Color.** Copies color from one area or object to another.

- **Pencil.** Draws free form lines.

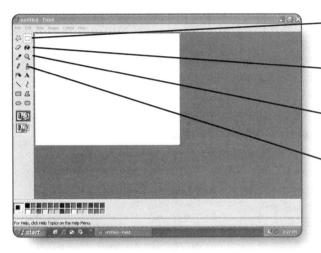

- **Select.** Selects a rectangular portion of the picture to edit.

- **Fill With Color.** Fills in an enclosed area with color.

- **Magnifier.** Magnifies or zooms in or out on a picture.

- **Brush.** Draws with a brush of a selected size and shape.

Other tools include the tools for drawing shapes such as lines, circles, or rectangles, or for typing text. A tool is selected by clicking once on its designated button.

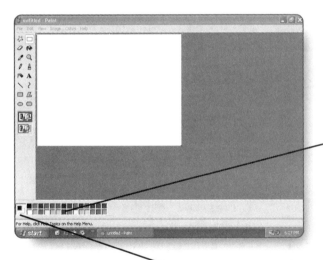

TIP

You can position the mouse pointer on top of each tool to see a description of it.

At the very bottom of the screen is the Color box. Clicking on a color with the left mouse button selects a color for the frame or line of an object. Clicking on a color with the right mouse button selects a color for the interior of a filled object.

The currently selected colors are displayed on the left side of the color box.

Drawing with the Paintbrush

The Paintbrush tool is a free-form drawing tool, which means it can have a variable shape or design.

Many tools, when selected, will display available options at the bottom of the Tool box. For example, if you select the Paintbrush, the various shapes, thickness, and angles will be available for you to choose from. If you select the Rectangle, you can choose from a rectangle with a frame only, filled with a frame, or filled only.

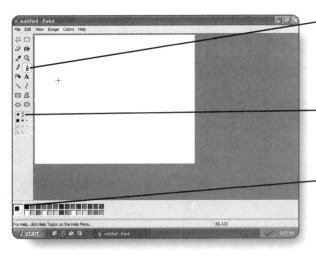

1. **Click** on the **Brush tool**. The Brush button appears "pushed in" to indicate that the tool is active. The mouse pointer will become a small black cross.

2. **Click** on a **brush shape** from the bottom of the Tool box. A dark blue box will appear around the brush shape.

3. **Click** on a **color** from the color box. The selected color will appear in the top of the two boxes on the left side of the color box.

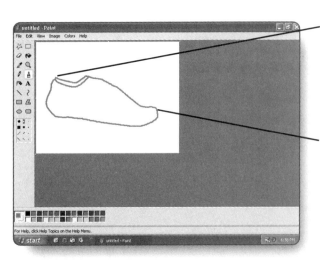

4. **Press and hold** the **mouse button** and **drag** the **mouse pointer** on the drawing screen to draw the desired shape or object. The drawing will appear onscreen as you move the mouse.

5. **Release** the **mouse button**. The completed drawn object will appear onscreen. (Please don't laugh at my drawing . . . I'm a writer, not an artist!)

TIP

If you make a mistake, click on Edit, and then Undo to reverse up to three previous actions.

Drawing a Rectangle or Circle

Unless you are a skilled artist, getting a good-looking drawing with the paintbrush is rather difficult. That's why the rectangle and other shapes are available to assist you.

1. **Click** on the **Rectangle tool**, the **Rounded Corner Rectangle tool**, or the **Ellipse tool**. The tool will appear selected and the mouse pointer will become a small cross.

NOTE

A tool stays selected until a new tool is chosen.

2. **Click** on a **fill style** from the bottom of the Tool box. A dark blue box will appear around the selection.

3. **Click** on a **color** from the color box for the shape's outline. The selected color will appear in the top of the two boxes on the left side of the color box.

4. **Right-click** on a **color** in the color box for the shape fill color. The selected color will appear in the bottom of the two boxes on the left side of the color box.

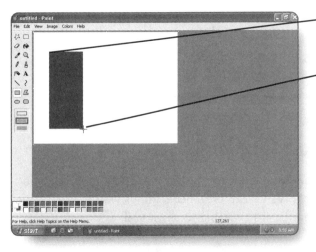

5. Click the **mouse** at the location you want the object to begin.

6. Drag the **mouse pointer diagonally** in the direction you want. The object will appear as you move the mouse.

7. Release the **mouse button** when the shape is the correct size.

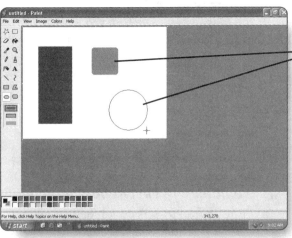

TIP

To draw a perfect square or circle, press and hold the Shift key as you draw the shape. Release the mouse button *before* you release the Shift key.

Filling in the Background Color

You can change the interior (fill) color of any closed-in area.

1. Click on the **Fill With Color tool**. The mouse pointer will look like a paint bucket.

2. Click on the desired **fill color** from the color box. The selected color will appear in the top of the two boxes on the left side of the color box.

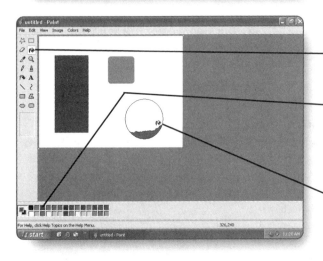

3. Click the **mouse pointer** inside the object to be filled. The interior of the object will take on the new color.

> **TIP**
> If you click in the background area of the drawing, the background changes to the new color.

Selecting and Moving an Object

Objects or shapes that have been drawn onscreen can be moved to a new location. The secret to moving an object is to select it first. With Microsoft Paint you can move all or just part of a drawn object.

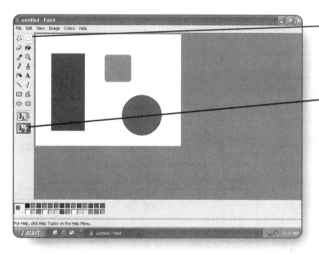

1. Click on the **Select tool** or the **Free-Form Select tool**. The mouse pointer will become a small black cross.

2. Select whether the **background** of the object you're going to move is to be solid in color or transparent.

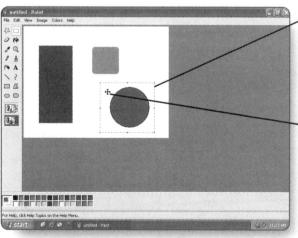

3. Click and **drag** around the area of the object to be moved. A dotted line (called the *selection box*) will appear around the area when you release the mouse button.

4. Position the **mouse pointer** in the middle of the selection box. The mouse pointer will become a small black cross with four arrowheads.

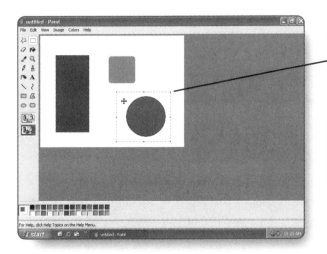

TIP

If you position the mouse pointer over one of the eight small black "handles" on the selection box it becomes a double-headed arrow. You can resize the object by clicking and dragging the box to the desired size.

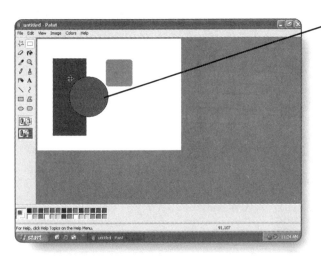

5. **Drag** the **selection box** to the desired location. The selected object will move.

6. **Release** the **mouse button**. The object remains selected and is ready for the next editing action.

TIP

To deselect an object, click on any other area of the drawing, or click on another tool.

7

Playing Around with the Games

I'm sure you've heard the expression, "All work and no play. . . ." Well, Microsoft has included many great games with Windows XP. You can play these games alone on your own computer, or with just a click of the mouse, you can play them against an opponent on the Internet.

Stand-alone games include FreeCell, Hearts, Solitaire, Pinball, Minesweeper, and Spider Solitaire. Games you can play over the Internet are connected through a server called the MS Gaming Zone. These include Backgammon, Hearts, Spades, and Reversi. In this chapter, you'll learn how to:

- Start the Spider Solitaire game
- Start Internet Hearts
- Chat with other Internet players

Starting Single-User Games

One of the single-user games is a cool variation of solitaire called Spider Solitaire. The object of Spider Solitaire is to remove all the cards from the playing area.

1. **Click** on **Start**. The Start menu will appear.

2. **Click** on **All Programs**. The Programs menu will appear.

3. **Click** on **Games**. The Games menu will appear.

4. **Click** on **Spider Solitaire**. The Spider Solitaire game will launch with an opening dialog box.

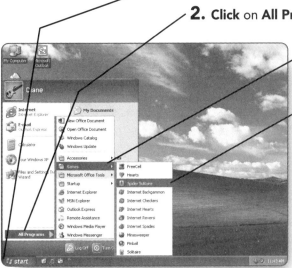

5. **Click** on the **level of difficulty** at which you want to play. The option will be selected. (Hint: From experience, start with Easy, One Suit.)

6. **Click** on **OK**. Let the games begin!

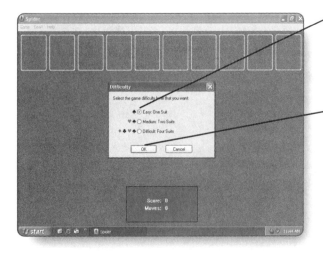

The game area is made up of ten columns of cards, each with one card turned up.

TIP

To move a card, click the card and drag it to the new location.

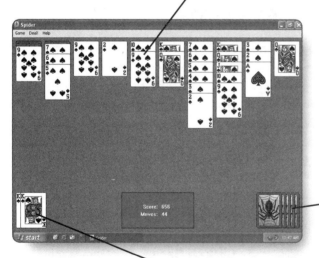

7. Move cards according to these rules:

- You can move a card from the bottom of a column to a free space.

- You can move a card from the bottom of a column to a card one higher, regardless of suit or color.

- You can move a set of cards all of the same suit, and in order, as if they were one card.

8. Click on the **turned down deck**, when there are no more moves to make. The next layer of cards is dealt.

To win, move the cards around until you line up each suit of cards in descending order, King to Ace. When you line up one suit, the line of cards slide down to the bottom of the screen, leaving room for you to arrange the next line of cards.

All finished?

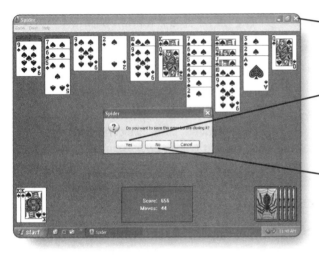

9. Click on the **Close box**. A dialog box asking whether you want to save the current game until next time will appear.

10a. Click on **Yes**. The current game will be saved before the program closes.

OR

10b. Click on **No**. The current game will not be saved before the program closes.

TIP

To return to the saved game, start Spider Solitaire and then click on Game, Open Last Saved Game.

Connecting to an Internet Game

You can play the game of classic hearts against yourself or other players on your network. You're not on a network? That's not a problem if you have Internet access. You can join other players across the world. Your identity is anonymous to other players.

1. Click on **Start**. The Start menu will appear.

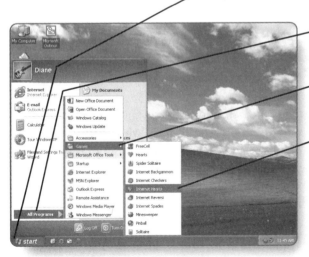

2. Click on **All Programs**. The Programs menu will appear.

3. Click on **Games**. The Games menu will appear.

4. Click on **Internet Hearts**. An MSN Gaming Zone dialog box will appear.

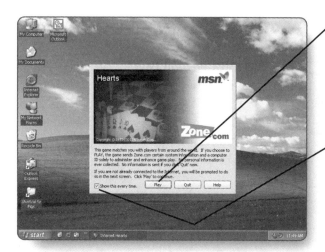

5. Click on **Play**. If you are not already connected to the Internet, a connection will be established.

> ### TIP
> To avoid seeing this dialog box in the future, remove the check mark from Show this every time.

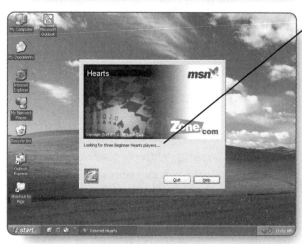

By default, Internet Hearts starts with a Beginner skill level. MSN Gaming Zone tries to match you up with three other Internet Hearts players with similar skills. When enough players have been contacted, the game board will open. You will be assigned a player number; no names are used, just player numbers.

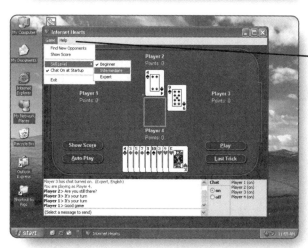

> ### TIP
> If you don't know how to play the game of hearts, click on the Help menu and look through the Hearts Help Topics.

Not a Beginner? You can change your skill level.

6. Click on **Game**. The Game menu will appear.

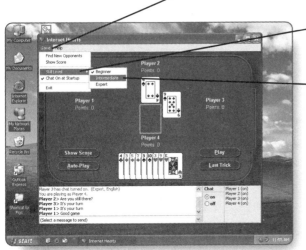

7. Click on **Skill Level**. The Skill Level sub-menu will appear.

8. Click on a **skill level**. The new skill level will not begin until the next time you start Internet Hearts.

NOTE

You may be prompted with a message box indicating that the new skill level will begin the next time you start Internet Hearts. Click on OK to continue with the current game.

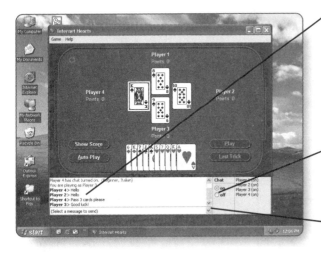

Chat is turned on by default when you start a game. With chat activated, you can select from key phrases to communicate with the other players.

TIP

Click on the Off button to turn off chat ability.

9. Click on the **phrase list**. A list of phrases will appear.

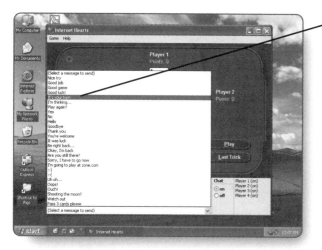

10. Click on a **chat phrase**. The phrase will appear in the chat window and is displayed to the other players. Other players' text is also displayed in the Chat window. If a player has his chat turned off, he will not be able to see your messages.

NOTE

Even if the other players speak a different language, the games translate the chat so it always appears in their language.

Exit the game in the same manner as other windows applications.

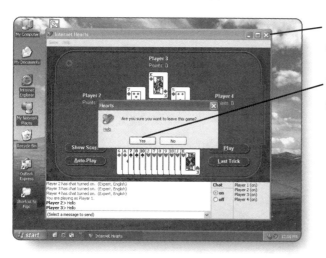

11. Click on the **Close box**. A confirmation message will appear.

12. Click on **Yes**. The Internet Hearts game window will close.

8

Discovering Multimedia

One of the most exciting reasons to use a computer today is *multimedia*. Multimedia is the capability of a computer application to combine with other media, such as video or sound. To enjoy the capabilities of multimedia, your computer needs a CD-ROM or DVD drive, a sound card, and speakers. In this chapter, you'll learn how to:

- Play a music CD
- Use the Media Player
- Listen to Internet radio
- Adjust the sound volume
- Add a media clip to a document

Using Media Player

Windows XP and the Windows Media Player can make beautiful music together. The Windows Media Player allows you to listen to CDs, tune in to Internet radio, download music and video from the Internet, or categorize and manage media stored on your computer.

Playing a Music CD

What's your style? No matter whether it's rock and roll, jazz, classical, or the blues, the Windows Media Player gives you several different ways to enjoy your music.

Starting a Music CD

Place your favorite music CD into the computer and listen while you work! With Internet access, the Windows Media Player can locate information about the album and artist you're currently playing.

1. Insert the audio **CD** into the CD-ROM drive. The Audio CD dialog box will open.

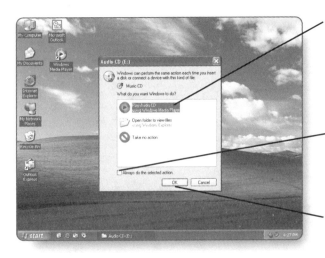

2. Click on **Play Audio CD using Windows Media Player**. The option will be selected.

> **TIP**
>
> To avoid seeing this dialog box in the future, click on Always do the selected action.

3. Click on **OK**. The Windows Media player will open and the audio CD will begin playing.

TIP

To Start the Media Player manually, click on the Windows Media Player button on the Quick Launch bar.

If you're not already connected to the Internet, you'll be prompted to connect. With an Internet connection, Windows XP can connect and provide more information about the disc you've inserted. See Chapter 22, "Surfing with Internet Explorer," to establish an Internet connection.

Windows Media Player searches the Internet for information on the current CD. After the Internet connection is established, the Windows Media Player identifies the following:

- The CD title
- The current song title
- The artist

Discovering Visualizations

Visualizations are the splashes of color and geometric shapes you see on the Windows Media Player that change with the beat of the audio currently playing. You can choose from dozens of visualizations.

1. Click on the **arrows** below the visualization window. The next available visualization will appear.

The visualization name appears next to the arrow.

2. Continue clicking on a **visualization window arrow** until you arrive at the visualization you want to use.

With each click, a different visualization will appear.

Choosing from the Playlist

Choose any song you want to hear from your CD. The right hand pane in the media player window lists each song on the current CD. If you connected to the Internet, Windows Media Player lists these tracks by name, otherwise the tracks are listed by number.

The current song name is highlighted.

1. Double-click on the **track** you want to hear. The track will begin playing.

TIP

Click on the **Show Playlist** button to hide or redisplay the playlist.

Working with the Media Player

Windows Media Player is an application that offers a single place to find, organize, and play digital media. It provides easy access to the most common digital media activities, including audio and video playback, CD playback and recording, Internet radio, and transfer of media files to portable devices and removable media.

The Windows Media Player window has many of the same buttons that you see on a standard CD player.

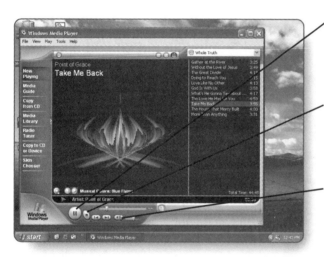

- **Pause/(Play)**. Stops the play, but remembers the current location. (This button turns into Play if the CD is not currently playing a song.)

- **Stop**. Stops the current song. The next time you click the Play button, the CD restarts at the beginning of the disc.

- **Mute**. Turns the volume on or off.

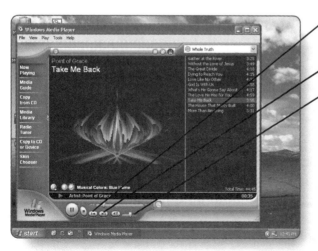

- **Previous Track**. Plays the preceding song.

- **Next Track**. Plays the next song.

- **Volume Control**. Controls the volume level.

Listening to Web Radio

With Internet access and the Windows Media Player, you can listen to music, news, or sports from thousands of live Internet radio stations from around the world.

1. **Click** on **Radio Tuner**. A list of preset radio stations will appear.

Selecting a Preset Radio Station

A number of various radio stations are preset with the Windows Media Player.

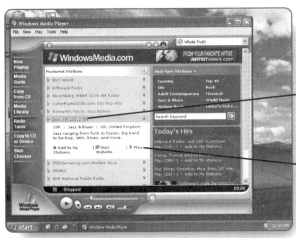

1. **Click** on a **radio station** from the presets window pane. A list of options will appear.

2. **Click** on **Play**. Internet Explorer will open and connect to a Web page associated with the radio station. In a short time, the radio broadcast will begin.

TIP

Click on the **Internet Explorer** button to view the Web page associated with the radio station.
---

3. **Click** on **Stop**. The radio broadcast will stop.

Searching for Radio Stations

Didn't find a preset station you like? You can search for other radio stations by their format or other variables.

1. Click on **Find More Stations**. A list of additional stations will appear.

2. Click on the **Browse by Genre** down arrow. A list of options will appear.

3. Click on your favorite **musical genre**. A list of available stations fitting your selections will appear.

4. Click on a **radio station**. A list of options will appear.

5. Click on **Play**. Internet Explorer will open and connect to a Web page associated with the radio station. In a short time, the radio broadcast will begin.

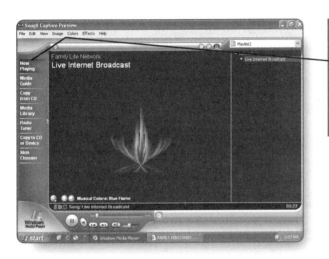

TIP

Click on Now Playing to see the visualizations and playlist (if available) for the currently selected radio station.

Applying Skins

Windows Media Player includes two different modes of viewing the player—full mode and compact mode. Up until now, you've been viewing the player in full mode, the non-customizable view that allows access to all Windows Media Player features. The second view, compact mode, uses Windows Media Player *skins*. Skins are files that customize the look and functionality of the Windows Media Player.

1. Click on **Skin Chooser**. A preview and list of skins will appear.

2. Click on a **skin name**. The skin name will be highlighted.

A preview of the skin appears in the right window pane.

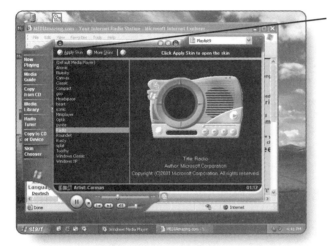

3. Click on **Apply Skin**. The Media Player will switch to compact mode with the skin appearing on your desktop.

The Media Player is displayed in compact mode with the selected skin.

The Control window is displayed.

4. Click on the **Control window icon**. A submenu will appear.

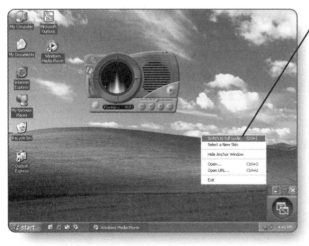

5. Click on **Switch to full mode**. The Media Player will return to full mode.

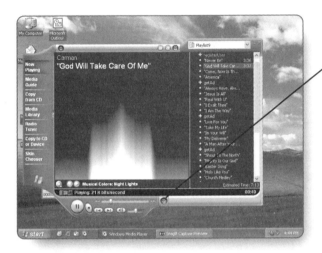

TIP

Click on the Switch to Skin mode button to return to Compact mode.

6. Click the **Close button**. The Media Player window will close.

Using the Windows Volume Control

It's almost like having a remote control right at your fingertips! The volume control allows you to choose different settings for the sounds and other audible objects you play on your computer. You'll learn how to assign sounds to your computer functions in Chapter 14, "Having Fun with the Control Panel."

1. Click on the **volume icon** in the Notification Area. The volume slider will appear.

TIP

If you can't see the volume icon, click on the arrow to display hidden icons.

2. **Click** and **drag** the **volume slider** up or down. The volume level will increase or decrease.

TIP

Click the **Mute check box** to mute all speaker volume.

---

3. **Click anywhere** on the **desktop**. The Volume slider will close.

4. **Double-click** on the **volume icon** in the Notification Area. The Master Out volume control window will open.

The Master Out window allows you to balance and adjust other mixer properties in addition to the volume. The options available in the Volume Control window vary with the type of sound card installed in your computer.

5. **Adjust** the **settings** as you desire.

6. **Click** on the **Close button**. The Master Out window closes.

TIP

You can also open the Master Out Volume Control window by clicking on Start, All Programs, Accessories, Entertainment, Volume Control.

Adding a Media Clip to a Document

Today's applications, such as Word, WordPerfect, Excel, Lotus 1-2-3, and many others, have the capability to embed media files within documents. Adding sound or video to a file sent electronically can add more pizzazz. The only limitation is that the person receiving the file must have multimedia capabilities (speakers and a sound card).

1. **Locate** the **media file** you want to include in your document. Use Windows Explorer or the Windows Search feature to help locate your desired file. If the file is located in My Documents, open the My Documents folder.

NOTE

Using the Windows Explorer window is discussed in Chapter 9, "Organizing Files and Folders."

2. **Right-click** on the **media file** you want to place in the document. A shortcut menu will appear.

3. **Click** on **Copy**. Although it looks like nothing happened, Windows copied the media file to the Windows Clipboard.

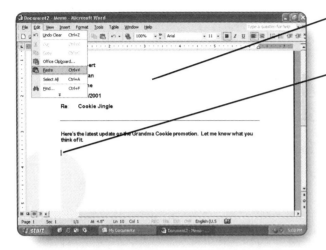

4. Create or open the **document** in which you want to place the media file.

5. Click the **mouse** where you want to place the media file. The insertion point will appear in the selected location.

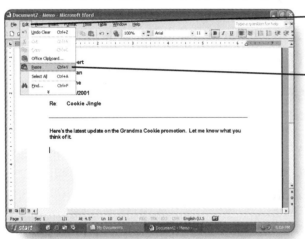

6. Click on **Edit**. The Edit menu will appear.

7. Click on **Paste**. An object box will appear in the document.

The appearance of the object in the document varies between applications and the type of media file.

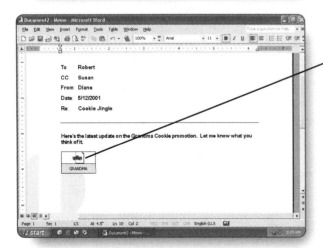

TIP
Double-click on the media clip to play it.

Part II Review Questions

1. What key can be pressed to clear the totals on the Windows calculator? *See "Using the Calculator" in Chapter 4*

2. What are the two types of Windows calculator that can be displayed? *See "Changing the Style of the Calculator" in Chapter 4*

3. Name two types of documents you can create with WordPad. *See "Starting WordPad" in Chapter 5*

4. In WordPad, pressing the Backspace key will delete text in which direction? *See "Deleting Text" in Chapter 5*

5. What key can you press to draw a perfect circle in Paint? *See "Drawing a Rectangle or Circle" in Chapter 6*

6. In a Paint drawing, what can you do when you position the mouse over any of the eight handles on a selection box? *See "Selecting and Moving an Object" in Chapter 8*

7. What Windows XP games can you play across the Internet, via the MS Gaming Zone? *See "Playing Around with the Games" in Chapter 7*

8. How do you win a game of Spider Solitaire? *See "Playing Spider Solitaire" in Chapter 7*

9. What can you do with the Windows Media Player? *See "Using Media Player" in Chapter 8*

10. What are Media Player skins? *See "Applying Skins" in Chapter 8*

PART III

Managing Files

Chapter 9
Organizing Files and Folders **109**

Chapter 10
Managing the Recycle Bin **129**

Chapter 11
Searching for Items **135**

9

Organizing Files and Folders

The process of organizing computer files has quite a history. First there was the DOS DIR command with all of its switches and syntax. Later came File Manager with Windows 3.x, and when Windows 95 came along with its graphic appearance, so did the Explorer. Each Windows upgrade made managing files easier than the previous version.

Windows, and the newest XP version, has done it again. The Windows graphical interface in Windows XP is more powerful yet. In this chapter, you'll learn how to:

- Explore My Computer
- Discover the Windows Explorer application
- View the contents of drives and folders
- Select, move, copy, and rename files and folders
- Modify the ways files and folders are displayed on your PC

Looking at My Computer

Windows organizes some of the specifics of your computer in a window called My Computer.

Exploring My Computer

From the My Computer window, you can see each disk drive on your computer and tell whether it is a floppy disk drive, a hard disk drive, or a CD-ROM drive. You can browse through your files and folders from each of these disk drives.

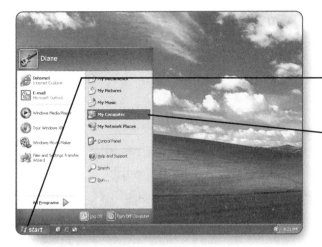

1. Click on the **Start menu**. The Start menu will appear.

2. Click on **My Computer**. The My Computer window will open.

TIP

If your Windows XP is an upgrade from a previous Windows version you can also double-click on the My Computer icon to open the My Computer Window.

Windows XP divides the drive and storage devices into separate areas on the screen. An icon will represent each drive or storage area on your computer.

NOTE

Depending on the configuration of your computer, your screen may be slightly different from the setup shown here. Windows automatically assigns drive letters to each storage device on your machine.

- **Drive C.** The local hard drive. Some computers have more than one hard drive. Hard drives vary greatly in capacity. The one shown here holds 9.3 gigabytes of information.

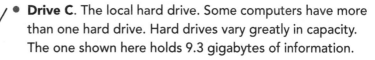

- **Drive A.** Holds a removable 3.5 inch floppy disk. Most floppy disk drives hold about 1.4 megabytes of information.

- **Drive D.** Holds a removable Zip disk drive. Zip drives hold up to 250mbs of storage. Not all computers come with a Zip disk drive. They are an optional purchase.

- **Drive E.** Holds a CD-ROM disk. This is the drive where you'll play your music CD's like you learned about in Chapter 8, "Discovering Multimedia." You'll also be able to load programs from CD or work with data. CD disks hold approximately 650 megabytes of information.

- **Network drives.** If you have drives mapped from other computers on your network, you'll also see them in the My Computer window. You'll learn more about mapping drives in Chapter 21, "Using a Network."

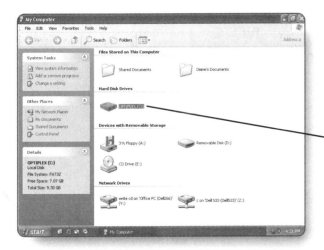

Viewing Disk Drive Contents

You'll need to open a disk drive icon to view its contents.

1. Double-click on a **drive icon**. The drive window will open.

If this is the first time you've opened the drive icon you may see a screen indicating that the files are hidden. If not, skip to step 3.

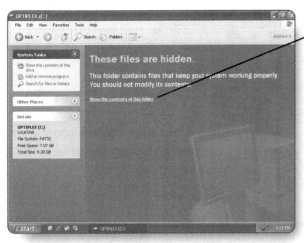

2. Click on **Show the contents of this folder**. A listing of all the folders, along with any files located in the top-level folder of the drive, will appear.

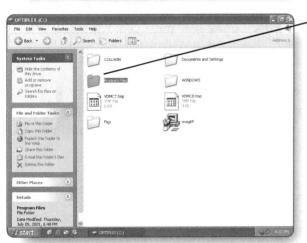

3. Double-click on a **folder**. A window for that folder will appear and show any files or other folders in it.

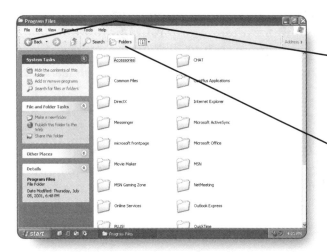

TIP

If you open the wrong folder, click on the Back button to return to the previous window.

4. Click on the **Folders button**. The Task pane on the left will close.

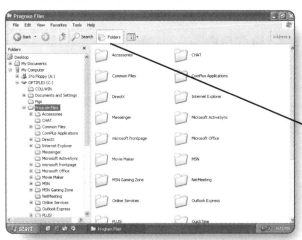

A window will open with a list of the drives and folders on the left and the contents of the selected drive or folder on the right. This is the Windows Explorer view, which you'll learn about later in this chapter.

5. Click on the **Folders button** again. The Explorer view will close and the Task pane will redisplay.

Browsing the Task Pane

Several Windows windows include a Task pane that provides quick access to other tasks you might want to use, based on the task you are currently using.

You can expand or collapse the various headings in a task pane.

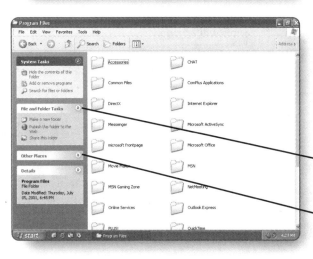

1. Click on the **Up arrows**. The task section will collapse.

2. Click on the **Down arrows**. The task section will expand.

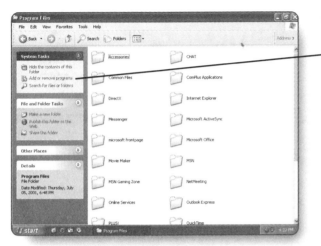

NOTE

Other chapters in this book will show you how to accomplish many of the tasks listed here.

3. Click on the **Close button**. The My Computer window will close.

Peeking in the Explorer Window

The Windows Explorer is a graphic illustration of the file and folder contents of the storage devices on, or connected to, your computer.

In the previous section, you learned how to display Explorer view. Another way is to open the Explorer window from the Start menu.

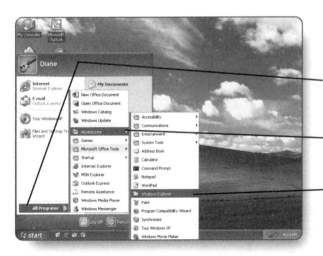

1. Click on the **Start button**. The Start menu will appear.

2. Click on **All Programs**. The Programs menu will appear.

3. Click on **Accessories**. The Accessories menu will appear.

4. Click on **Windows Explorer**. The Explorer window will open.

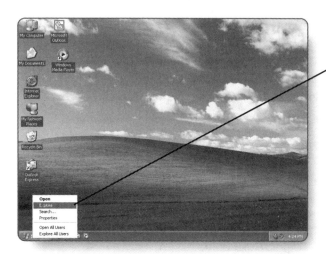

TIP

Another quick way to open Explorer is to right-click the Start button, and then click on Explore from the shortcut menu.

NOTE

Your Explorer window may not display all the elements listed in this section. You'll learn how to change the look of the Explorer window later in this chapter.

TIP

Click on any folder in the Folders window to view its contents.

Identifying Explorer Components

An assortment of information is displayed in the Explorer window, including the following:

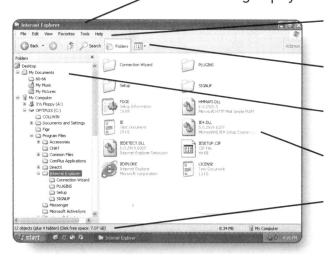

- **Title Bar**. Contains the title of the current drive or folder being displayed.

- **Menu bar.** Contains Explorer's drop-down menus.

- **Toolbar.** Contains shortcuts to commonly used features.

- **Folders window.** Displays available drives and folders on your computer.

- **Files window.** Displays the contents of the selected drive or folder.

- **Status bar.** Displays such information as the number and size of selected files.

Expanding Folder Levels

You'll notice that in the Folders window many items have a plus sign next to them. This indicates that there are more folders within them. It's like a tree with its branches—each branch expands from a larger one.

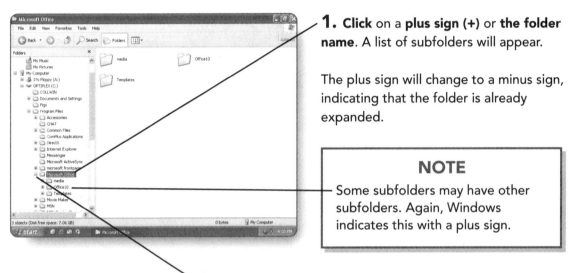

1. **Click** on a **plus sign (+)** or **the folder name**. A list of subfolders will appear.

The plus sign will change to a minus sign, indicating that the folder is already expanded.

NOTE

Some subfolders may have other subfolders. Again, Windows indicates this with a plus sign.

2. **Click** on the **minus sign (-)**. The subfolder will collapse and a plus sign will reappear.

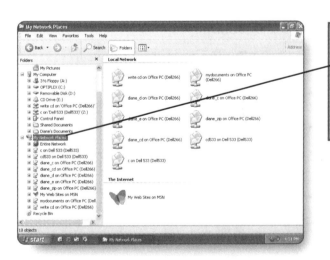

TIP

Open the My Network Places icon from the Folders window to view the contents of folders on another computer.

Selecting Files and Folders

To open, copy, move, or otherwise manipulate a file or folder, you must first select it. You can also select multiple files at once, even if those files are not adjacent. Selected files are highlighted in a different color.

1. Open the **folder** that has the file or folder with which you want to work. The contents will appear on the right side of the screen.

2. Click on the desired **item**. The item will be selected. The status bar will indicate information on the selected item.

3. Press and hold down the **Shift key**. Using the Shift key allows you to select a sequential group of files.

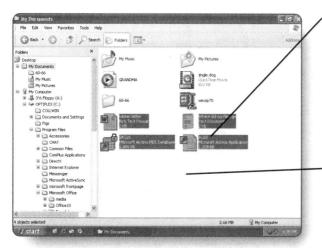

4. Click on **another item**. All items between the first and second clicks will be selected.

5. Release the **Shift key**. Notice that the status bar has been updated to reflect the additional selections.

6. Click on a **blank area** of the window. The items will be deselected.

Instead of the Shift key, you can use the Ctrl key to select files and folders that are not adjacent to each other.

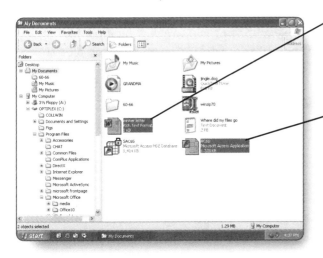

7. Click on an **item**. The item will be selected.

8. Press and hold down the **Ctrl key**.

9. Click on another **item**. Only the two clicked items will be selected.

10. Release the **Ctrl key**. Notice that the status bar indicates the additional selections.

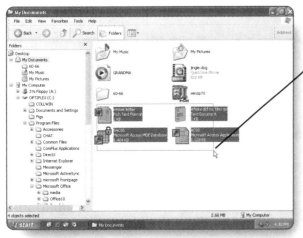

TIP

You can also select one or more adjacent files by clicking next to (but not on top of) the first file and dragging across all the desired files.

Moving or Copying Files and Folders

Files or folders can be moved or copied from one location to another. For example, you can copy a file from your hard drive to a floppy disk. Or you can move a file you've been working on to a network drive. Whether you are working with a file or a folder, the steps are the same.

NOTE

If you move or copy a folder, all the contents of that folder are moved or copied as well. In addition, if the folder contains subfolders, the subfolder structure is also moved or copied to the new location.

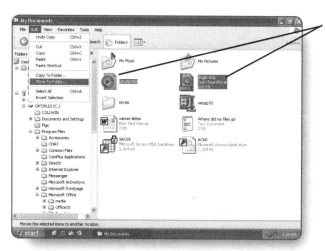

1. Select the **item(s)** to be moved or copied. The item(s) will be highlighted.

2. Click on the **Edit menu**. The Edit menu will appear.

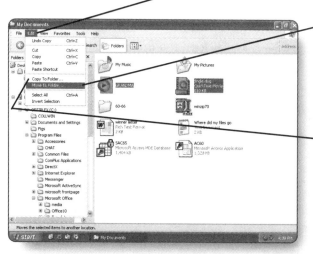

3a. Click on **Move To Folder**, if you want to move the selected item. The Browse For Folder dialog box will open.

OR

3b. Click on **Copy To Folder**, if you want to copy the selected item. The Browse For Folder dialog box will open.

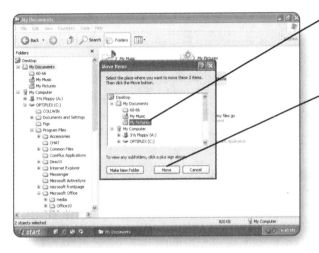

4. **Locate and click** on the **drive** or **folder** in which you want to place the file. The drive or folder will be selected.

5. **Click** on **Move** or **Copy** (Depending on which option you selected in step 3). The Browse For Folder dialog box will close and the files will appear in the new location.

TIP

Another way to move a file to a different folder is to drag the selected file until it is on top of the desired folder.

Creating New Folders

For organizational purposes, it's nice to have your own folders to separate your data. For example, most Windows programs store the data files you create in a folder called *My Documents*—but it might be handy to have folders within the My Documents folder to separate memos from proposals.

1. **Click** on the **drive** or **folder** in which you want to create a subfolder. The folder will open and the folder contents will appear.

2. **Click** on **File**. The File menu will appear.

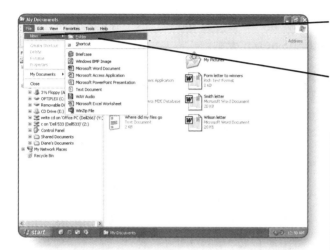

3. Click on **New**. The New submenu will appear.

4. Click on **Folder**. A new folder will appear in the Files window.

TIP

Another method to create a new folder is to right-click in the Files window and choose New, and then choose Folder.

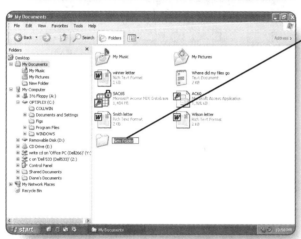

5. Type a **name** for the new folder. The words "New Folder" will be replaced with the name you type.

6. Press the **Enter key**. The new folder and its name will be accepted and displayed.

Renaming Files and Folders

If you have incorrectly named a file or folder, you can easily rename it using the Windows Explorer.

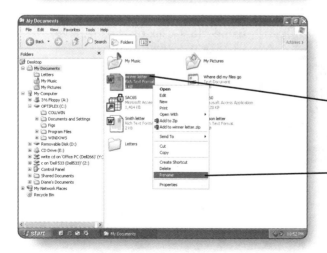

1. Right-click the **file or folder** you want to rename. A shortcut menu will appear.

2. Click on **Rename**. The file or folder name will remain selected and a blinking insertion point will appear at the end of the current name.

3. **Type** the **new file or folder name**. The old name will be replaced with the new name.

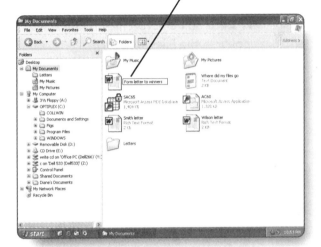

NOTE

If the original file name has an extension (a period and three characters at the end), be sure to include that extension with the new file name. If you don't, Windows could lose the association for the file and not know which program to use when opening it. For example, if the file was originally called MYMEMO and you are renaming it MEMO TO BOB SMITH, that's fine; but if it was originally MYMEMO. DOC, you should rename it MEMO TO BOB SMITH.DOC.

4. **Press** the **Enter key**. Your changes will be accepted.

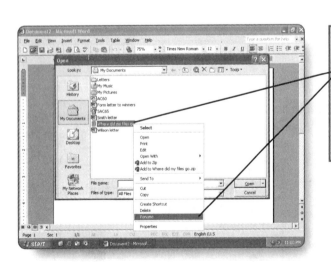

TIP

You can also rename a file from any Open or Save As dialog box in a Windows program. Select the file name, right-click on the file, and click on Rename.

Modifying the Explorer Display

The Explorer window has several different toolbars that can be displayed. Toolbars make it easier to get to your programs, files, folders, and favorite Web pages.

Displaying Toolbars

By default, Explorer displays only the Standard Buttons toolbar. To display or turn off a toolbar, look in the View menu.

1. Click on **View**. The View menu will appear.

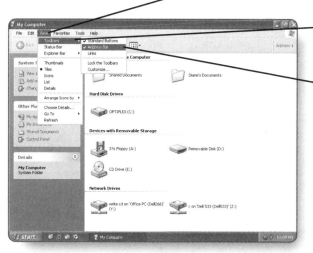

2. Click on **Toolbars**. The Toolbars submenu will appear.

3. Click on any desired **toolbar**. The toolbar will appear onscreen.

- **Standard Buttons.** Shows toolbar buttons such as Back, Forward, Up, Search, Folders, and Views.

- **Address Bar.** Indicates the current folder being displayed. With this toolbar, you can type a Web page address without opening Internet Explorer first.

- **Links.** Provides shortcuts to important Web sites.

Moving Toolbars

The Standard toolbar may prevent you from seeing the features of other toolbars. If you can't see a toolbar's features, you may want to move it to a better location. First, however, you'll need to unlock it. By default, toolbars are locked in their position to prevent accidental moving.

TIP

A check mark (✔) beside an item indicates the choice is active. Clicking on the item again removes the check mark and hides the toolbar.

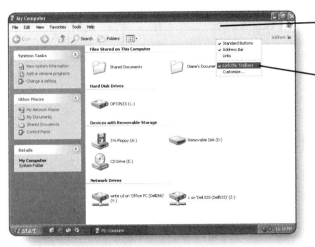

1. Right-click anywhere on a **toolbar**. A shortcut menu will appear.

2. Click on **Lock the Toolbars**. The option will be deselected.

3. Press and hold the **mouse pointer** over the toolbar name. The mouse pointer will turn into a four-headed arrow.

4. Press and drag the **toolbar** down about ½ inch until the toolbar changes shape.

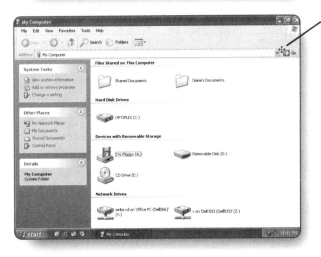

5. Release the **mouse button**. The toolbar will expand.

Changing the Way Files Are Displayed

There are five different ways of looking at your files in the Files window:

- **Tiles View.** Shows the file name and optional extension beneath a large, easy-to-see icon associated with the file. Available file information is listed under each icon. Files are listed in a horizontal, multiple-column format.

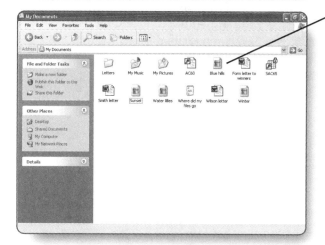

- **Icons View.** Shows the file name and optional extension beside a smaller icon associated with the file. No file information is displayed. Files are listed in a horizontal, multiple-column format.

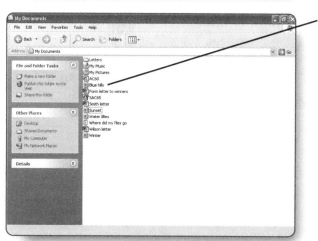

- **List View.** Icons are even smaller than Icons view but the files are listed in a vertical-column format.

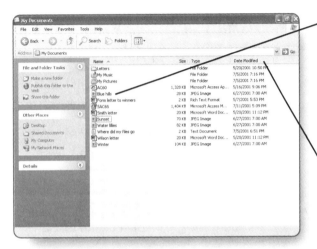

- **Details View.** Displays more information about the files, including the size, type, last modification date, and, optionally, the attributes of the file. Files are listed in a vertical, single-column format.

TIP

You can change the display width of any column in Details view by positioning the mouse over the bar on the right side of the column description and clicking and dragging the mouse until the column is the desired width.

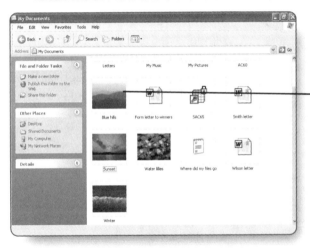

- **Thumbnails View.** Displays graphics files as the files would appear, rather than as an icon.

Choose one of the five ways of looking at your files.

1. Click on **View**. The View menu will appear.

2. Click on an **option**. The Files window will change to the selected view.

TIP

You can also click on the Views button to select your icon view choice.

Sorting Files

By default, files are sorted in alphabetical order by file name. You can also sort them by type, size, or date. Headings are displayed at the top of each column.

1. Click on **View**. The View menu will appear.

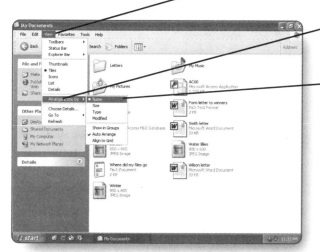

2. Click on **Arrange Icons by**. The Arrange Icons by submenu will appear.

3. Click on **Name**, **Type**, **Size**, or **Modified**. The files in the Files window will be displayed in the order you selected.

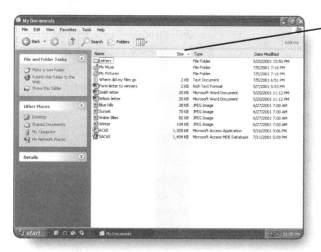

TIP

If you are in Details view, click on any heading to sort by that column in ascending order. Click on the same heading again to sort by that column in descending order.

Modifying Folder Options

By changing the folder options, you can decide whether a file should be accessible with a single-click or double-click, which type of files to display, and whether the file names should display an extension.

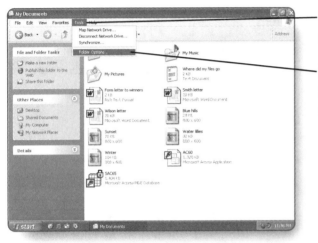

1. Click on **Tools**. The Tools menu will appear.

2. Click on **Folder Options**. The Folder Options dialog box will open with the General tab displayed.

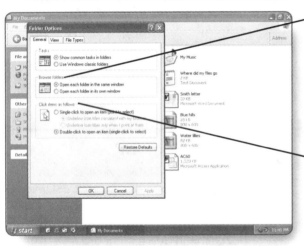

● In the Browse folders option, you can set the option so that each time you open a folder, the folder opens in a separate window. The option can also be set so that each time you open a folder, the folder opens in the existing window.

● In the Click items as follows section, you can determine whether to single-click or double-click to activate an icon.

3. Click on an **option**. The option will be selected.

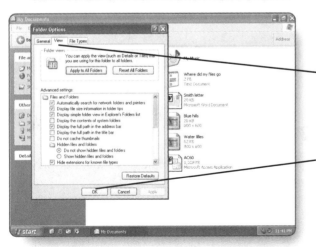

TIP

Optionally, you can click on the View tab to set more display options, including showing file extensions.

4. Click on **OK**. The Folder Options dialog box will close, and the view changes to your specifications.

10

Managing the Recycle Bin

Everyone has a trash can into which they throw unwanted items. It's the same in Windows XP: on your desktop is an icon that looks like a small trash can—the Windows Recycle Bin. The Recycle Bin is an area that temporarily holds unwanted items. In this chapter you'll learn how to:

- Delete files and folders
- Restore deleted items
- Empty the Recycle Bin

Deleting Files and Folders

You'll want to clean up your computer periodically by deleting old data files. Make sure you know exactly which file you want to delete. It's a bad idea to delete a file or folder just because you don't know what it is or does. The file could be critical to making your computer, or one of its applications, function correctly.

Deleting Items from a Window

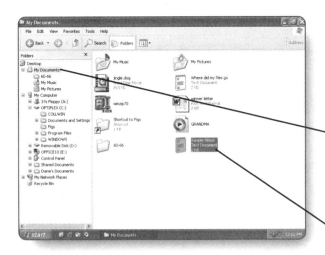

Items can be deleted using the Windows Explorer, or from any open window. When you delete files or folders from your hard drive, Windows places them in the Recycle Bin.

1. Open the **drive and folder** that has the file or folder you want to delete. The file name will appear on the right side of the screen.

2. Click on the **file or folder** you want to delete. The file name will be selected.

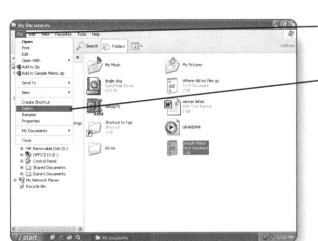

3. Click on the **File menu**. The File menu will appear.

4. Click on **Delete**. A Confirm File Delete dialog box will open.

TIP

Optionally, select a file and press the Delete key on the keyboard.

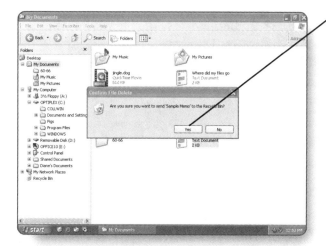

5. Click on **Yes**. The file will be deleted from its folder and placed in the Recycle Bin, unless you are deleting a file from a removable disk such as a floppy disk. Those files are *not* placed in the Recycle Bin; they are permanently deleted.

Deleting Items from an Application

You can also delete a file from most open Windows applications.

1. Click on **File**. The File menu will appear.

2. Click on **Open or Save As**. The Open or Save As dialog box will open.

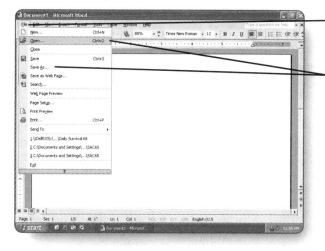

3. Right-click on the unwanted **file name**. A shortcut menu will appear.

4. Click on **Delete**. The confirmation message will appear.

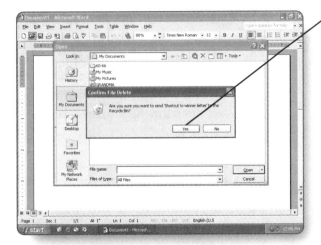

5. Click on **Yes**. The file will be deleted.

Deleting an Item From the Desktop

Unwanted shortcuts, files, and other items can easily be deleted from the Windows desktop.

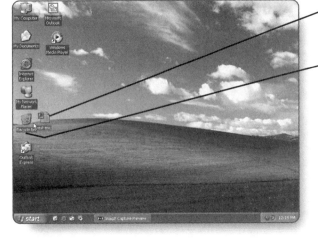

1. Click on the unwanted **item**. The item will be highlighted.

2. Drag the **item** until it is on top of the Recycle Bin. The item will be placed in the Recycle Bin.

NOTE

If you highlight the item and press the Delete key (instead of dragging it directly to the Recycle Bin), a confirmation message will appear.

Recovering an Item from the Recycle Bin

If you want to recover an item from your trash can at home or work you can just reach in and pull it out. You work with the Windows Recycle Bin the same way. Since items remain in the Recycle Bin until you empty it, this "just in case" feature can save you a great deal of grief when you realize you deleted the wrong file or deleted a file too soon.

1. Double-click on the **Recycle Bin icon**. The Recycle Bin window will open, displaying the contents of the Recycle Bin.

NOTE

When the Recycle Bin is empty, the trash can icon looks empty. When the Recycle Bin has items in it, pieces of paper stick out the top of the can.

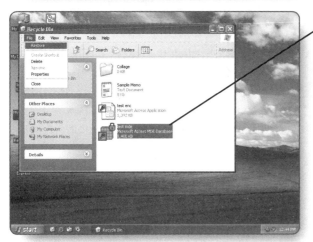

2. Click on the **item** you want to recover. The item will be highlighted.

3. Click on **File**. The File menu will appear.

4. Click on **Restore**. The file will be removed from the Recycle Bin and placed in the folder from which it was originally deleted.

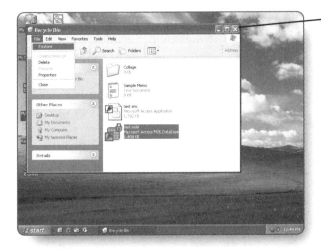

5. Click on the **Close button**. The Recycle Bin window will close.

Emptying the Recycle Bin

Items stored in the Recycle Bin are using disk space on your computer. It's a good idea to periodically empty the Recycle Bin. Be aware, though, that once the Recycle Bin has been emptied, the items that were in it are permanently deleted.

1. Right-click the **Recycle Bin**. A shortcut menu will appear.

2. Click on **Empty Recycle Bin**. A confirmation message will appear.

3. Click on **Yes**. The files are permanently deleted from the computer. The Recycle Bin is now empty.

11

Searching for Items

Programs and documents sometimes get buried quite deep in the folder structure of your hard drive. In order to work efficiently you must know how quickly to find files on your computer. With Windows XP you can let your computer do all the searching for you, whether you're trying to locate a specific file, a group of files, or even a name from the Windows Address Book. In this chapter, you'll learn how to:

- Find a file or folder
- Look for a file by date
- Search for a name in the Address Book

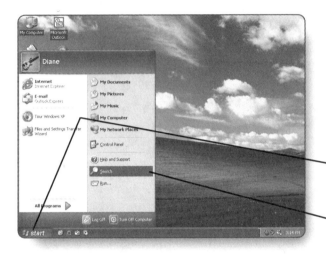

Finding a File or Folder

Windows has a powerful tool called Search to help you locate those misplaced files and folders.

1. Click on the **Start button**. The Start menu will appear.

2. Click on **Search**. The Search results window will open.

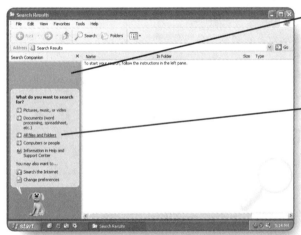

On the left side of the Search Results window you'll see the Search Companion (an animated character) and a list of search options.

3. Click on **All files and folders**. A list of search criteria will appear.

You can search for a file (or folder) based on the name of the file or the contents in the file. For example, you can look for a file with the word "bear" in the title or for a document with the word "bear" in its contents. If you search for the word "bear" in the body text, Windows will also list any documents with "bear" in the title.

4a. Type any or all of the **file name** or **folder name**. The text is displayed in the All or part of the file name text box.

OR

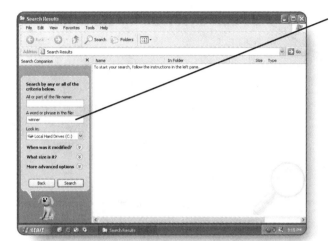

4b. **Click** in the **A word or phrase in the file text box** and **type** the requested **word** or **phrase.** This tells the Search companion to look beyond the file name into the actual documents.

NOTE

If you type multiple words in either text box, Windows will find all files that have any of those words in the file name or contents.

You have the option of specifying where to look for the text. You can search any specific disk drive or the entire computer.

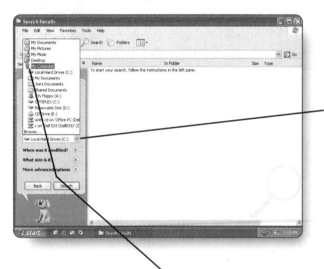

5. **Click** on the **down arrow** next to the Look in list box. A list of locations will appear.

6. **Click** on a **drive or folder**. The selection will appear in the list box.

TIP

If you want to search all of your available drives (including network drives), choose My Computer.

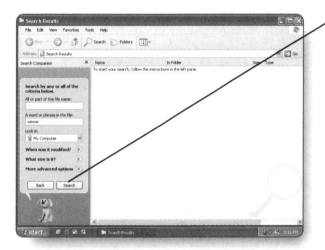

7. Click on **Search**. The search will begin.

> ### NOTE
> If you are searching in the body of the document, the search may be quite lengthy depending on how many files are stored on the searched disk or folder.

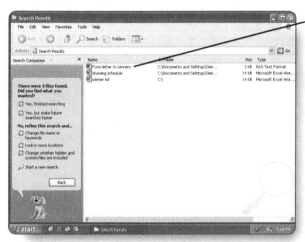

The results of the search are displayed on the right side of the window. The name of the file is listed, as well as its folder location, size, type, and the date it was last modified.

> ### TIP
> Double-click on a file to open it in the application it was created.

Looking for a File by Date

You can also find files based on the date on which they were created or even by the last time you modified them. For example, you might need to find a file you worked on last week. Let Windows do the work for you!

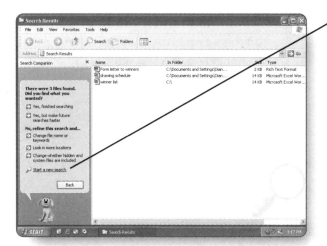

1. **Click** on **Start a New search**. The Search Companion will return to the original window.

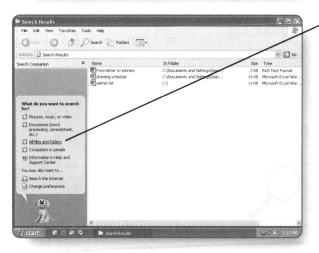

2. **Click** on **All files and folders**. A list of search criteria will appear.

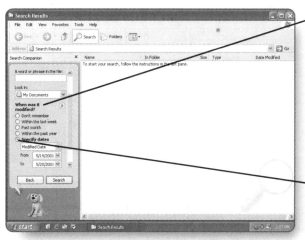

3. **Click** on **When was it modified?** A list of options will appear.

You can specify four types of time frames: Specific dates (for example June 3rd through July 16th), within the last week, past month or within the past year.

4. **Click** on **Specify Dates**. Options for searching by date will appear.

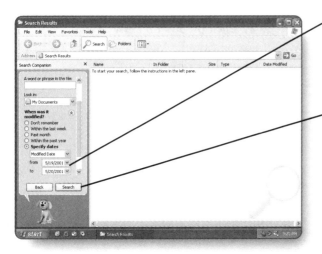

5. In both the From and To boxes, **click** on the **down arrows** and **click** on a **date** to begin and end the search. The option will be selected.

6. Click on **Search**. The search will begin.

All files meeting your date criteria are displayed in the right pane of the search window.

7. Click on the **Close button**. The Search Results window will close.

Searching for People in the Address Book

You can use the Find feature to search the Windows Address Book for a particular person's name, address, phone numbers, or e-mail addresses. Adding information to the Address Book is covered in Chapter 25, "Using the Windows Address Book."

1. **Click** on the **Start button**. The Start menu will appear.

2. **Click** on **Search**. The Search results window will open.

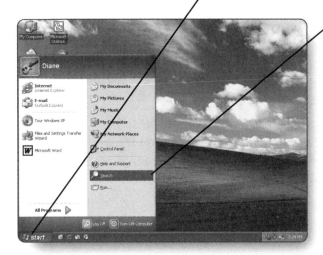

3. **Click** on **Computers or People**. Another message will display in the Search Companion window.

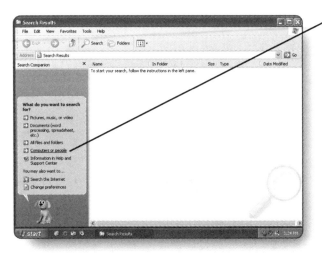

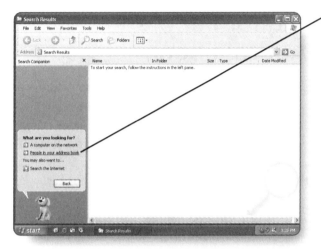

4. Click on **People in your address book**. The Find People dialog box will open.

There are a several ways you can search the Address Book:

- Type any part of a name. For example, to find anyone with George as part of his first or last name, type **George** in the Name: text box.

- Type any part of a e-mail address. For example, to find everyone whose e-mail address is at America Online, type **AOL** in the E-mail: text box.

- Type in both the name and e-mail fields to be more specific. For example, to find your friend George who subscribes to America Online, type **George** in the Name: text box AND type **AOL** in the E-mail: text box.

4. Type the **information** you are searching for in the appropriate text boxes.

5. Click on **Find Now**. The search will begin.

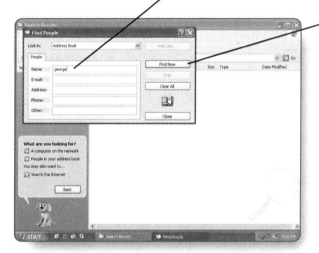

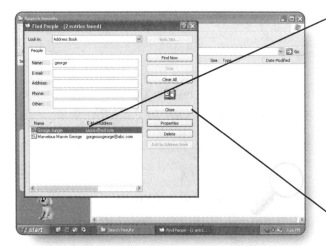

The Find People dialog box expands and any Address Book entries that match the requested criteria are displayed at the bottom.

TIP

Double-click on a name to see the entire Address Book entry.

6. Click on **Close**. The Find People dialog box will close.

7. Click on the **Close button**. The Search Results window will close.

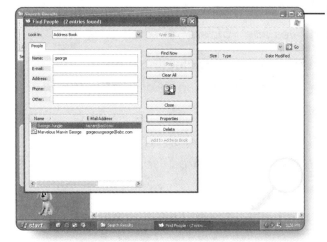

Part III Review Questions

1. What icon do you open to view a list of disk drives on your computer? *See "Exploring the My Computer Icon" in Chapter 9*

2. What does a Task Pane do? *See "Browsing the Task Pane" in Chapter 9*

3. What program is a graphic illustration of the files and folder contents of your computer? *See "Looking in the Explorer Window" in Chapter 9*

4. What key can you press down to assist when selecting a sequential group of files? *See "Selecting Files and Folders" in Chapter 9*

5. What key can you press down to assist when selecting a non-sequential group of files? *See "Selecting Files and Folders" in Chapter 9*

6. What type of information is displayed when you show your files in Detail View? *See "Changing the Way Files Are Displayed" in Chapter 9*

7. When a file is deleted, where is it placed? *See "Deleting Items From a Window" in Chapter 10*

8. How do you empty the Recycle Bin? *See "Emptying the Recycle Bin" in Chapter 10*

9. How do you specify you want to search for a file on all drives, including network drives? *See "Finding a File or Folder" in Chapter 11*

10. When searching for a file by modification date, what are the four time frames you can specify? *See "Looking for a File by Date" in Chapter 11*

PART IV

Customizing Windows

Chapter 12
Customizing the Desktop **147**

Chapter 13
Tinkering with the Control Panel **159**

Chapter 14
Having Fun with the Control Panel. . . . **179**

Chapter 15
Setting Accessibility Options **189**

12

Customizing the Desktop

If you upgraded from a previous version of Windows I'm sure you've noticed that there are many different items on the Windows desktop. In Chapter 1, "Discovering Desktop Components," you took a brief look at some of the desktop items, such as My Network Places, My Computer, the Taskbar, and the Notification Area. You'll find you will use the right mouse button quite a bit when working with these and other items on the Windows desktop. In this chapter, you'll learn how to:

- Display desktop icons
- Create new desktop folders
- Move, delete and rename icons
- Create a shortcut
- Customize the Taskbar

Displaying Desktop Items

Windows XP, when installed new and not as an upgrade, does not display any desktop icons except for the Recycle Bin. Many users like the new cleaner look, while others prefer to have their commonly used icons displayed on the desktop.

If your desktop doesn't have the My Computer and other icons, you can easily place them on your desktop.

1. Right-click on a **blank area** of your desktop. A shortcut menu will appear.

2. Click on **Properties**. The Display Properties dialog box will open.

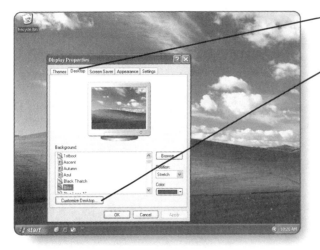

3. Click on the **Desktop tab**. The Desktop tab will appear in front.

4. Click on **Customize Desktop**. The Desktop Items dialog box will open.

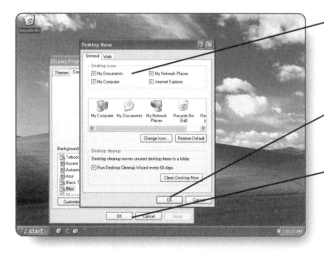

5. Click on the **item(s)** you want to display on your desktop. A check mark will appear next to the selected items.

6. Click on **OK**. The Desktop Items dialog box will close.

7. Click on **OK**. The Display Properties dialog box will close.

Creating Desktop Folders

In Chapter 9, "Organizing Files and Folders" you learned how to create a new folder in the Explorer window. Occasionally you might want a folder to organize some of the icons that appear on your Windows desktop.

1. Right-click on a **blank area of the desktop**. A shortcut menu will appear.

2. Click on **New**. The New submenu will appear.

3. Click on **Folder**. A new folder will appear on the desktop ready to be named.

4. **Type** a **name** for the new folder. The words "New Folder" will be replaced with the text you type.

5. **Press** the **Enter key**. The folder will be ready to use.

Creating a Shortcut

It can be annoying to dig through the profusion of selections on the Start menu just to get to your favorite program. Why not create a shortcut on your desktop? You can even create a shortcut for a document that you use frequently.

1. **Locate** the **file or item** for which you want to create a shortcut. (Hint: Use the Windows Explorer.)

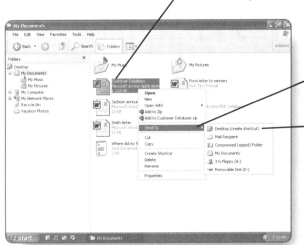

2. **Right-click** on the **item**. A shortcut menu will appear.

3. **Click** on **Send to**. The Send to shortcut menu will appear.

4. **Click** on **Desktop (create shortcut)**. Windows will place a shortcut icon on the desktop.

When you double-click on a shortcut, Windows will open the creating program and that specific file for you.

Modifying Icons

Icons appear all over the desktop— some icons you may want and some you may not. Icons can be moved or deleted with a click of the mouse.

Moving an Icon

If you want to move an icon to a different location, a feature called *Auto Arrange* must be turned off. If Auto Arrange is activated, you can move an icon but it may not remain where you move it.

1. **Right-click** over a **blank area of the desktop**. A shortcut menu will appear.

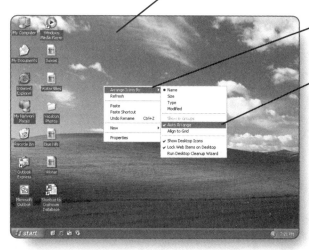

2. **Click** on **Arrange Icons by**. The Arrange Icons submenu will appear.

3a. If there is a check mark already next to it, **click** on **Auto Arrange**. The feature will be deactivated and the shortcut menu will close.

OR

3b. **Click anywhere** on the desktop, if no check mark appears next to Auto Arrange. The shortcut menu will close with no changes made.

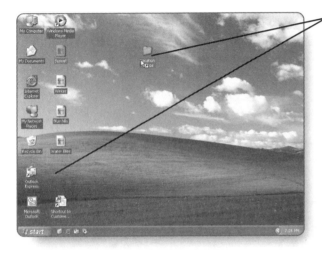

4. Click and drag the **icon** you want to move. The icon will move with the mouse pointer.

5. Release the **mouse button**. The icon will remain in the new location.

> **TIP**
>
> To move an icon into a folder on the desktop, drop the icon on top of the folder.

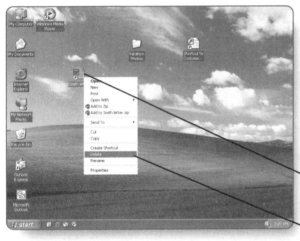

Deleting an Icon

If the icon you want to delete has a small black arrow in the lower-left corner of it, you will not be deleting the program or document to which the icon refers. You will be deleting only the shortcut to the program or document.

1. Right-click on the **icon** you want to delete. A shortcut menu will appear.

2. Click on **Delete**. The Confirm File Delete dialog box will open.

3. Click on **Yes**. The icon will be deleted and placed in the Recycle Bin.

> **TIP**
>
> To avoid the confirmation message, drag the unwanted items directly to the Recycle Bin.

Changing an Icon

Shortcuts that you create have an icon associated with them. If you've created a shortcut to a document, the icon used is the one associated with the document's program icon. You can select from other icons.

Shortcuts can be identified by a small arrow in the lower-left corner of the icon itself.

1. Right-click on the **icon** you want to change. A shortcut menu will appear.

2. Click on **Properties**. The Properties dialog box will open.

3. Click on the **Shortcut tab**, if necessary. The Shortcut tab will come to the front.

4. Click on **Change Icon**. The Change Icon dialog box will open.

5. Click on the **icon** you want to use. The icon will be highlighted.

NOTE

If you have other icon software on your computer, click on the Browse button to navigate to the folder that contains the other icons.

6. Click on **OK**. The Properties dialog box will appear again.

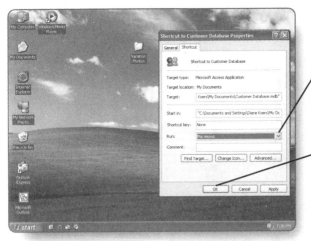

TIP

To always have a full screen when you launch the shortcut, click on the Run down arrow and then select Maximized.

7. Click on **OK**. The Properties dialog box will close, and the current icon will be replaced with the newly selected one.

Renaming an Icon

With the exception of the Recycle Bin, you can rename the text that displays under any icon on your desktop.

1. Right-click on the **icon** you want to change. A shortcut menu will appear.

2. Click on **Rename**. The current icon name will be highlighted.

3. Type a **new name** for the icon. The new name will replace the existing name.

4. Press the **Enter key**. The change will be accepted.

Customizing the Taskbar

With Windows XP you can control the actions of the Taskbar. You can decide when and where the Taskbar is displayed or even add more toolbars to the Taskbar.

Unlocking the Taskbar

It's so easy to move the Taskbar that many users found themselves moving it accidentally. To prevent accidental movement, Windows XP locks the taskbar in place. You can easily unlock it so that you can place it where you want.

1. Right-click on the **Taskbar**. A shortcut menu will appear.

2. Click on **Lock the Taskbar** to remove the check mark from the Lock the Taskbar option. The Taskbar will be unlocked.

Moving the Taskbar

By default, the Taskbar is located at the bottom of the screen. However, you can move it to any side of your screen.

NOTE

A locked Taskbar cannot be moved.

1. Press and **hold** the **mouse button** on a blank area of the Taskbar.

NOTE

Be sure the mouse pointer remains a white arrow and not a double-headed black arrow. Performing Step 2 with a double-headed black arrow results in the Taskbar being resized.

2. Drag the **Taskbar** to the desired side of the screen. The Taskbar will appear at the new location.

3. Release the **mouse button**. The Taskbar will remain at the new location.

Changing Taskbar Options

You can also control the behavior of the Taskbar.

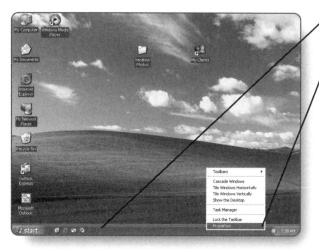

1. **Right-click** on the **Taskbar**. A shortcut menu will appear.

2. **Click** on **Properties**. The Taskbar and Start Menu Properties dialog box will open.

Some Taskbar display options include:

- **Lock the Taskbar.** Prevents accidental relocation of the Taskbar.

- **Auto-hide the Taskbar.** Allows the Taskbar to be hidden until you point to the location where the Taskbar usually resides, at which the Taskbar reappears.

- **Group similar Taskbar buttons**. Displays buttons for files opened in the same program in the same area of the Taskbar. If too many buttons are on the Taskbar, then all the buttons for the same program are combined into one button that you can click on to access any of the files.

- **Show Quick Launch**. Allows display of the Quick Launch bar. You learned about the Quick Launch bar in Chapter 1, "Discovering Desktop Components."

- **Keep the Taskbar on top of other windows.** Guarantees that the Taskbar is always visible, even when running a program in a maximized window.

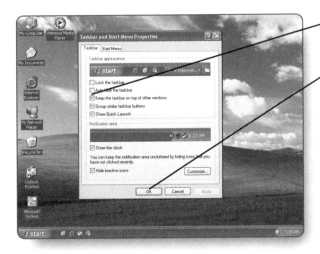

3. Click on the desired **options**. A check mark will appear in each selected choice.

4. Click on **OK**. The dialog box will close and the new options will be applied.

13

Tinkering with the Control Panel

How do you make your mouse less sensitive? How do you set the current date? You'll find the answers to these questions, as well as others related to fine-tuning your computer, in the Control Panel. In this chapter, you'll learn how to:

- Change the current date and time
- Change the way the mouse works
- Add new software and Windows components
- Set up multiple users

Opening the Control Panel

You can access the Control Panel from the Start menu or from the My Computer icon.

1. **Click** on the **Start button**. The Start menu will appear.

2. **Click** on **Control Panel**. The Control Panel window will open displaying commonly-used Control Panel options.

Windows XP groups options that are similar in category. In this book, we'll work with the Control Panel by switching to classic view.

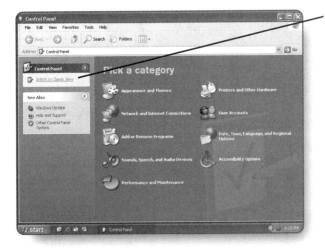

3. **Click** on **Switch to Classic View**. All available Control Panel options will appear.

Changing the Current Date and Time

It's important to have the correct date and time, especially when you need to insert the current date into a document on which you are working.

1. Double-click on **Date and Time.** The Date and Time Properties dialog box will open.

From here you have four options that you can set:

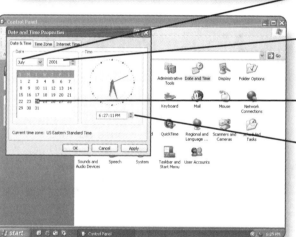

- **The current month**. Click on the down arrow to choose the current month.

- **The current year**. Click on the up/down arrows to select the current year.

- **The current day**. Click on the current day of the month.

- **The current time**. Click on the portion of the time you want to change, then click on the up/down arrows.

2. Make any desired **changes** to the date or time.

NOTE
Be sure you make adjustments according to your time zone. Windows knows when time changes (such as Daylight Savings Time) occur and will adjust the time accordingly. Click on the Time Zone tab to select your zone.

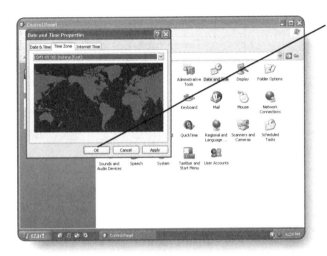

3. Click on **OK**. The Date and Time Properties dialog box will close.

> ## TIP
>
> A quick way to access the Date and Time Properties dialog box is to double-click on the current time in the Notification Area.

Changing Mouse Response

The mouse settings are stored in the Control Panel. You can make the mouse respond according to your preferences; for example, you can temper the motion of the mouse, select different pointers, or even reverse the mouse buttons.

1. Double-click on **Mouse**. The Mouse Properties dialog box will open.

The choices displayed in the Mouse Properties dialog box vary depending on the brand of mouse you have installed on your computer. The selections displayed in this section are specific to the Microsoft PS2 mouse.

Changing Basic Mouse Responses

The left mouse button is by default the primary key to selections, while the right mouse button is used to display a shortcut menu. This is easiest to perform if you use your right hand. Some people prefer to reverse the buttons and use their left hand.

1. If necessary, **click** on the **Buttons tab**. The Buttons tab will appear in front.

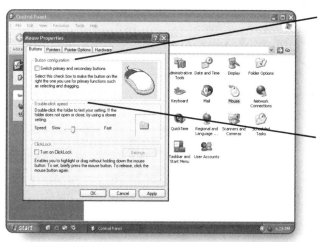

- **Choose** your **main mouse button**. Some mice properties ask you to specifically use left or right, while others, such as the one in this figure, simply ask you if you want to reverse the buttons.

- **Select** the **speed** at which a double-click initiates action. If you have difficulty making a double-click to take the action you intend, you might try slowing down the double-click speed.

TIP
Test the double-click speed by double-clicking in the test area. If you can easily make the icon change, you have correctly set your double-click speed.

Changing Mouse Pointers

Instead of the traditional hourglass or arrowhead on the mouse pointer, how about a drum or a dinosaur? You can choose from a variety of pointers.

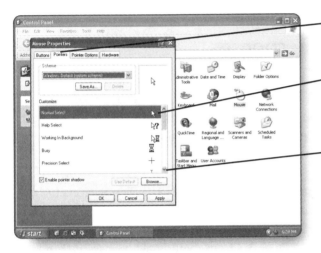

1. Click on the **Pointers tab**. The Pointers tab appears in front.

You'll see the current selection of mouse pointers for various tasks. You can choose from many others.

2. Click on the **down arrow** in the scheme box. A list of pointer schemes will appear.

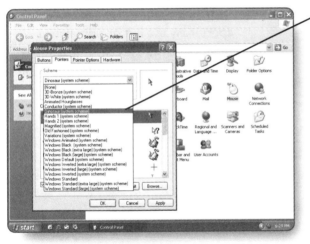

3. Click on a **scheme**. The pointer examples will appear.

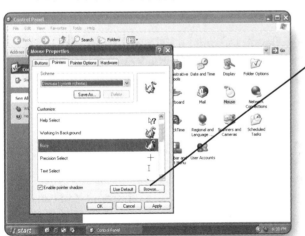

TIP

To change an individual pointer, click on the pointer you want to change, then click on the Browse button to locate and select the desired mouse pointer.

Changing Mouse Visibility

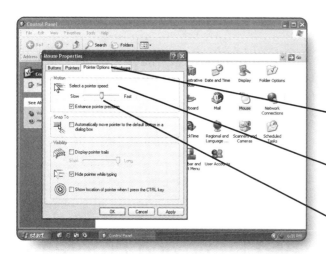

Changing the visibility of the mouse arrow can be very helpful, especially when using a laptop computer. Sometimes the mouse appears to get "lost."

1. Click on the **Pointer Options tab**. The Pointer Options tab will appear in front.

If your mouse moves faster than you'd like it to, change the speed.

2. Click and drag the **slide bar** to make the mouse move faster or slower across the screen.

Other options you can change include:

- **Snap To.** When a dialog box opens, the mouse pointer automatically moves to the default (usually the OK) button.

- **Display pointer trails.** This option shows a comet-like trail as you move the mouse arrow. This one is especially handy on notebook computers.

- **Hide the pointer while typing.** The pointer reappears when you move the mouse.

- **Show the location of the pointer when you press the Ctrl key.** A series of gray circles helps you quickly locate the mouse.

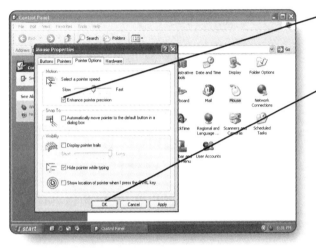

3. Click the **check box** next to any desired choice. A check mark will appear in the box.

4. Click on **OK**. The new options are applied and the Mouse Properties dialog box will close.

Adding and Removing Programs

Most newer applications start the install process automatically when you insert the CD into the CD-ROM drive, however some applications require you to start the process manually.

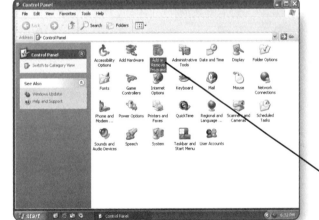

When it comes time to install or uninstall software on your computer, the Control Panel Add or Remove Programs icon simplifies the process. This is also the place to go when you need to add or remove Windows components.

1. Double-click on **Add or Remove Programs**. The Add or Remove Programs Properties dialog box opens.

Installing a New Program

Windows applications must go through an installation process; you cannot just copy them from a disk. When installing a new software program, follow the manufacturer's instructions or the following steps.

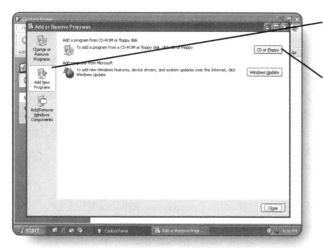

1. **Click** on **Add New Programs**. Add program options will display.

2. **Click** on **CD or floppy**. The Install Program from Floppy Disk or CD-ROM wizard will begin.

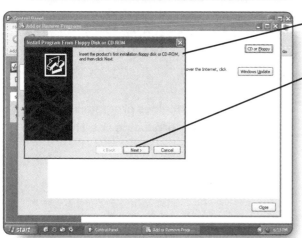

3. **Insert** the **software installation disk** or **CD** into the appropriate drive.

4. **Click** on **Next**. The next screen will appear.

Windows searches the floppy disk drive first; then, if it doesn't find any type of installation or setup program, it searches the CD-ROM drive. The suggested setup program that it finds is usually the correct program.

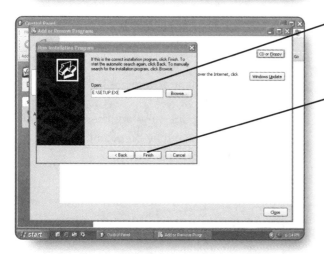

5. If necessary, **type** the correct **setup program location**. You can click on the Browse button to locate it if needed.

6. **Click** on **Finish**. The installation will begin. You may need to answer individual questions from the software manufacturer. It's probably a good idea to accept the installation selections offered by the manufacturer.

Uninstalling a Program

If you have a program you no longer want on your computer, you usually can use the Windows uninstaller to remove it. This is usually the cleanest way to remove a program, because Windows not only deletes the program files, but also cleans the Windows registry of any markers related to that program. Also, any extra files frequently stored in the Windows directory will safely be removed.

1. From the Add or Remove Programs window, **click** on **Change or Remove Programs**. A list of presently installed programs will display.

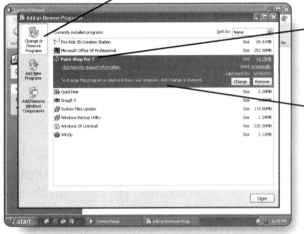

2. Click on the **program** you want to uninstall. The selected item will be highlighted.

Windows provides program information including approximate size and frequency of usage.

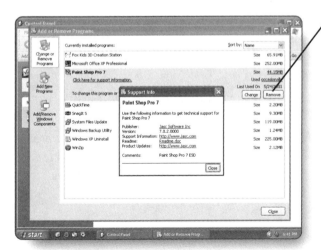

3. Click on **Remove**. A confirmation dialog box will open. (Depending on the application you've selected, the button may say Change/Remove.)

Depending upon the application you're removing, you may be prompted to insert the original CD.

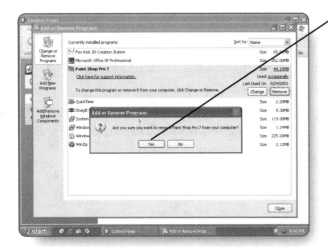

4. Click on **Yes**. Windows will begin the uninstall process.

> ### NOTE
>
> When a program is uninstalled and deleted, it is not placed in the Recycle Bin. There is no Undo step available. If you want the program back, you must reinstall it.

Adding Windows Program Components

By default, Windows doesn't install all possible features. If you want these additional features, you must add them through the Control Panel Add or Remove Programs option.

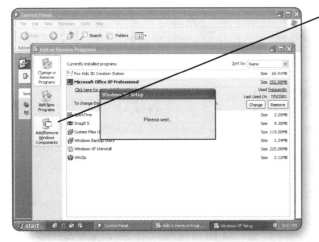

1. Click on the **Add/Remove Windows Components**. Windows will search for the components already installed on your PC.

The Windows components Wizard dialog box will open with a list of currently installed Windows component categories displayed.

Windows uses the following designations to indicate if any, all, or no parts of a category are already installed:

- Items with no check mark in the check box indicates no parts of that category are installed.

  - Items with a check mark in a gray check box indicates only part of the category is installed.

  - Items with a check mark in a white check box indicates that the entire category is already installed.

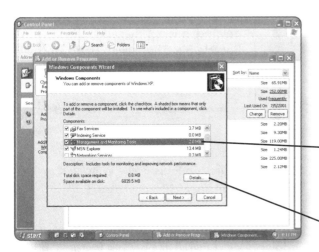

2. **Click** on the **category** you want to install or remove. The category is selected.

3. If available, **click** on **Details**. The dialog box for the selected category will open.

4. **Click** on as many **components** of that category that you want to install. A check mark will appear in the check box. To remove a Windows component, remove the check mark from the items you want to uninstall.

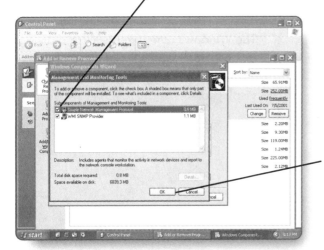

NOTE
Some components require additional choices to operate correctly. Windows Setup tells you if this is the case.

5. **Click** on **OK**. The category dialog box will close.

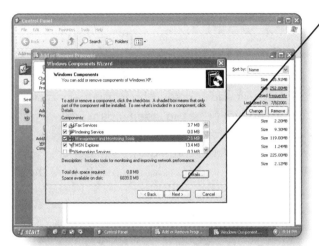

6. Click on **Next**. The Windows Components Wizard will begin the install or uninstall process. You may be prompted to insert the Windows CD into the CD-ROM drive.

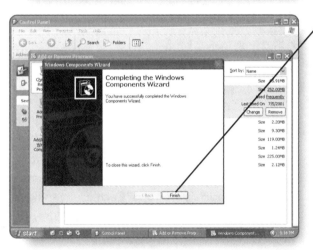

7. Click on **Finish**. The Windows Component Wizard will close.

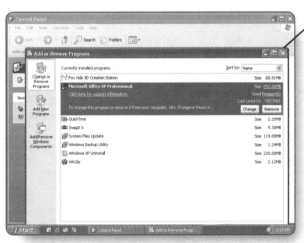

8. Click on **Close**. The Add or Remove Programs window will close.

NOTE
You may be prompted to restart Windows.

Managing Users

In Chapter 1, "Discovering Desktop Components," you learned how to switch user accounts. User accounts personalize Windows for each person who is using a particular computer by giving him or her an independent view of his or her own files, a list of favorite Web sites, and recently visited Web pages. Documents created by each user are stored in their own My Documents folder, separate from the documents of others who also use the computer. Users are maintained through the Control Panel.

1. Double-click on **User Accounts**. The User Accounts window will open.

Adding Users

Windows XP sets up one user the first time you access the computer. You can later add other users. Each user can have his or her own account name, picture, password, and other settings.

1. Click on **Create a New Account**. The User Accounts wizard will begin.

Existing user name and rights are displayed.

2. Type a **name** for the new user. This is the name that will appear on the Windows welcome screen and in the Start menu. No two users can have the exact same name.

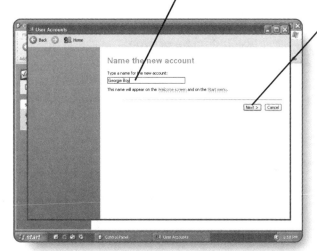

3. Click on **Next**. The Pick an account type screen will appear.

There are two types of user accounts. The one you created when your first started Windows XP is an administrator account that has full access to every function in Windows. Other users can also be administrators or have limited capabilities. Administrator-only functions include installing programs and hardware, modifying user accounts including other than your own, and making system-wide changes. Limited accounts allow the user to change only a few settings.

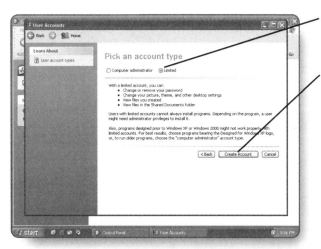

4. Click on an **account type**. The option will be selected.

5. Click on **Create Account**. The new account will appear in the user list.

Changing User Options

You can assign a password to each user or change the picture, name, or account type. Only administrators can change the account name or type.

1. Click on the **account name** you want to modify. A user options screen will appear listing available changes.

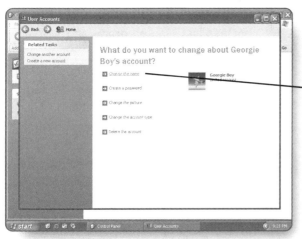

Changing the User Name

You can easily rename any user account.

1. Click on **Change the name**. You'll be prompted to provide a new user name.

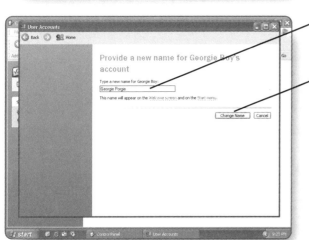

2. Type the **new user name**. The new name will replace the existing name.

3. Click on **Change name**. The user options window will appear.

Creating a Password

If you want to restrict the user ability to access the machine, assign a password.

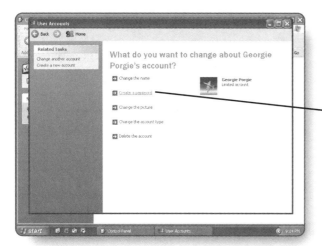

1. Click on **Create a password**. The password screen will appear.

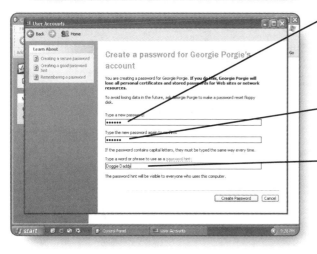

2. Type the **password**. A series of dots will appear.

Passwords are case-sensitive.

3. Retype the **password** in the second box. Doing so confirms your password.

4. In the third box, **type** a **hint** (*not* the password). If the user forgets his password, he can see the hint to remind him.

5. Click on **Create Password**. The user options window will appear.

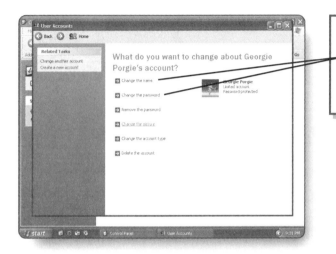

TIP

To change or remove a user password, click on the appropriate option.

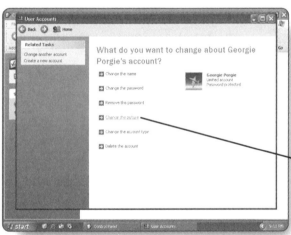

Changing the User Picture

When a user account is created, Windows automatically assigns a graphic picture. You can select from a number of other pictures including your own images.

1. **Click** on **Change the picture**. A selection of pictures will appear.

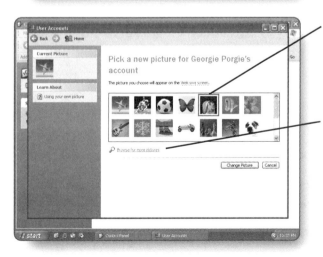

2a. **Click** on a **picture**. A blue border will surround the selected picture.

OR

2b. **Click** on **Browse for more pictures**. The Open dialog box will open.

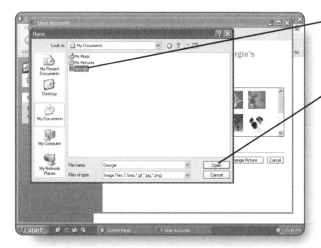

3. Locate and click on the **picture** you want to use. The file name will be selected.

4. Click on **Open**. The selected picture will be applied to the user account and the user options window will appear.

Deleting Users

If you no longer want a user on the system, you can delete the user and his or her created files and folders. Only an administrator can delete user accounts.

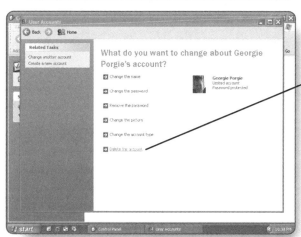

1. Click on **Delete the account**. An inquiry about keeping the user files will appear.

Windows can save the user desktop settings and My Documents contents but cannot preserve e-mail messages, favorites, and other settings.

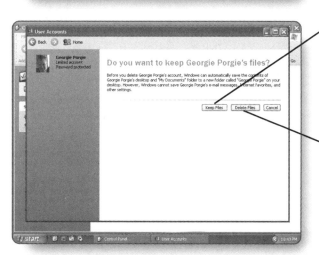

2a. Click on **Keep Files**. A confirmation message will appear. The files will appear in a folder on the desktop.

OR

2a. Click on **Delete Files**. A confirmation message will appear.

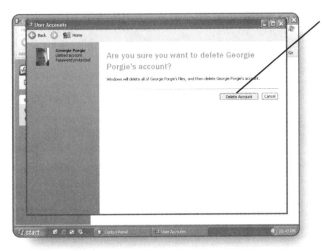

3. Click on **Delete account**. The user account will be deleted.

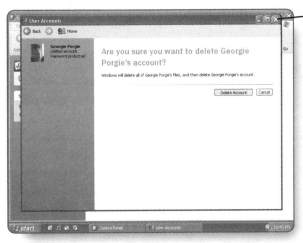

4. Click on the **Close box**. The User Accounts window will close.

5. Optionally, **click** on the **Close box** to close the Control Panel window.

14

Having Fun with the Control Panel

In the previous chapter you learned how to use some of the system support items that Control Panel offers. Now you'll learn how to use the Control Panel to maximize the fun you can have with your computer. Do you want something prettier than the standard Windows desktop? How about changing the sound you hear every time a message appears? In this chapter, you'll learn how to:

- Change sounds
- Choose a wallpaper
- Change desktop colors
- Change screen resolution

Changing Sounds

You might hear a sound when you attempt to complete a particular task in Windows. It could sound like a ding or a chord, even a drum roll or an owl. These sounds are controlled through the Windows Control Panel.

TIP

To open the Control Panel, click on Start, Control Panel.

1. Open the **Control Panel**.

2. Double-click on **Sounds and Audio Devices**. The Sounds and Audio Devices Properties dialog box will open.

TIP

If you don't see the Sounds and Audio Devices icon, click on Switch to Classic View.

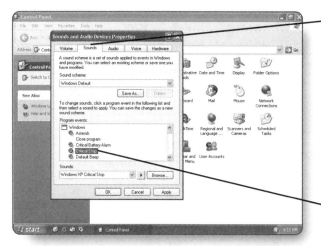

3. Click on the **Sounds tab**. The Sounds tab will move to the front.

The Program Events area lists various Windows events, such as closing a program or the appearance of a warning message. An icon indicates those events that already have a sound assigned to them.

4. Click on a **Program Event**. The event is selected.

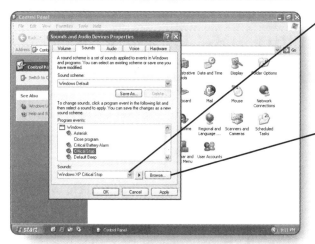

5. Click on the **down arrow** next to the Sounds list box. A list of available sounds will appear.

TIP
If you've downloaded or purchased other sounds, click on the Browse button to locate and select those sounds.

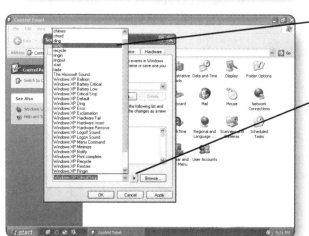

6. Click on the **sound name** you want to associate with the event. The sound name will appear in the Sounds list box.

7. Click on the **play arrow**. A preview of the sound will play.

8. Repeat Steps 4 through **6** for each event you want to change.

9. Click on **OK**. The Sounds and Audio Devices Properties dialog box will close.

Enhancing Your Display

If you've used previous version of Windows, by now you've noticed major changes to the appearance of Windows XP. Brighter colors and different icons are a few differences.

If the choices provided by Microsoft are just not your style, you can change them.

1. Double-click on **Display** in the Control Panel window. The Display Properties dialog box will open.

Changing Backgrounds and Colors

The Windows background is the main area displayed on your screen. Many different graphic types and .html files can be displayed as background for your Windows desktop. You can even use your scanned photo of that special person. Windows XP also includes many choices from which you can select.

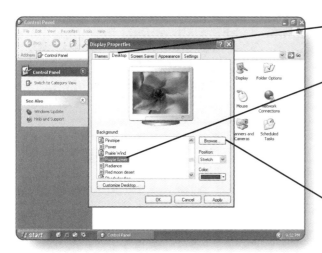

1. Click on the **Desktop tab**. The Desktop tab will move to the front.

2. Click on a **background** from the selections provided. A sample of the background will appear in the Preview box.

TIP

If you don't find a background image that you like, click the Browse button and navigate to the folder that contains the image you want to display. Double-click on the image you want to use.

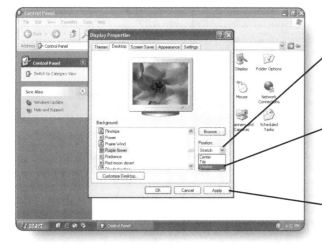

3. Click on the **down arrow** next to the Position list box. A list of choices will appear.

4. Click an **option**. These affect the way the background image will display on your screen.

5. Click on **Apply**. Your new background selection will be applied.

Selecting a Screen Saver

Screen savers display moving images that appear on your screen when the computer is idle for a specified amount of time. You can choose from the abundance of screen savers included with Windows or you can purchase many different themes from third-party software manufacturers.

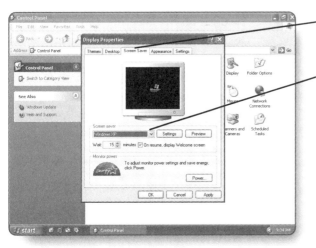

1. Click on the **Screen Saver tab**. The Screen Saver tab will move to the front.

2. Click on the **down arrow** of the Screen Saver list box. A list of available choices will appear.

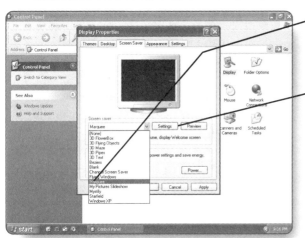

3. Click on the **screen saver** you want to use. Your selection will appear in the Screen Saver list box.

4. Click on **Settings.** A Screen Saver Properties dialog box specific to the screen saver you have selected will open.

From here, you can set various options, such as speed, sound, and sometimes color or size. The options will vary with each screen saver.

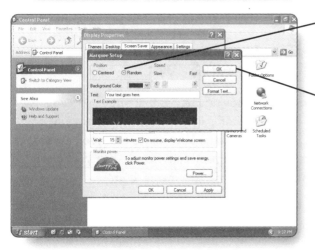

5. Change any desired **options** in the Screen Saver Properties dialog box. The options will be selected.

6. Click on **OK**. The Screen Saver Properties dialog box will close.

You can determine the number of minutes that elapse before the screen saver starts. An average time is 10 to 15 minutes.

7. **Click** on the **up** or **down arrow** next to the Wait spin box. The number represents the number of minutes.

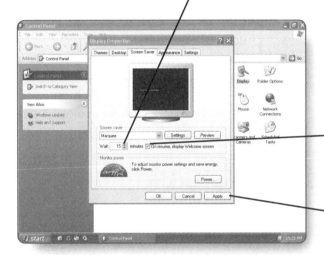

When you resume using the computer after the screen saver kicks in, Windows can return to the screen as you left it before the screen saver, or it can return to the Welcome screen.

8. Optionally, **click** on **On resume, display Welcome screen**. The check mark will be removed.

9. **Click** on **Apply**. Your new screen saver selections will be applied.

Changing the Colors of Your Windows

You can adjust the appearance of your screen by changing the colors that are displayed in any Windows program. Windows includes some pretty (and some not-so-pretty) color combinations from which you can choose. Color schemes affect everything from the color of a window title bar to the text displayed in a menu.

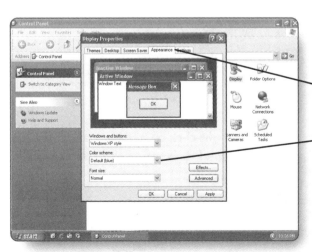

1. **Click** on the **Appearance tab**. The Appearance tab will appear in front.

2. **Click** on the **down arrow** next to the Color scheme list box. A selection of color schemes will appear.

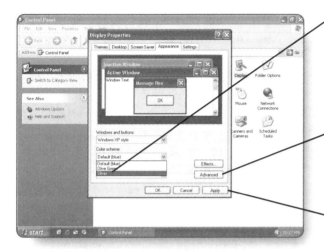

3. Click on the **color scheme** you want to use. Your selection will appear in the Color scheme list box.

TIP

Click on Advanced to modify the color of each individual window component.

4. Click on **Apply**. The new color settings are applied.

Changing Screen Resolution

The *screen resolution* (sometimes called *video resolution*) is the measure of how many individual dots, called *pixels*, make up the display. The higher the resolution, the smaller and finer objects appear on screen. A small monitor usually works best with a 600 x 800 resolution (although some children's games and other programs require an even smaller resolution), while larger monitors can use up to 1024 x 768 or more. (I keep my 17" monitor at 600 x 800.)

Color depth is the measure of how many colors can be shown onscreen. Color depth can run from 2 colors to Highest color which can show millions of colors at the same time.

Right-clicking on the desktop is a faster way to access the Display settings found in the Control Panel.

1. Right-click on a **blank area of the Windows desktop**. A shortcut menu will appear.

2. Click on **Properties**. The Display Properties dialog box will open.

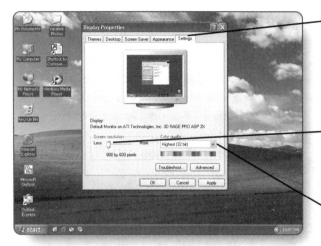

3. Click on the **Settings tab**. The Settings tab will come to the front.

The available resolutions and color depths depend on your video card and monitor.

4. Drag the **Screen resolution slider bar** to the left or right to decrease or increase the video resolution.

5. Click on the **down arrow** in the Color quality box. The available color depths for your machine will appear.

6. Click on a **color depth**. The color depth will display.

7. Click on **OK**. The screen will change and a message box will display.

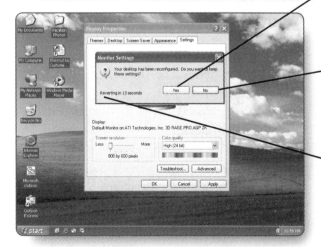

8a. Click on **Yes**. The screen will remain at the new selections.

OR

8b. Click on **No**. The screen will revert to the previous settings.

NOTE

If you don't answer the dialog box within 15 seconds, Windows will automatically revert to the previous settings.

Lowering Resolution with Compatibility Mode

Some applications, especially children's games, may require a lower resolution of 256 colors or in 640 x 480 resolution.

Windows XP generally requires higher resolutions, but through the Compatibility mode feature, you can use those applications. You first learned about Compatibility mode in Chapter 2, "Using Windows Programs."

1. **Right-click** on the **game icon** or other program you want to run in 256-color mode. A shortcut menu will appear.

2. **Click** on **Properties**. The Properties dialog box will open.

3. **Click** on the **Compatibility tab**. The Compatibility tab will move to the front.

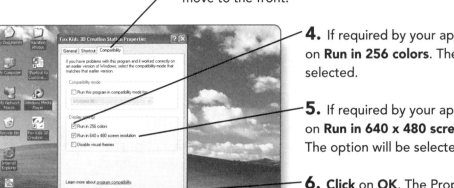

4. If required by your application, **click** on **Run in 256 colors**. The option will be selected.

5. If required by your application, **click** on **Run in 640 x 480 screen resolution**. The option will be selected.

6. **Click** on **OK**. The Properties dialog box will close.

Now when you run the game, the new settings will take effect and Windows will return to your default settings when you finish running the application.

15

Setting Accessibility Options

Windows XP offers many enhancements designed to make using a PC easier if you have certain physical limitations. Accessibility features include enhancements for easier keyboard and mouse input for those with mobility impairments, as well as features for users who are visually- or hearing-impaired. In this chapter you'll learn how to:

- Open a magnified window
- Use the Narrator utility
- Set-up and use the on-screen keyboard
- Activate the SoundSentry

NOTE

While the Accessibility options included with Windows XP provide a minimum level of functionality for users with special needs, some users will need utility programs with more advanced features. You can obtain lots of help and information by searching for "accessibility" at the Microsoft Web site at www.microsoft.com.

Working with the Magnifier

The Magnifier utility magnifies a portion of the screen, making it more readable for those with low vision.

1. Click on **Start**. The Start menu will appear.

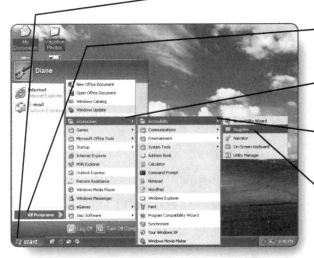

2. Click on **All Programs**. The All Programs menu will appear.

3. Click on **Accessories**. The Accessories submenu will appear.

4. Click on **Accessibility**. The Accessibility submenu will appear.

5. Click on **Magnifier**. A separate magnified window will open on your screen along with an informational dialog box.

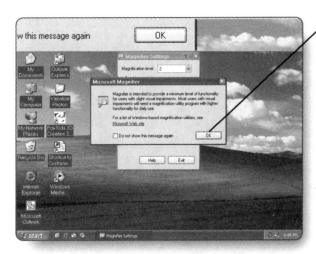

6. Click on **OK**. The informational dialog box will close.

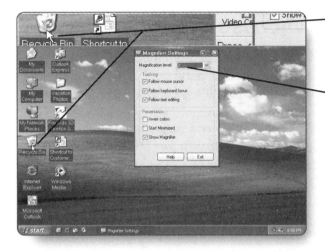

As you move your mouse across the screen, the magnifier window reflects the area surrounding the mouse pointer.

7. Change any desired **settings**, including magnification. The new settings will take immediate effect.

TIP

Click on the minimize button if the settings box is in your way.

8. Click and drag the **magnifier window edge** to resize it. The mouse pointer takes the shape of a double-headed black arrow.

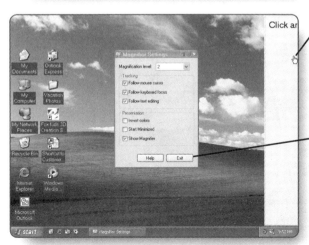

9. Click and drag the **magnifier window body** to move it to a new location. When you release the mouse button, the magnifier window will remain in the new location.

10. When you've finished, **click** on **Exit**. The magnification window will close.

Using Microsoft Narrator

Narrator is a text-to-speech program that can help people with low vision set up the computer by reading aloud the contents of the active window, menu options, or text.

Narrator speaks only English and works best with Notepad, WordPad, Control Panel options, Internet Explorer, the Windows desktop, and Windows setup.

1. Click on **Start**. The Start menu will appear.

2. Click on **All Programs**. The All Programs menu will appear.

3. Click on **Accessories**. The Accessories submenu will appear.

4. Click on **Accessibility**. The Accessibility submenu will appear.

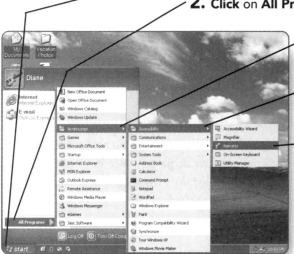

5. Click on **Narrator**. A Microsoft Narrator dialog box will open and the narrator voice will begin reading the box contents.

6. Click on **OK**. The Narrator dialog box will close.

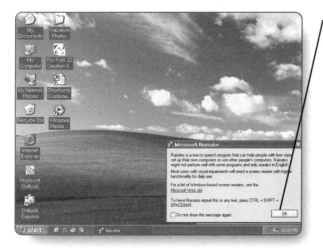

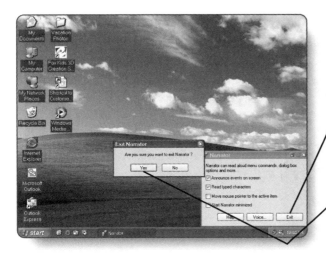

As you click on items on the desktop or any application supported by Narrator, the narrator voice will read the description of the selected or displayed item.

7. When you are finished with the Narrator, **click** on **Exit**. A confirmation box will open.

8. **Click** on **Yes**. The Narrator dialog box will close.

Displaying the On-Screen Keyboard

The On-Screen keyboard is a utility which displays a keyboard on the screen and allows users to type data using a pointing device or joystick. This is particularly useful for users with mobility impairments.

1. **Click** on **Start**. The Start menu will appear.

2. **Click** on **All Programs**. The All Programs menu will appear.

3. **Click** on **Accessories**. The Accessories submenu will appear.

4. **Click** on **Accessibility**. The Accessibility submenu will appear.

5. **Click** on **On-Screen Keyboard**. The keyboard will display on the screen, along with an information dialog box.

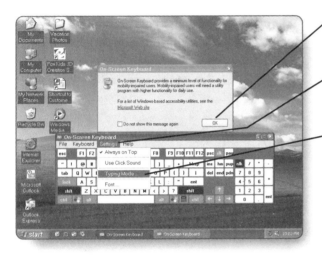

6. Click on **OK**. The informational dialog box will close.

7. Click on **Settings**. The Settings menu will appear.

8. Click on **Typing Mode**. The Typing Mode dialog box will open.

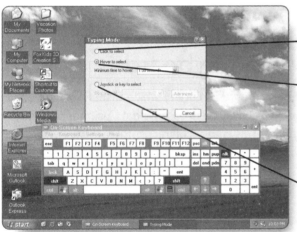

Three different modes are available.

- **Click**. Click the on-screen keys to type text.

- **Hover**. Use a mouse or joystick to point to a key for a predefined period of time, and the selected character will be typed automatically. You can also click the on-screen keys.

- **Joystick or key to select (Scan)**. The on-screen keyboard is continually scanned. When the row with the character you want to use is highlighted, you press the spacebar. The keyboard will then scan each key on the row. Again, you press the spacebar to select the character and it will be typed on screen.

9. Click on a **mode**. The option will be selected.

10. Click on **OK**. The Typing Mode dialog box will close.

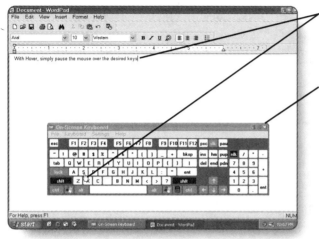

You can now launch the program you want to use and begin using the on-screen keyboard.

11. **Click** on the **Close button** when you are finished with the on-screen keyboard. The keyboard will close.

Activating the SoundSentry

If you have hearing difficulties, the SoundSentry can assist you by displaying visual warnings for system sounds. The SoundSentry is available through the Accessibility Wizard or the Control Panel Accessibility Options.

1. **Click** on **Start**. The Start menu will appear.

2. **Click** on **All Programs**. The All Programs menu will appear.

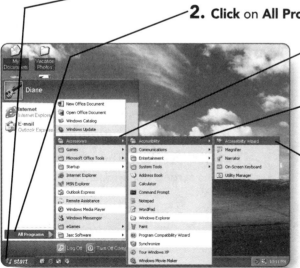

3. **Click** on **Accessories**. The Accessories submenu will appear.

4. **Click** on **Accessibility**. The Accessibility submenu will appear.

5. **Click** on **Accessibility Wizard**. The Accessibility Wizard will open.

6. Click on **Next**. The Text Size screen will appear.

7. Click on the **smallest text size** you can read. A border will surround the selected text.

8. Click on **Next**. The Display Settings screen will appear.

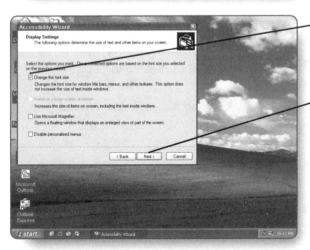

9. Click on any desired **display setting options**. The selected options will have a check mark.

10. Click on **Next**. The Set Wizard Options screen will appear.

This is the screen where the Wizard determines the type of assistance you might need.

11. Click on **I am deaf or have difficulty hearing sounds from the computer**. The option will be selected.

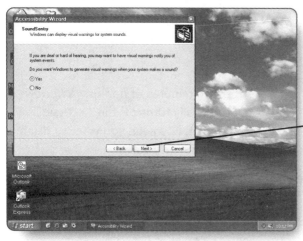

TIP

Optionally, click on any other options that apply to you.

12. Click on **Next**. The SoundSentry screen will appear.

Windows can display visual warnings for computer sounds.

13. Click on **Yes**. The option will be selected.

14. Click on **Next**. The Show Sounds screen will appear.

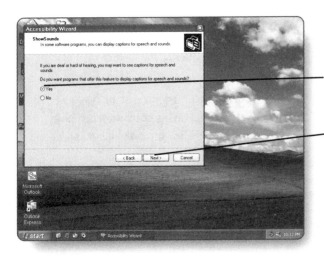

Windows can display captions for speech and sounds.

15. **Click** on **Yes**. The option will be selected.

16. **Click** on **Next**. The final Accessibility Wizard screen will appear.

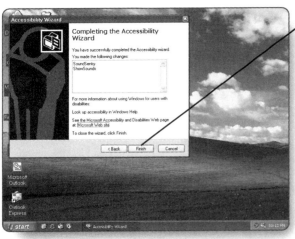

17. **Click** on **Finish**. The Sound Sensor will flash messages on the screen as needed.

After five minutes of non-use, Windows automatically turns off the Accessibility features. If, however, you want to disable the SoundSentry earlier, use the Accessibility Options icon in the Control Panel.

18. **Open** the **Control Panel** (Hint: **Click** on **Start**, **Control Panel**).

19. **Double-click** on **Accessibility Options**. The Accessibility Options dialog box will open.

20. **Click** on the **Sound tab**. The Sound tab will move to the front.

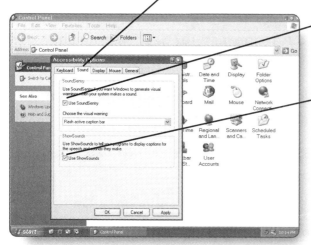

21. **Click** on **Use SoundSentry**. The check mark will be removed and the feature deactivated.

22. **Click** on **Use ShowSounds**. The check mark will be removed and the feature deactivated.

TIP

Take a few moments to explore some of the other options available in the Accessibility Options dialog box.

23. **Click** on **OK**. The Accessibility Options dialog box will close.

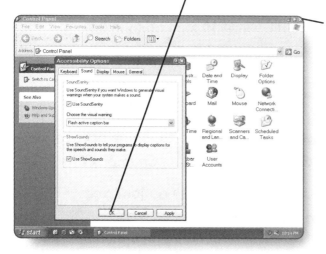

24. **Click** on the **Close button**. The Control Panel window will close.

Part IV Review Questions

1. How can you turn off the Auto Arrange feature? *See "Moving an Icon" in Chapter 12*

2. If you delete a shortcut, are you deleting the program or document to which it refers? *See "Deleting an Icon" in Chapter 12*

3. What icon located on your desktop cannot be renamed? *See "Renaming an Icon" in Chapter 12*

4. What does Auto-hide the Taskbar do to the Windows taskbar? *See "Changing Taskbar Options" in Chapter 12*

5. When are mouse trails handy to use? *See "Changing Mouse Visibility" in Chapter 12*

6. Why should you use the Uninstall process to remove a program? *See "Uninstalling a Program" in Chapter 13*

7. Which type of user account has full access to every function in Windows? *See "Adding Users" in Chapter 13*

8. What do screen savers do? *See "Selecting a Screen Saver" in Chapter 14*

9. What does setting a higher screen resolution do to the objects on your screen? *See "Changing Screen Resolution" in Chapter 14*

10. Who might want to use the Narrator accessibility option? *See "Using Microsoft Narrator" in Chapter 15*

PART V

Discovering the Windows Tools

Chapter 16
   Working with Printers **203**

Chapter 17
   Preparing for Disasters—
   Backing up Your Data **225**

Chapter 18
   Troubleshooting Problems **237**

Chapter 19
   Improving System Performance **249**

16

Working with Printers

Printing is still the most common way to distribute information to others. When you work with a Windows-based program, all the printing is controlled by Windows—not by the individual software program. This promotes consistency and the ability to resolve printing issues in one central area. In this chapter, you'll learn how to:

- Install a new printer
- Share a printer
- Connect to a network printer
- Make a printer the default printer
- Control printing jobs
- Fax a document

Installing a Local Printer

Most of the time, when you hook up a printer to your computer Windows' Plug and Play feature will detect the new printer and automatically install the necessary printer settings. Occasionally, however, you must manually tell the computer what type of printer you're using. Windows includes the Add Printer Wizard to assist you in installing a new printer.

NOTE

If your printer came with a setup disk, use that setup program instead of the following procedure to configure your printer. It may install some special utilities that you might want.

1. Open the Control Panel window. (Hint: **Click** on **Start**, **Control Panel**) The Control Panel window will open.

2. Double-click on **Printers and Faxes**. The Printers and Faxes dialog box will open.

TIP

If your screen doesn't look like the one shown here, click on Switch to Classic view on the left side of the screen.

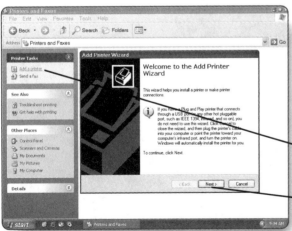

3. Click on **Add a Printer**. The Add Printer Wizard will open.

4. Click on **Next**. The Local or Network Printer screen will appear.

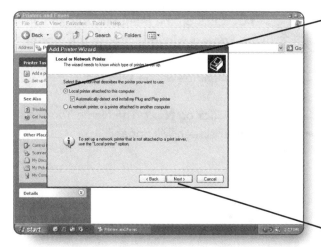

5. Click on **Local Printer attached to this computer**. The option will be selected.

NOTE

Hooking up to a network printer is discussed in the section entitled "Connecting to a Network Printer" later in this chapter.

6. Click on **Next**. Windows will try to automatically detect your printer.

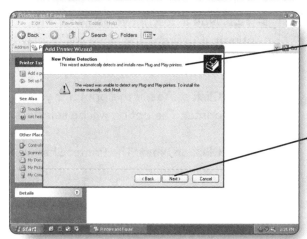

If your printer is a Plug and Play-compliant printer, Windows will automatically detect it and no further interaction will be required on your part.

7. Click on **Next**. The Select a Printer Port screen will appear.

Many printers are physically connected through the LPT1 printer port or the USB port.

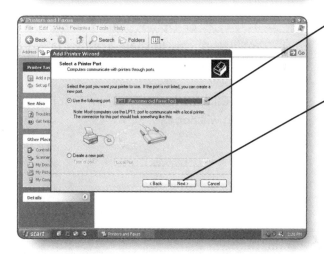

8. Click on the **down arrow** and **select** the **printer port** you will use. The selection will appear on the screen.

9. Click on **Next**. The Install Printer Software screen will appear.

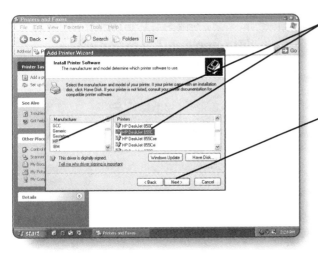

10. Click on the **Manufacturer** and, in the Printers window, **choose** the **model** of your printer. The manufacturer and model names will be selected.

11. Click on **Next**. The Name Your Printer screen will appear.

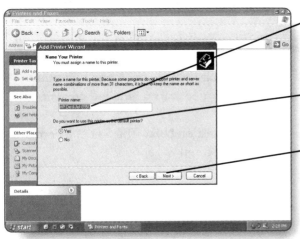

12. Type a descriptive **name** for the printer, if desired. The name will display in the Printer Name text box.

13. Click on **Yes**, if this printer is your main printer. The option will be selected.

14. Click on **Next**. The Printer Sharing screen will appear.

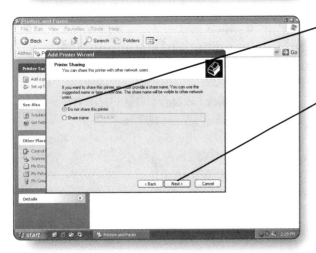

15. Click on **Do not share this printer**. You'll learn how to share a printer later in this chapter.

16. Click on **Next**. The Print Test Page screen will appear.

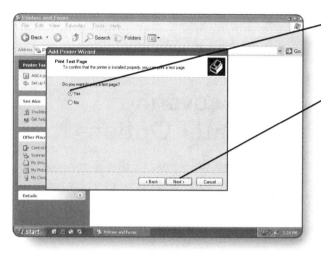

17. **Click** on **Yes** if you want to print a test page to check the connections to your printer. The option will be selected.

18. **Click** on **Next**. The final printer wizard screen will appear.

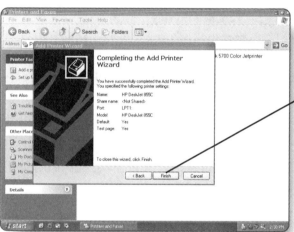

All of the specifications you selected for your printer will appear on the final screen.

19. **Click** on **Finish**. The necessary files will be copied to your computer and you might be prompted to insert the Windows CD-ROM or another specified disk.

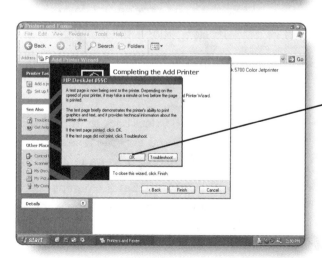

If you elected to print a test page, a dialog box opens, asking you if the test page printed correctly.

20. **Click** on **OK** if the page printed correctly. If the test page didn't print correctly, the Printing Troubleshooter can assist in resolving the problem. The Printer Wizard dialog box will close.

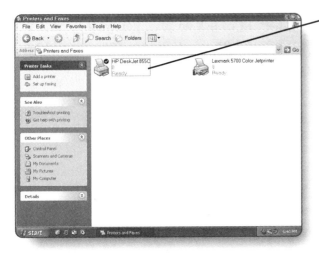

An icon representing the new printer will appear in your printer folder.

Discovering Printer Options

Printers have options that determine the default page and paper settings for a specific printer.

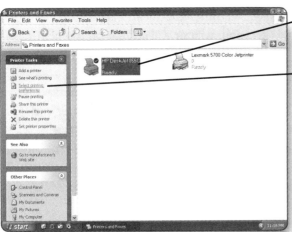

1. **Click** on the **printer** you want to modify. The printer will be selected.

2. **Click** on **Select printing preferences**. A Printing Preferences dialog box specific to your printer will open.

These options will apply to all documents. Most applications allow you to change these settings for a particular document.

3. **Explore and click** on any desired **settings**. The options will be selected.

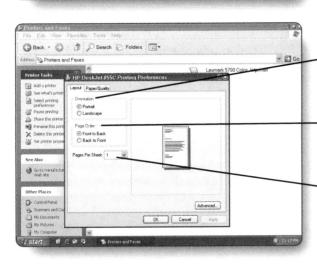

- **Orientation**. Select landscape if you want to print along the longer edge of the paper.

- **Page Order**. Select back to front if you want to print the pages in reverse order; for example print page 2 then 1.

- **Pages Per Sheet**. Set the number of copies of every document you want the printer to print.

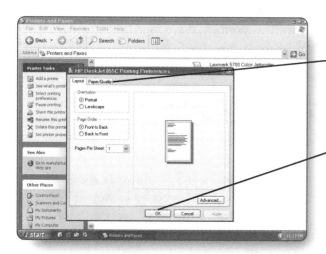

TIP
Click on the Paper/Quality tab to set the paper location and quality of print.

4. Click on **OK** when you have finished making changes. The Preferences dialog box will close.

Sharing a Printer

If you want to share your printer with others on your network, you must first tell the printer it has permission to be used by others. You'll learn about networks in Chapter 20, "Using a Network."

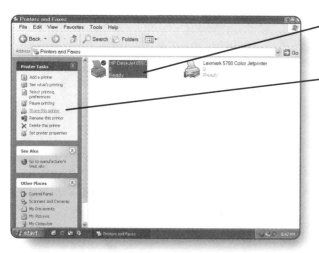

1. Click on the **printer** that you want to share. The printer will be highlighted.

2. Click on **Share this printer**. The printer Properties dialog box will open with the Sharing tab in front.

3. Click on **Share this printer**. The option is selected and the Share name will become available.

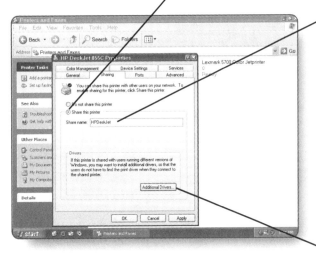

4. Type a **name** for the printer in the Share Name text box. This is the name others will use to recognize that this is your printer.

If all users on your network are using Windows XP, proceed to step 7; however, if the other users on your network are using a version of Windows other than Windows XP, you'll want to also perform the following steps:

5. Click on **Additional Drivers**. The Additional Drivers dialog box will open.

6. Click on the **Windows versions** the other users are using. A check mark will appear next to the selected versions.

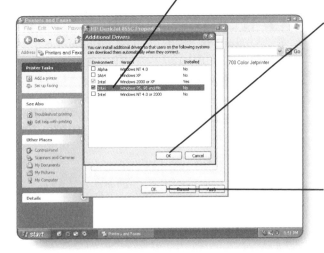

7. Click on **OK**. Windows will attempt to install the additional software.

NOTE

You may be prompted for a Windows CD or printer disk.

8. Click on **OK**. The Properties dialog box will close.

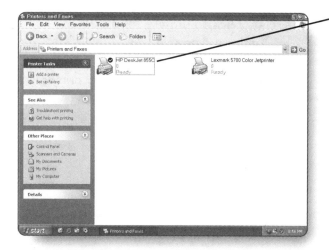

A shared printer is represented with a small hand under it.

Connecting to a Network Printer

If you want to print to a printer across a network, the printer must be a shared printer.

1. Click on **Add a printer**. The Add Printer Wizard will open.

2. Click on **Next**. The Local or Network printer screen will appear.

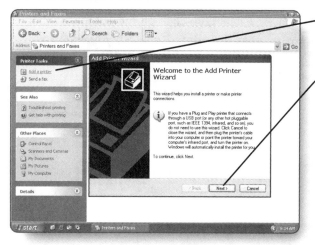

3. Click on **A network printer, or a printer attached to another computer**. The option will be selected.

4. Click on **Next**. The Specify a Printer screen will appear.

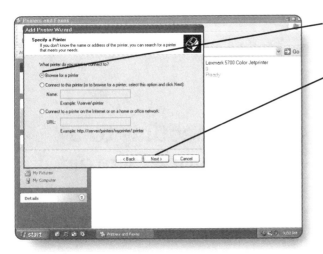

5. Click on **Browse for a printer**. The option will be selected.

6. Click on **Next**. The Shared printer list will appear.

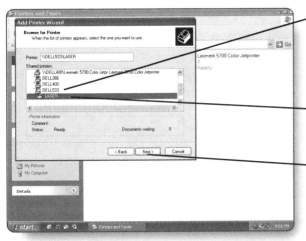

7. Double-click on the **computer** that has the printer to which you want to connect. A list of available printers will appear.

8. Click on the **printer** you want to use. The printer will be highlighted.

9. Click on **Next**. The Default Printer screen will appear.

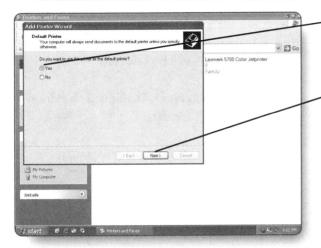

10. Click on **Yes** if this printer is to be your main printer. The option will be selected.

11. Click on **Next**. The final Printer Wizard screen will appear.

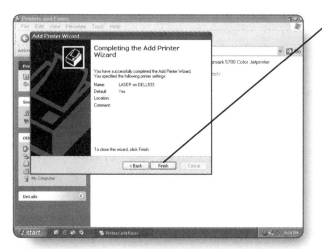

12. **Click** on **Finish**. The Add Printer Wizard closes, and the necessary files are copied to your computer. You may be prompted to insert the Windows CD-ROM or other specified disks.

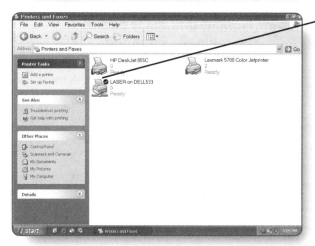

A printer icon is displayed in the Printers and Faxes window. A network printer is designated by what looks like a cable running underneath it.

Making a Printer the Default

You might have several printers to which you can print, including a fax or other device. One of these must be set as a default printer. The default printer is the one Windows assumes you want to print to unless you tell it otherwise.

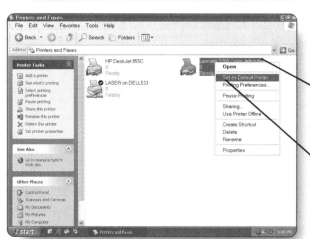

1. **Right-click** on the **printer** to be the default printer. A shortcut menu will appear.

2. **Click** on **Set as Default Printer**. The shortcut menu will close.

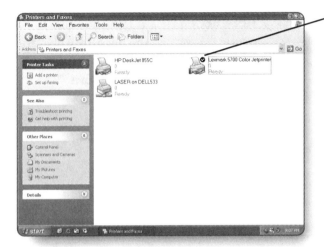

A check mark will appear on the printer icon to indicate it is the default printer.

Creating a Desktop Shortcut to the Printer

Having a printer icon on the desktop allows for "drag-and-drop" printing.

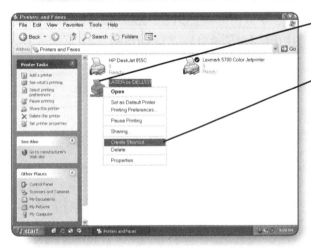

1. Right-click on the **printer icon**. A shortcut menu will appear.

2. Click on **Create Shortcut**. A message dialog box will open.

3. Click on **Yes**. The Shortcut dialog box will close.

NOTE

To take advantage of drag-and-drop printing from the Windows desktop, Windows Explorer, or any Windows Open or Save File dialog box, click on the document you want to print and drag it to the printer shortcut icon. The document prints with any default settings installed for that printer.

Controlling Print Jobs

Sometimes printing problems occur, or you need to stop a job from printing either temporarily or permanently, or you need to "rush" a job ahead of others waiting in line. Printing is controlled through the print *queue*.

When you choose to print a document, the printer icon appears in the Notification Area. If no printer is displayed in the Notification Area, you're too late—the job has already gone to the printer.

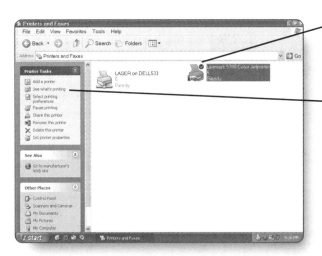

1. **Click** on the **printer** you want to control. The Printer icon will be highlighted.

2. **Click** on **See what's printing**.

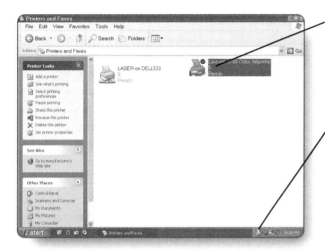

Windows displays the number of print jobs waiting to print.

TIP

Optionally, double-click on the printer icon in the Notification Area.

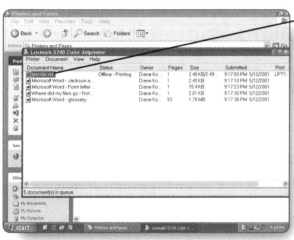

The job currently being printed is at the top of the list.

Pausing a Print Job

In many cases, you can use the Printer window to temporarily stop, or pause, a print job.

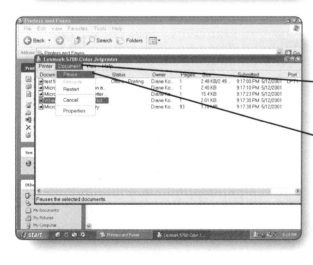

1. Click on the **print job** you want to pause. The job will be selected.

2. Click on **Document**. The Document menu will appear.

3. Click on **Pause**. The selected print job will be marked as paused.

Deleting a Print Job

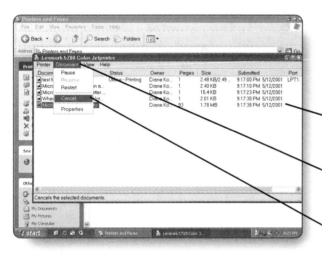

If you want to completely stop the printing of a particular print job, you can delete the print job from the Printer window.

1. Click on the **print job** you want to stop. The job will be selected.

2. Click on **Document**. The Document menu will appear.

3. Click on **Cancel**. A confirmation message will appear.

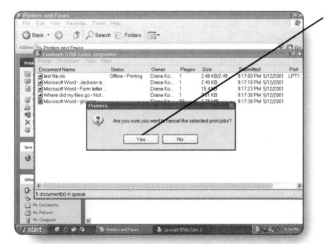

4. Click on **Yes**. The print job will be deleted from the print queue.

Faxing from the Computer

If you have a fax/modem installed in your computer, you can fax a document directly from your PC.

Installing the Fax Component

By default, Windows may not install the software needed to fax, but you can easily add it through the Printers and Faxes window.

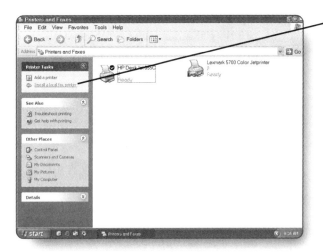

1. **Click** on **Install a local fax printer** or **Set up faxing**. Windows will install and configure the necessary fax components.

NOTE
You may be prompted to insert your Windows XP CD.

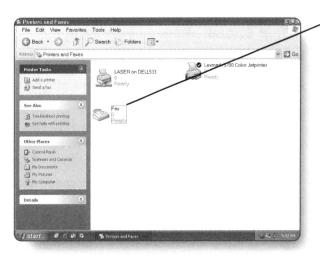

The fax will be listed as another printer in the Printers and Faxes window.

Faxing a Document

Faxing is actually printing, but it allows printing to another printer across the telephone line.

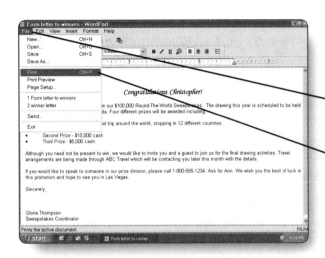

1. Create or **open** the **document** you want to fax. The document will appear on screen.

2. Click on **File**. The File menu will appear.

3. Click on **Print**. The current application printer dialog box will open.

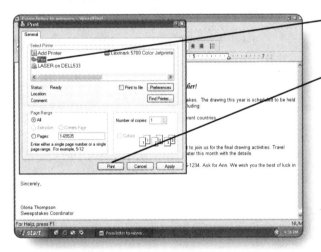

4. Click on **Fax** from the list of available printers. The Fax printer will be selected.

5. Click on **Print** or **OK** (depending on the application).

If this is the first time you've faxed from Windows, the Fax Configuration Wizard will open.

If you've previously entered information in the Fax Configuration Wizard, skip the next section and go to "Using the Send Fax Wizard" later in this chapter.

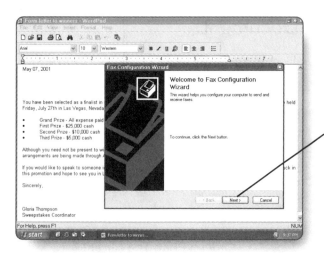

Configuring the Fax

The Fax Configuration Wizard prompts you for information it will store for future faxing.

1. Click on **Next**. The Sender Information screen will appear.

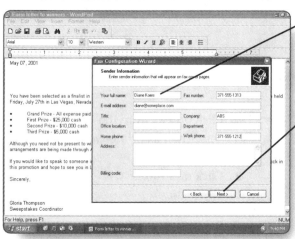

2. Enter your **name, phone number** and **other information** into the appropriate boxes. All information is optional.

3. Click on **Next**. The Select Device screen will appear.

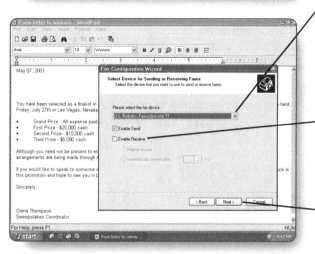

4. Click on the **down arrow** and **select** the **appropriate device** from the available options.

TIP

Optionally, click on the Enable Receive box if you want to receive faxes on your PC.

---

5. Click on **Next**. The TSID screen will appear.

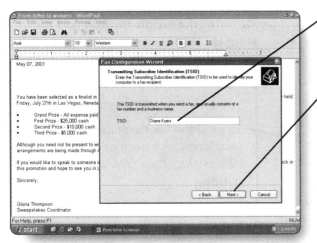

6. Enter your name or **fax number**. This is the information that will print at the top edge of the faxed page.

7. Click on **Next**. The final Fax Configuration screen will appear.

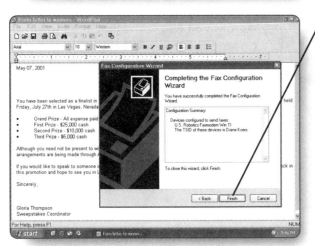

8. Click on **Finish**. The Fax Configuration Wizard will close and the Send Fax Wizard will begin.

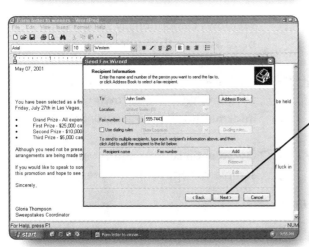

Using the Send Fax Wizard

The Send Fax Wizard will prompt you for the recipient information.

1. Click on **Next**. The Recipient Information screen will appear.

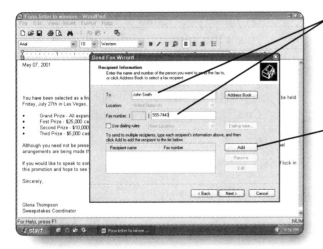

2. Enter the **recipient name and fax number**. The information will appear on the screen.

TIP

To send the fax to multiple recipients, type each person's information, then click on the Add button.

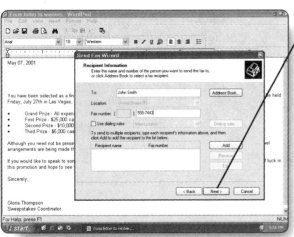

3. Click on **Next**. The Preparing the Cover page screen will appear.

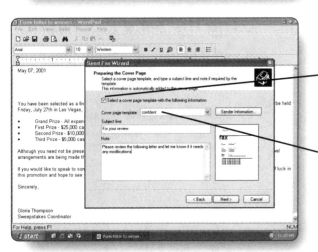

Windows can optionally send a cover page along with the document.

4. Click on **Select a cover page template with the following information**. The option will be selected.

5. Select a **cover page template**. A sample will appear in the preview box.

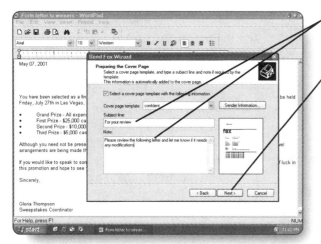

6. Enter the desired **information** for the cover page.

7. Click on **Next**. The Schedule screen will appear.

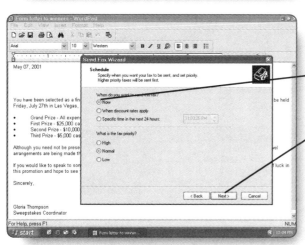

You have the option of sending the fax immediately or at a specified time.

8. Click on an **option**. The option will be selected.

9. Click on **Next**. The final Send Fax Wizard screen will appear.

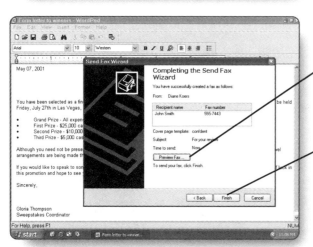

TIP

Click on Preview Fax to see the cover page and document prior to sending.

10. Click on **Finish**. The fax will be sent according to your specifications.

The Fax monitor keeps you apprised of the fax progress.

TIP

To display the Fax Console which tracks and manages faxes sent and received, click on Start, All Programs, Accessories, Communications, Fax, Fax Console.

17

Preparing for Disasters—Backing Up Your Data

"Stuff happens" whether we like it or not. When it comes to your computer, however, a little preplanning can go a long way when a disaster such as hardware failure, lighting strikes, power surges, or virus corruption occurs. In this chapter you'll learn how to:

- Install the backup utility
- Backup your important files
- Restore files from a backup

Installing the Backup Program

Windows includes a great backup program, but it isn't installed by default. Unfortunately, Microsoft hid this little program, so you'll need to locate it and load it before you can use it. The backup application is stored in the Windows CD. The good news is that you'll only have to install the backup program once.

1. Click on **Start**. The Start menu will appear.

2. Click on **Control Panel**. The Control Panel will open.

3. Double-click on **Add or Remove Programs**. The Add or Remove Programs window will open.

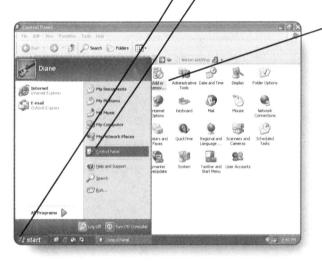

4. Click on **Add New Programs**. The Add New Programs options will appear.

5. Click on **CD or Floppy**. The Install Program From Floppy Disk or CD-ROM Wizard will start.

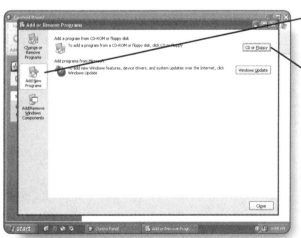

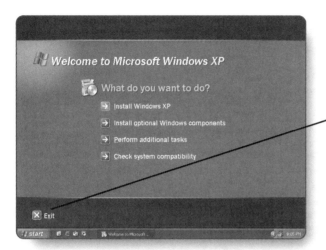

6. **Insert** the **Windows XP CD** into your CD-ROM drive.

NOTE

If the Welcome to Microsoft Windows XP screen appears, click on Exit.

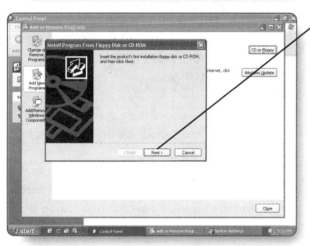

7. **Click** on **Next**. The Run Installation Program screen will appear.

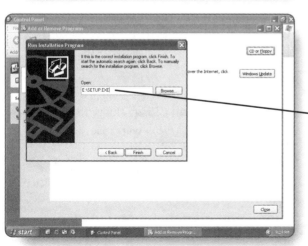

Windows will locate a program called Setup, which is the program that loads Windows. This is *not* the program you need to load backup.

8. **Click** the **insertion point** at the end of the text in the Open text box. A blinking insertion point will appear.

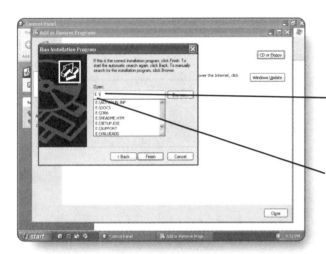

Make sure you have a blinking insertion point and not highlighted text before proceeding to the next section.

9. Press the **backspace key** until the word SETUP.EXE is deleted. A drop-down list may appear.

Only the letter specifying your CD-ROM drive will remain in the text box. Yours may not be the letter E.

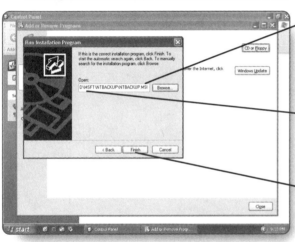

10. After the E:\, **type** the following **text** exactly as you see it here: **VALUEADD\MSFT\NTBACKUP\ NTBACKUP.MSI**

Don't be alarmed if you can't see all the text you just typed. It's there, hidden in the text box.

11. Click on **Finish**. Windows will install the backup utility program. A dialog box will appear when the installation is complete.

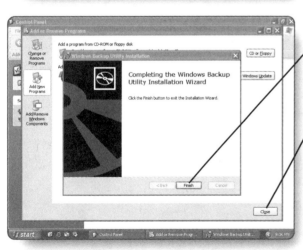

12. Click on **Finish**. The Windows Backup Utility Installation Wizard will close.

13. Click on **Close**. The Add or Remove Programs window will close.

14. Click on the **Close button**. The Control Panel window will close.

Backing Up Files

Backing up your critical data is one of the cheapest forms of insurance you can have. By backing up your important files to some disk other than your hard disk, you ensure that you will have copies of them available should something bad happens to your computer. Backing up makes copies of your data and places it on a different medium such as a tape, floppy, or zip disk.

1. Click on **Start**. The Start menu will appear.

2. Click on **All Programs**. The All Programs menu will appear.

3. Click on **Accessories**. The Accessories submenu will appear.

4. Click on **System Tools**. The System Tools submenu will appear.

5. Click on **Backup**. The Backup or Restore Wizard will open.

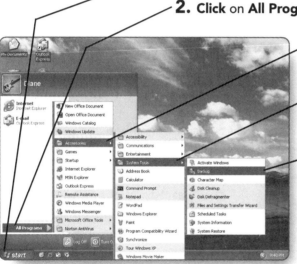

6. Click on **Next**. The Backup or Restore screen will appear.

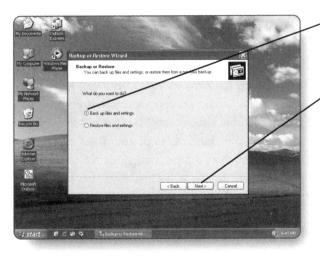

7. If not already selected, **click** on **Back up files and settings**. The option will be selected.

8. Click on **Next**. The What to Back Up screen will appear.

From here you must decide which files to back up. It's usually not necessary to back up your entire hard disk. Most of the hard disk's content probably came from programs you can reinstall whenever needed. Therefore, most people back up only their data.

9. Click on a **backup option**. The following describes the back up options.

● Back up just the files and settings for you, the current user. This includes all files in the My Documents folder.

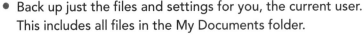

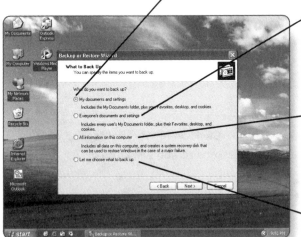

● Back up the My Documents files and personalized settings for all users. Windows stores documents and settings for each user independent of each other.

● Back up all information on this computer. You won't want to use this if you're going to back up to floppy or zip disks. (You'd probably need a stack of disks as tall as your desk!)

● Let me choose what to back up. Use this option if you want to back up files different from the options above.

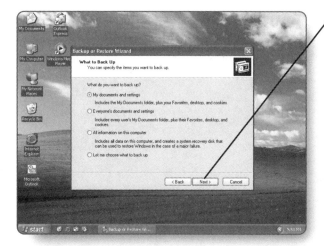

10. Click on **Next**. The Backup Type, Destination and Name screen will appear.

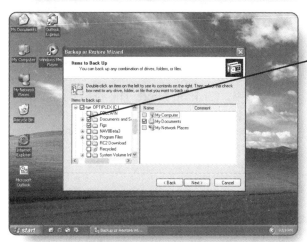

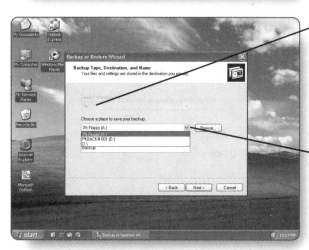

If you have tape drive installed on your computer, the Select a Backup type will allow you to choose to backup to a tape or to a file on disks. The computer used in this example does not have a tape backup available.

11. Click on the **down arrow** next to Choose a place to save your backup. A list of available disk drives will appear.

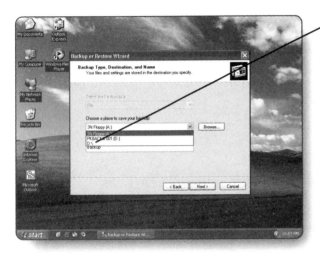

12. Click on **disk drive letter** (if backing up to a file), where to save the data. The option will be selected.

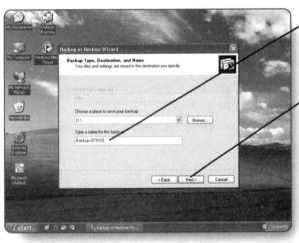

13. Type a **filename** for the backup. I recommend using the date as part of filename.

14. Click on **Next**. The final Backup or Restore screen will appear.

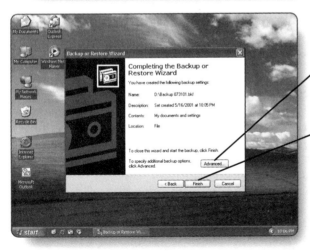

TIP

Optionally, click on Advanced to explore additional backup options.

15. Click on **Finish**. The backup process will begin.

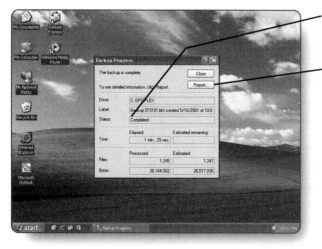

A Backup Progress dialog box will keep you apprised of the backup progress.

16. Click on **Close**. The Backup Progress dialog box will close.

Restoring Files

In the event something happens to your computer, you'll be very glad you backed up your critical data files. Backed up files are stored in a special format, so you can't use them directly. The Restore function places them back in their original locations and formats.

1. Click on **Start**. The Start menu will appear.

2. Click on **All Programs**. The All Programs menu will appear.

3. Click on **Accessories**. The Accessories submenu will appear.

4. Click on **System Tools**. The System Tools submenu will appear.

5. Click on **Backup**. The Backup or Restore Wizard will open.

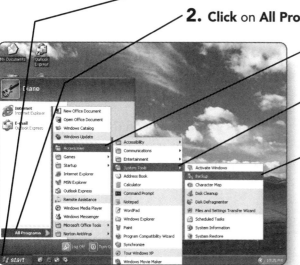

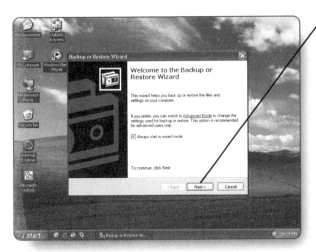

6. **Click** on **Next**. The Backup or Restore screen will appear.

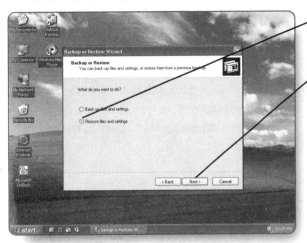

7. **Click** on **Restore files and settings**. The option will be selected.

8. **Click** on **Next**. The What to Restore screen will appear.

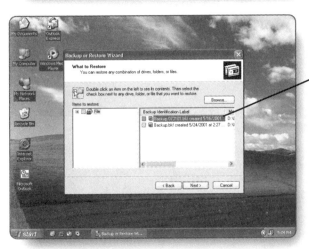

A listing of available backups will be displayed.

9. **Double-click** on the **backup set name** you want to restore. A tree of files included on the backup will appear.

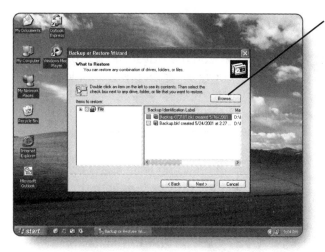

If there has been a total disaster and you have had to rebuild your PC and reload everything, the backup file may not be listed. If that's the case, click on Browse to enter the location where the backup resides.

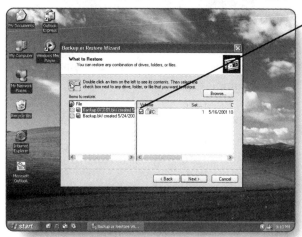

10. Click on the **files** you want to restore. A check mark will appear next to selected files.

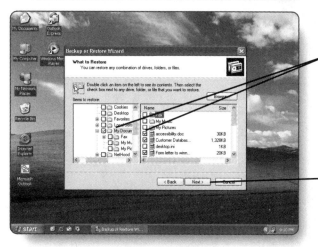

TIP

If you want to restore only a portion of the backup, double-click on folders until you see the files you want to restore, then click on the desired file check boxes.

11. Click on **Next**. The final Wizard screen will appear.

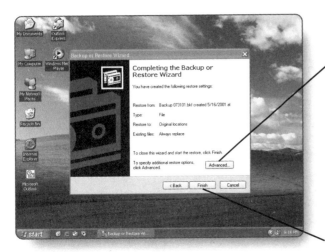

TIP

Click on the Advanced button to specify different restore options than the ones displayed on the final Wizard screen.

12. If restoring from a disk or tape, **insert** the **disk or tape** into the computer drive.

13. Click on **Finish**. The Restore Process dialog box will open.

The Restore Process dialog box will advise you when the restore process is complete.

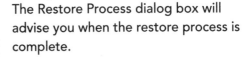

14. Click on **Close**. The Restore Process dialog box will close.

18

Troubleshooting Problems

Someday you may start up Windows and find that a program will not run or a device won't function. If this happens, try to troubleshoot the problem yourself before you call in an expert. In this chapter, you'll learn how to:

- Scan your hard disk for errors
- Restore your system to a previous setting
- Update Windows with the latest features and fixes

Scanning for Hard Disk Errors

Your hard disk does a good job of keeping track of which files are stored on which physical area of the disk, but it's not perfect. Sometimes mistakes creep in that cause mysterious problems when running Windows. Programs may lock up, or Windows may stop responding anymore.

When you experience problems with Windows, one thing to do is check each hard disk for errors.

1. Double-click on the **My Computer icon**. The My Computer window will open.

2. Right-click on your **hard drive icon**. A shortcut menu will appear.

NOTE
If you have more than one hard disk, do one at a time.

3. Click on **Properties**. The Properties dialog box will open.

4. Click on the **Tools tab**. The Tools tab will move to the front.

5. Click on the **Check Now button**. The Check Disk dialog box will open.

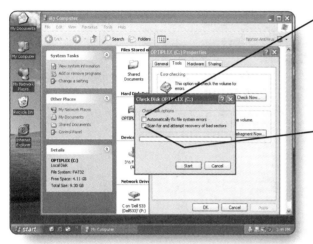

6a. Optionally, **click** on the **check box** next to Automatically fix file system errors. The option will be selected.

OR

6b. Optionally, **click** on the **check box** next to Scan for and attempt recovery of bad sectors. The option will be selected.

NOTE

Selecting Scan for and attempt recovery of bad sectors will take a little longer during the scan, but is worth doing, as any useable data located in bad sectors of the disk may be recovered.

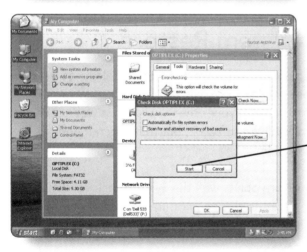

7. Click on **Start**. If you did not opt for either of the two automatic options in step 6a and 6b, the scan will begin.

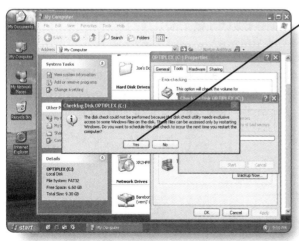

If you selected either of the two options in steps 6a or 6b, you will see a box saying that you cannot perform the check now. It offers to schedule the check to occur the next time you start the computer. If you see this, click on Yes and then restart your computer.

When the scan is complete, a dialog box will open.

8. Click on **OK**. The dialog box will close.

9. Click on **OK**. The Properties dialog box will close.

Using System Restore

We all have moments when we'd like to be able to go back in time. Suppose you loaded a new software program and it disrupted how some of your other applications work. Sure, you could uninstall the software, but that may not entirely resolve the problems.

By creating restore points with the System Restore feature, you can turn back the clock and return your computer settings to the way they were before the problems began.

Creating a Restore Point

Restore points are basically snapshots of the state of your system. Windows creates automatic restore points a couple of times a day, but you may want to create your own restore point before you install new hardware or software on your system.

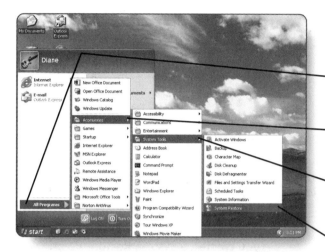

1. Click on **Start**. The Start menu will appear.

2. Click on **All Programs**. The All Programs menu will appear.

3. Click on **Accessories**. The Accessories submenu will appear.

4. Click on **System Tools**. The System Tools submenu will appear.

5. Click on **System Restore**. The Welcome to System Restore window will open.

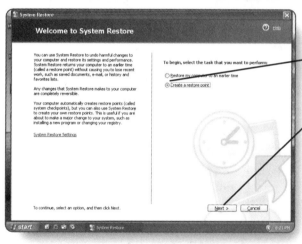

6. Click on **Create a restore point**. The option will be selected.

7. Click on **Next**. The Create a Restore Point screen will appear.

8. Type a **name** for the restore point. Use a description such as "Before an update" or "Before I installed Quake III." (Windows will automatically add the date and time.)

9. Click on **Create**. Windows will create a restore point.

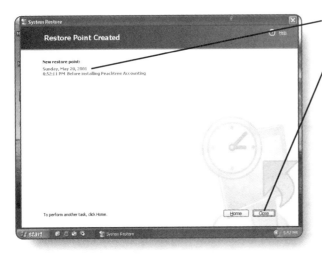

Windows confirms the restore point creation.

10. Click on **Close**. The System Restore window will close.

Restoring Your System

Uh-oh—something's not quite right. You installed that new game and now your screen is acting flaky or you cannot access a program. Now is the time you'll be glad you created a System Restore Point.

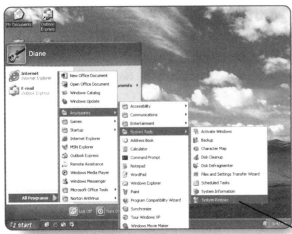

TIP

While System Restore does not remove any data, it will remove system changes since the last update—both those you want to get rid of and those you might want to keep. Thus, it should be used as an emergency procedure, not casually.

1. Follow steps 1-5 in the previous section, "Creating a Restore Point." The Welcome to System Restore window will open.

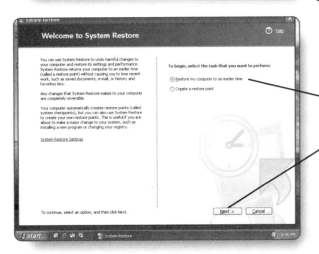

2. Click on **Restore my computer to an earlier time**. The option will be selected.

3. Click on **Next**. The Select a Restore Point screen will appear.

The calendar allows you to choose on what date you want to restore your system.

4. Click on a **date**. A list of all restore points created that day will appear.

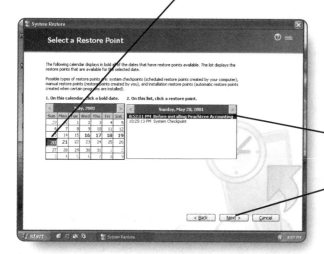

NOTE

System Checkpoints are those created automatically by Windows.

5. Click on a **restore point**. The restore point will be selected.

6. Click on **Next**. A Confirm Restore Point Selection window will appear.

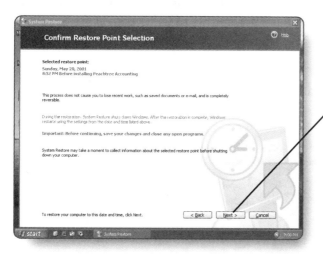

Restoring your system does not affect any document data; however, make sure to close all open applications and documents.

7. Click on **Next**. The restoration process will begin.

Windows will shut down and your computer will restart. A confirmation message will appear.

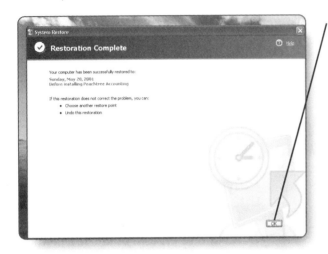

8. Click on **OK**. The System Restore window will close.

Getting Windows Updates

The Windows Update function is a Web-based service you can use to update your Windows system software. This function scans your computer for outdated system files and allows you to replace them with the most recent versions. You must have an Internet connection available to use this service and you must be logged on as an administrator.

Getting an Windows Update Manually

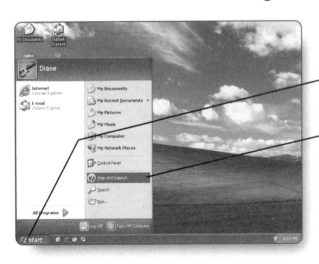

You can check for updates and manually update your system files at any time.

1. Click on **Start**. The Start menu will appear.

2. Click on **Help and Support**. The Help and Support Center screen will open.

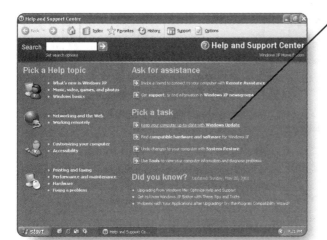

3. Click on **Keep your computer up-to-date with Windows Update**. The Welcome to Windows update screen will appear.

NOTE

If you are not already connected to the Internet, you will be prompted to connect.

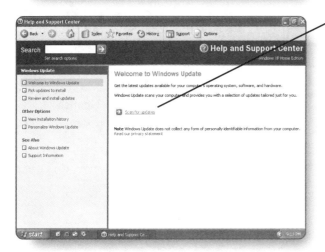

4. Click on **Scan for updates**. A list of available updates will appear.

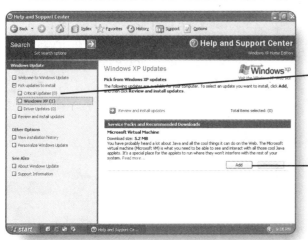

Your choices will vary from the ones shown in this figure.

Some may be classified as critical updates, meaning you really *should* choose them to make your computer function better.

5. Click on the **Add button** under any option you want to update. The item will be marked for update.

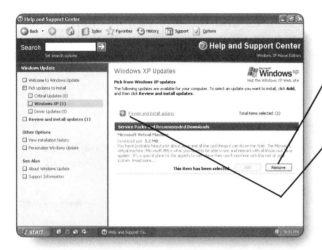

6. **Click** on **Review and install updates**. The Total Selected Updates screen will appear.

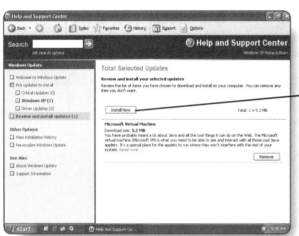

7. **Review** the **Total Selected Updates screen** to confirm the components you selected to update.

8. **Click** on **Install Now**. A License Agreement dialog box will open.

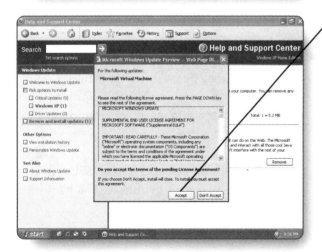

9. **Read** the **license agreement**, then **click** on **Accept**. The update process will begin. A status window will indicate the update progress.

Depending on the type of update, you may be prompted to restart your computer.

10a. **Click** on **OK**. The computer will restart.

OR

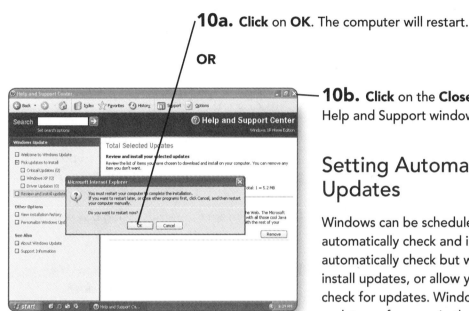

10b. **Click** on the **Close button**. The Help and Support window will close.

Setting Automatic Updates

Windows can be scheduled to automatically check and install updates, automatically check but wait for you to install updates, or allow you to manually check for updates. Windows stores your update preferences in the Control Panel, System area.

1. **Click** on **Start**. The Start menu will appear.

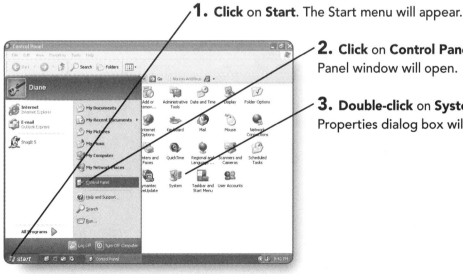

2. **Click** on **Control Panel**. The Control Panel window will open.

3. **Double-click** on **System**. The System Properties dialog box will open.

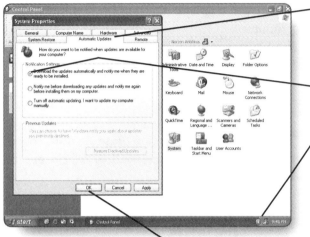

4. **Click** on the **Automatic Updates tab**. The Automatic Updates tab will come to the front.

5. **Click** on a **Notification Settings option**. The option will be selected.

If you choose either of the first two options, a yellow update notification message will appear in the status bar. You'll be able to click on the update message to proceed with the update.

6. **Click** on **OK**. The System Properties dialog box will close.

7. **Click** on the **Close button**. The Control Panel window will close.

19

Improving System Performance

Windows comes with several utilities that help your system run faster and better by organizing the files on the hard disk efficiently and by removing files that you don't need. In this chapter you'll learn how to:

- Defragment your hard disk for better performance
- Remove unwanted files with Disk Cleanup
- Schedule maintenance tasks

Defragmenting Your Hard Drive

When a file is stored, the computer puts it in the first available space on the disk drive. If there's not enough room for the entire file, the rest of the file is put into the next available space. A file is *fragmented* when it is split into more than one location on your hard drive. *Defragmenting* your hard drive rearranges the way data files are stored on your hard disk. Programs and documents are organized so that the entire program or document you want can be read with a minimum number of physical movements of the disk drive. This can substantially improve the performance of your computer by decreasing the amount of time needed to retrieve a file.

TIP

It's a good idea to run the defragment program every couple of months, or after you delete large amounts of data or programs from your hard drive.

---

1. Double-click on the **My Computer icon**. The My Computer window will open.

2. Right-click on your **hard disk drive**. A shortcut menu will appear.

3. Click on **Properties**. The Properties dialog box will open.

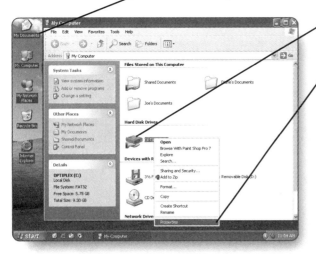

4. Click on the **Tools tab**. The Tools tab will move to the front.

5. Click on **Defragment Now**. The Disk Defragmenter window will open.

TIP
You can also open the Defragmenter window by clicking on Start, All Programs, Accessories, System Tools, Disk Defragmenter.

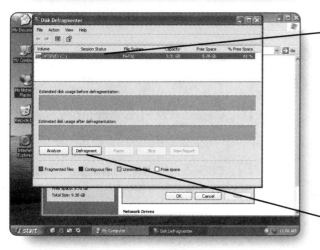

6. Click on the **drive letter** that you want to defragment. The drive letter will be selected.

NOTE
If you have more than one hard disk, do one at a time.

7. Click on **Defragment**. The defragmenting process will begin.

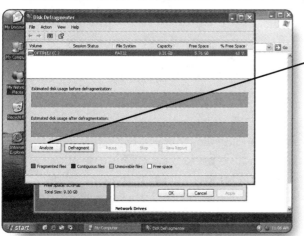

TIP
Click on Analyze if you want Windows to first check and see if the disk needs defragmenting.

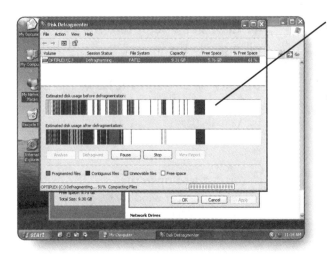

As the defragmentation process continues, you will see red areas gradually replaced with blue ones. Blue indicates contiguous files; red indicates fragmentation. White areas are unused space.

Don't be alarmed if the process repeats itself or takes a little time. When the process is complete, a message box will open.

8. **Click** on **Close**. The message box will close.

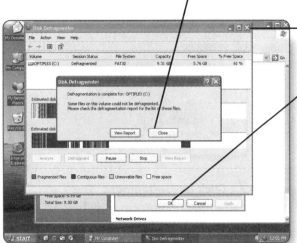

9. **Click** on the **Close button**. The Disk Defragmenter window will close.

10. **Click** on **OK**. The Properties dialog box will close.

11. **Click** on the **My computer window Close button**. The My Computer window will close.

Using Disk Cleanup

If you are running short on hard disk space or want to get rid of unnecessary files, Disk Cleanup can help by analyzing your system and recommending files that you can safely delete without affecting Windows performance. These deletion candidates may include temporary files that are no longer needed, downloaded Internet pages, installation files, and others.

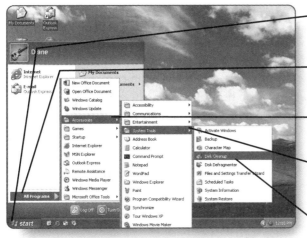

1. Click on **Start**. The Start menu will appear.

2. Click on **All Programs**. The All Programs menu will appear.

3. Click on **Accessories**. The Accessories submenu will appear.

4. Click on **System Tools**. The System Tools submenu will appear.

5. Click on **Disk Cleanup**. A Disk Cleaning dialog box will open.

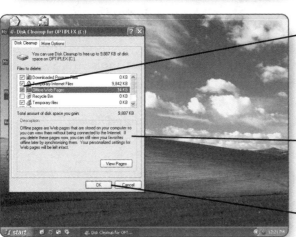

6. Click in the **check box** next to the file types you want to delete. A check mark will appear in selected items.

TIP

Click on any file to read a description of the file type.

7. Click on **OK**. A confirmation box will open.

8. Click on **Yes**. The Cleanup process will begin. A status bar will indicate the progress and the Disk Cleanup will close upon completion.

Automatically Scheduling Tasks

Many system tasks can be scheduled to run automatically at a time when you normally are not using the computer. These scheduled tasks can be housekeeping chores, such as defragmenting, or they can be opening your favorite software application.

1. Click on **Start**. The Start menu will appear.

2. Click on **All Programs**. The All Programs menu will appear.

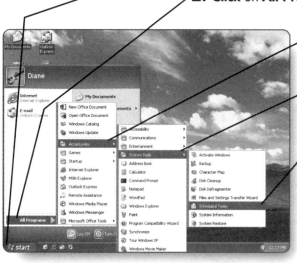

3. Click on **Accessories**. The Accessories submenu will appear.

4. Click on **System Tools**. The System Tools submenu will appear.

5. Click on **Scheduled Tasks**. The Scheduled Tasks window will open.

6. Double-click on **Add Scheduled Task**. The Scheduled Task Wizard will open.

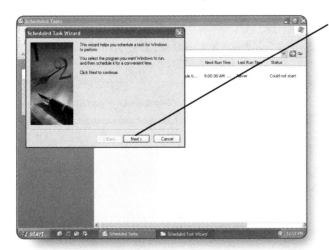

7. Click on **Next**. A list of available applications will appear.

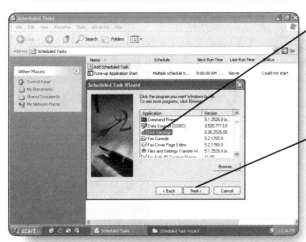

8. Click on the **program** you want to schedule. The item will be selected.

Scheduled tasks will be created one at a time with the Scheduled Task Wizard.

9. Click on **Next**. A list of timing intervals will appear.

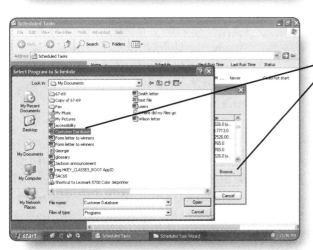

TIP

If you want to open an application with a specific document, click on the Browse button to locate and select the desired document.

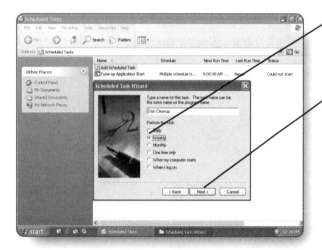

10. Click on an **interval** at which to schedule the task. The option will be selected.

11. Click on **Next**. More controls will appear to further define when you want the task to run.

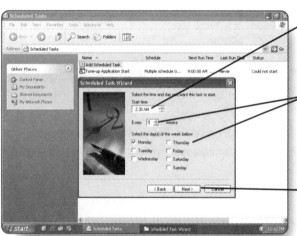

12. Enter a **start time** in the Start time list box. Be sure to choose if you want the task to start in the AM or PM.

13. Make your other **selections** from the controls provided. The exact controls displayed will vary, depending on the frequency of the scheduled task.

14. Click on **Next**. The next screen will prompt you for a user name and password.

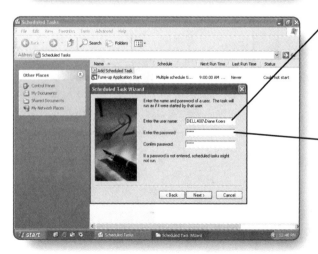

15. If necessary, **enter** a **user name**. Usually, the default name is the preferred choice. You learned about managing users in Chapter 13, "Tinkering with the Control Panel."

16. Optionally, **enter** a **password** in the password text box. A series of asterisks will appear. If you don't have a password when you log on to Windows, you won't need to enter the password here. You can leave the box blank.

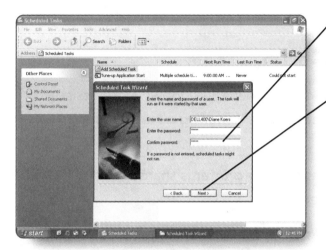

17. If you did enter a password in step 16, **re-enter** the **password** in the Confirm password text box.

18. Click on **Next**. A confirmation box will appear.

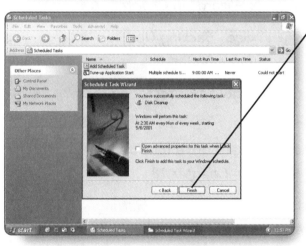

19. Click on **Finish**. The task will be scheduled.

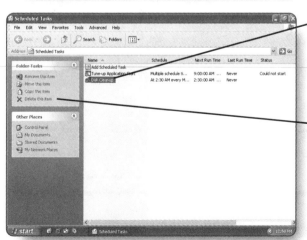

The task appears in the Scheduled Tasks window. You can modify any task by double-clicking on it.

TIP

To delete a scheduled task, select the task then click on Delete this item.

20. Click on the **Close button**. The Scheduled Tasks window will close.

Part V Review Questions

1. What is the name of the tool furnished with Windows XP to assist you with installing a new printer? *See "Installing a New Printer" in Chapter 16.*

2. How can you visually tell whether your printer is shared? *See "Sharing a Printer" in Chapter 18.*

3. Can you send a cover sheet with a document you fax from your computer? *See "Using the Send Fax Wizard" in Chapter 16*

4. Why should you back up your files? *See "Backing Up Files" in Chapter 17*

5. Why can't you use backed up files without first restoring them? *See "Restoring Files" in Chapter 17*

6. When might you want to check your hard drive for potential errors? *See "Scanning for Hard Disk Errors" in Chapter 18*

7. What does the Windows Update feature do? *See "Getting Windows Updates" in Chapter 18*

8. What happens to a file when it is fragmented? *See "Defragmenting Your Hard Drive" in Chapter 19*

9. What types of files might Disk Cleanup delete from your system? *See "Using Disk Cleanup" in Chapter 19*

10. What types of tasks can be scheduled to run automatically? *See "Automatically Scheduling Tasks" in Chapter 19*

PART VI

Connecting to Other Computers

Chapter 20
Using a Network. 261

Chapter 21
Connecting to the Internet. 277

Chapter 22
Surfing with Internet Explorer 287

Chapter 23
Working with Outlook Express. 303

Chapter 24
Using the Windows Address Book 325

Chapter 25
Discovering Windows Messenger. 337

20

Using a Network

If you have multiple machines in your home, Windows XP is an ideal operating system to use for creating a peer-to-peer network. It uses the Networking Wizard to connect network-capable machines and printers and makes them available to the workgroup. In this chapter, you'll learn how to:

- Browse other computers
- Create a Network Place
- Open or save a file to a network drive
- Map to and disconnect from a network drive
- Share your computer drives and folders

Preparing to Network

Before you actually tell the machines to talk to each other, you'll need some special equipment.

The first requirement is that all machines must have a network card in the system. If you don't have one, you'll need to purchase one and have it installed by a reliable technician.

Secondly, you'll need a method of connecting the machines. The most common method is via a cable connected from one network card to another. Some homes are pre-wired so the cables can connect through jacks placed in the walls. Others simply run the cable around the walls of the house. Other methods of connecting the two machines might be via a special piece of hardware plugged into an electrical socket or even a wireless system that uses radio frequency technology.

If you are connecting more than two machines, you'll also need a piece of hardware called a *hub*. Each computer cable will plug into the hub. If you have cable modem service or DSL Internet service, the service will also connect to the hub.

All of these items are usually available at a shop that sells computer hardware. Installing this hardware and setting the network configuration is done on an individual basis depending on the exact equipment and components you have, therefore it is beyond the scope of this book. I recommend you contact a reliable computer technician to assist with the connectivity process.

Working with My Network Places

The My Network Places window is similar to Windows Explorer. It displays and helps you manage files. The difference is that the My Network Places window also displays files on *other* computers.

Browsing Other Computers

In order to browse other computers, those computers must allow sharing. If they don't, you won't be able to see their contents. Later in this chapter, you'll learn how to set up computers to allow sharing.

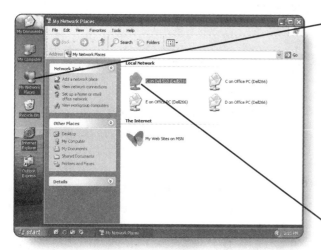

1. Double-click on **My Network Places**. The My Network Places Window will open.

Notice that in this figure a computer called Dell 266 has three different hard drives shared: C:, D:, and E:, while the computer called Dell 533 has only a C: drive to share. Each drive on a computer must be shared independently.

2. Double-click on the **computer location** you want to view. A different window will appear.

The window will display the contents of the specified computer.

From here you can work with the folders and files on that drive as if it were a drive on your own PC. Expect access to a network shared drive to be a little slower than your local drive. See Chapter 9 "Organizing Files and Folders" for a refresher.

TIP
Close the browsed window by clicking on the Close button.

Browsing the Entire Workgroup

The collection of your computers is called a workgroup. Traditionally, home users have a single workgroup, while some businesses have multiple workgroups. For example, a business might have all the accounting computers in a workgroup called ACCTG, while the marketing computers might be in a workgroup called MARKET.

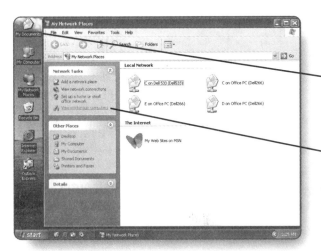

You can browse all the computers in your workgroup.

1. Double-click on **My Network Places**. The My Network Places Window will open.

2. Click on **View workgroup computers**. Icons representing all computers in your workgroup will appear.

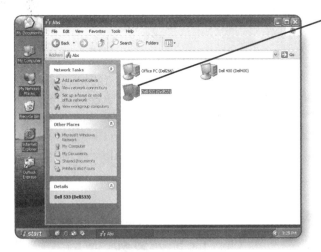

3. Double-click on any **icon**. A list of shared drives and printers on that computer will appear.

NOTE

Depending on how your network is configured, you may be prompted for your username and password.

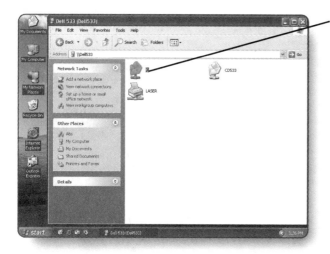

4. Double-click on any **drive**. A list of the folders on that drive will open.

From here you can work with the folders and files on that drive as if it were a drive on your own PC. See Chapter 9, "Organizing Files and Folders" for a refresher.

Creating a Network Place

When you add other computers to your workgroup, you'll probably want to also add the new computer's hard disk drive to your My Network Places. A network place is a shortcut to a network drive; creating a network place saves you from having to wade through multiple levels of workgroups and computers each time to find a particular drive.

1. Double-click on **My Network Places**. The My Network Places window will open.

2. Click on **Add a network place**. The Add Network Place Wizard will open.

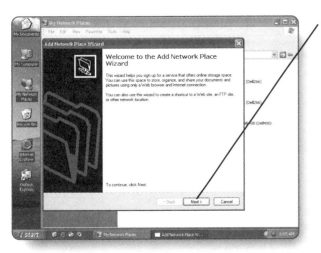

3. Click on **Next**. The next screen will appear.

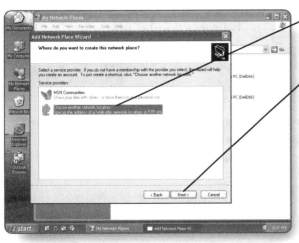

4. Click on **Choose another network location**. The option will be highlighted.

5. Click on **Next**. You'll be prompted for the network location.

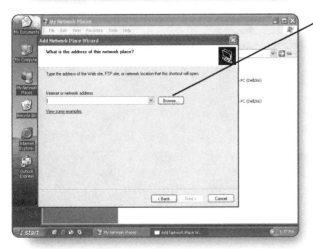

6. Click on **Browse**. The Browse For Folder dialog box will open.

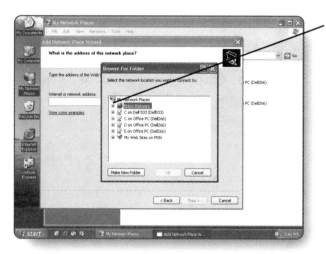

7. Click on the **plus sign** next to Entire Network. The plus sign will turn into a minus sign and a list of workgroup types will appear. Most home networks will only have one type of workgroup listed.

8. Click on the **plus sign** next to the workgroup types. The plus sign will turn into a minus sign and a list of workgroup names will appear.

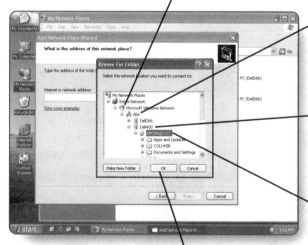

9. Click on the **plus sign** next to the workgroup name. The plus sign will turn into a minus sign and a list of all computers in the workgroup will appear.

10. Click on the **plus sign** next to the computer you want to add to My Network Places. A list of shared drives will appear.

11. Click on the **shared drive** you want to add. The drive name will be highlighted.

12. Click on **OK**. The Browse For Folder dialog box will close.

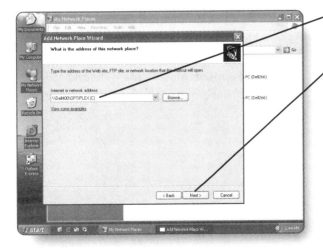

The network address will appear in the Internet or network address text box.

13. Click on **Next**. The What do you want to name this place? screen will appear.

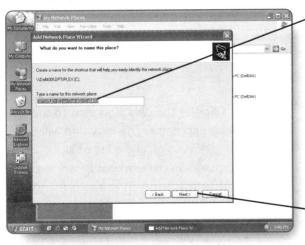

The name determines how you see the icon in the My Network places box.

TIP

Optionally, type a new, more descriptive name for the new location. (For example, **Susan's computer** or **Jerry's CD-ROM Drive**.)

14. Click on **Next**. The final Wizard screen will appear.

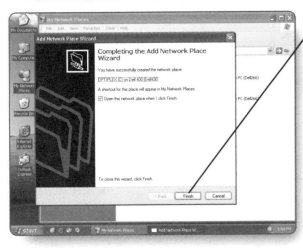

15. Click on **Finish**. The Wizard screen will close.

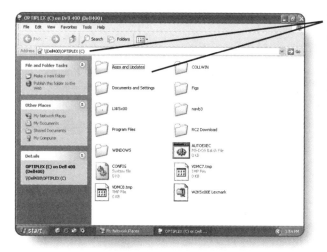

Windows automatically opens a window to the newly networked drive.

The newly created location will appear in the My Network Places window.

Choosing a Network Drive in an Application

You may want to open files from a network drive or save files to one. Most programs enable you to select from your My Network Places folder from within the Open or Save dialog boxes.

Start the following steps from within an application, with the Open dialog box open. In most programs, you can display the Open dialog box by opening the File menu and clicking on Open. You would follow the same steps to save a file to a network drive, except click on File, Save instead of Open.

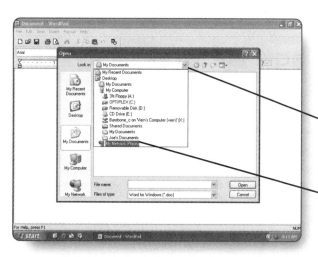

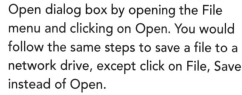

1. Click on the **down arrow** next to the Look in list box. A drop down list of locations will appear.

2. Click on **My Network Places**.

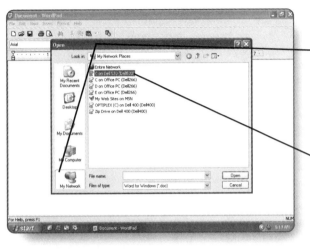

TIP

Optionally, if the application allows it, click on the My Network Places icon instead of following steps 1 and 2.

A list of network locations will appear.

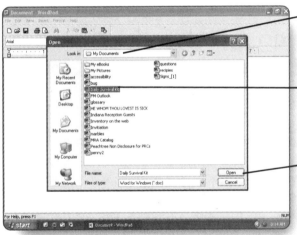

3. Navigate to the **network folder** containing the file you want to open or in which you want to save.

4. Click on or **type** the **file name** you want to open or save. The file name will be highlighted.

5. Click on **Open (or Save)**. The file will be either opened and appear on the screen, or saved to the network folder.

Mapping a Network Drive

Some applications do not allow you to select files from the My Network Places, but require that you specify a drive letter instead. This is called *mapping*. Mapping is sort of like tricking the application into working with network drives by assigning a drive letter. If that needed information is stored on a network drive, you'll need to assign a drive letter to it—for example G:—rather than the network address of \\bob\c_drive.

1. Double-click on **My Network Places.** The My Network Places window will open.

TIP
Optionally, open the My Computer window instead of the My Network Places.

2. Click on **Tools.** The Tools menu will appear.

3. Click on **Map Network Drive.** The Map Network Drive Wizard will open.

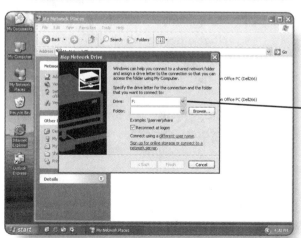

Windows will suggest assigning the next available drive letter to the mapped drive. You can accept this choice or select your own drive letter.

4. Click on the **down arrow** next to the Drive list box. A list of available drive letters will appear.

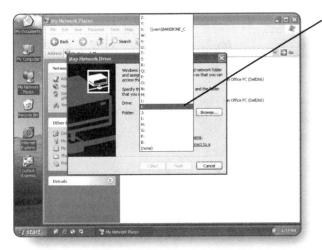

5. Click on a **drive letter** you want to assign to this network location. The selected letter will appear in the Drive list box.

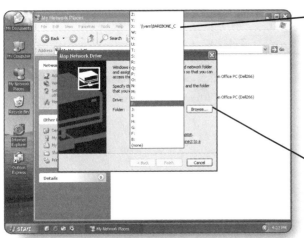

Currently mapped drive connections appear next to the letter to which they are assigned.

Now you need to specify which network drive or folder you want to assign to the selected drive letter.

6. Click on **Browse**. The Browse For Folder dialog box will open.

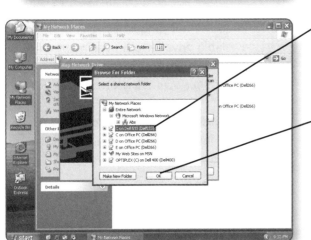

7. Navigate to and **select** the **drive** or **specific folder** to which you want to assign the drive letter. The drive or folder name will be highlighted.

8. Click on **OK**. The Browse For Folder dialog box will close.

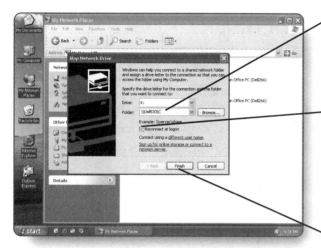

The network path will appear in the Folder text box.

TIP

Deselect the Reconnect at logon check box if you do not want this location to be mapped to the selected drive letter every time you log on to the network.

9. Click on **Finish**. The Wizard will close and the contents of the selected drive or folder will appear.

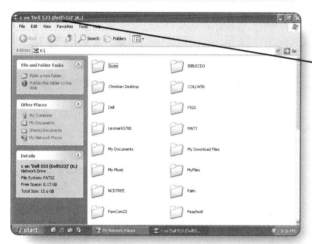

The title bar lists the network path and the newly mapped drive letter.

NOTE

For some unknown reason, and at the most unexpected times, Windows occasionally forgets where a mapped drive is located. In those cases, you'll need to redo the mapping steps above.

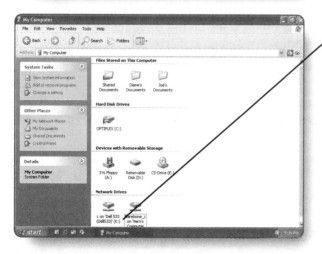

The mapped drive as it appears in the My Computer window.

Disconnecting from a Network Drive

If you no longer want a particular drive mapped, you can cancel it by disconnecting a network drive. This does not change your ability to access network resources—it merely cancels the shortcut to the mapped drive.

1. Double-click on **My Computer**. The My Computer window will open.

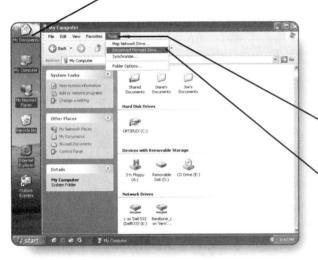

> ### TIP
> Optionally, open the My Network Places window instead of the My Computer.

2. Click on **Tools**. The Tools menu will appear.

3. Click on **Disconnect Network Drive**. The Disconnect Network Drive dialog box will open.

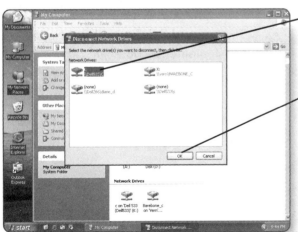

4. Click on the **drive icon** you want to disconnect. The drive icon will be highlighted.

5. Click on **OK**. The Disconnect Network Drive dialog box will close.

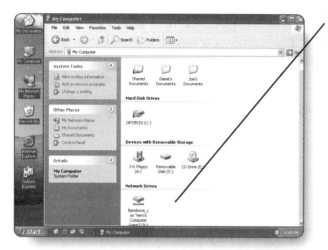

The drive icon will no longer appear in the My Computer window.

Sharing Your Computer with Others

If you want to allow other users on the network to access your computer, you must give Windows permission to share the drive or folder. You can choose to share hard drives, zip drives, CD-ROM drives, specific folders, or even printers. Keep in mind that by sharing your files and folders, you are giving other users of your computer and others on your network permission to open, edit, rename or delete those files.

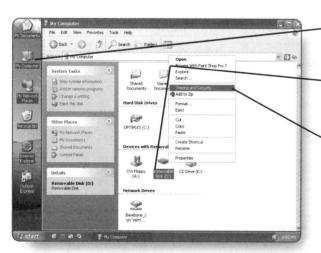

1. **Double-click** on **My Computer**. The My Computer window will appear.

2. **Right-click** on the **drive** you want to share. A shortcut menu will appear.

3. **Click** on **Sharing and Security**. The Sharing and Security dialog box will open.

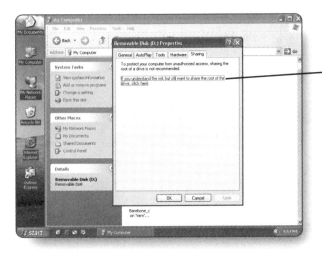

Windows will warn you of the risk of sharing drives and folders.

4. **Click** on **If you understand the risk but still want to share the root of the drive, click here**. The sharing options will become available.

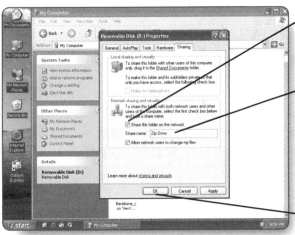

5. **Click** on **Share this folder on the network**. A check mark will appear in the check box.

6. **Type** a **name** for the shared drive. This will allow others to easily identify the drive they are accessing. If other users on your network are not using Windows XP, keep the name to less than 12 characters.

7. **Click** on **OK**. The Sharing and Security dialog box will close.

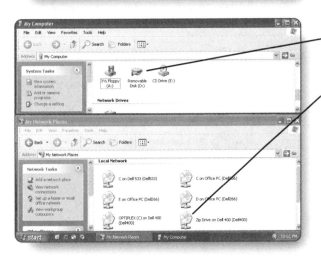

Shared drives are indicated with a hand under the icon.

The shared drive as it appears in My Network Places.

21

Connecting to the Internet

Whether you plan on surfing the Internet or just need to send an e-mail message, you need to get connected. Windows provides several tools to assist you with your online connectivity needs. In this chapter, you'll learn how to:

- Set up an Internet connection
- Configure an e-mail account
- Connect with a dial-up connection
- Start your Web browser

Setting Up an Internet Connection

The New Connection Wizard helps you configure your Windows XP to your Internet Service Provider (ISP).

Starting the New Connection Wizard

If you do not have an ISP account, the New Connection Wizard will help you choose a provider and sign up.

1. Click on **Start**. The Start menu will appear.

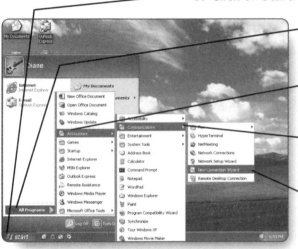

2. Click on **All Programs**. The All Programs menu will appear.

3. Click on **Accessories**. The Accessories submenu will appear.

4. Click on **Communications**. The Communications submenu will appear.

5. Click on **New Connection Wizard**. The Welcome to the New Connection Wizard will begin.

6. Click on **Next**. The Network Connection Type screen will appear.

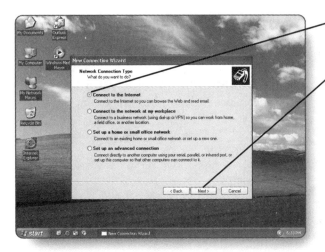

7. Click on **Connect to the Internet**. The option will be selected.

8. Click on **Next**. The Getting Ready Screen will appear.

If you don't already have an ISP, proceed to the next section. If you do already have an Internet account, skip the next section and jump ahead to the "Setting Up an Existing Internet Account" section.

Signing Up for a New Internet Account

There are two ways to go about signing up for an Internet account. One is to shop around in your area to find a provider who offers service at a reasonable price. If you choose this method, skip to the section "Setting Up an Existing Internet Account" later in this chapter.

Optionally, you can choose from among the providers that Microsoft suggests for your area. Most of these are large national providers who offer good service.

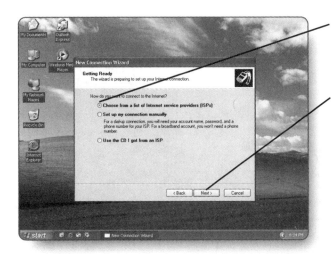

1. Click on **Choose from a list of Internet service providers (ISPs)**. The option will be selected.

2. Click on **Next**. The next screen will appear.

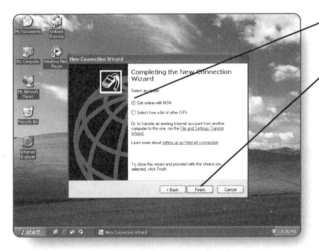

3. Click on an **option**. For our example, we'll go online with the MSN service.

4. Click on **Finish**. The Use MSN Explorer? dialog box will open.

In order to view pages on the Internet, you'll need a Web browser. You can use Microsoft Internet Explorer, MSN Explorer, Netscape, or any Web browser you choose. For the remainder of this exercise, we'll use the new MSN Explorer.

5. Click on **Yes**. The Welcome to MSN Explorer window will open.

6. Click on **Continue**. MSN prompts you for your location.

7. **Click** on an **down arrow** and **select** your **country** from the Country/Region list box. Your country will appear in the list box.

8. **Click** on **Continue**. The next sign up screen will appear.

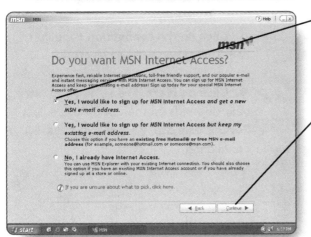

9. **Click** on **Yes, I would like to sign up for MSN Internet Access and get a new MSN e-mail address**. The option will be selected.

10. **Click** on **Continue**. The check your dialing options screen will appear.

From this point on, the screens will vary depending on choices you made in the previous steps. The ISP you choose will prompt you for information about your phone service, your name, and other identifying information, including credit card information for billing purposes. Answer any requested questions and make sure your phone line is connected to the modem connection of your computer. You will be connected to the MSN network and given a screen name to use when connecting. You'll also be prompted to supply a password to use when signing on.

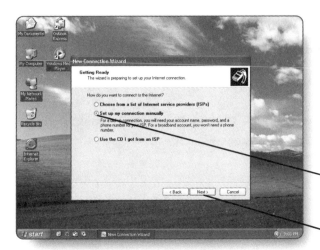

Setting Up an Existing Internet Account

If you already have an Internet account, you'll need to supply information to the New Connection Wizard about connecting to your existing ISP.

1. **Click** on **Set up my connection manually**. The option will be selected.

2. **Click** on **Next**. The Internet Connection screen will appear.

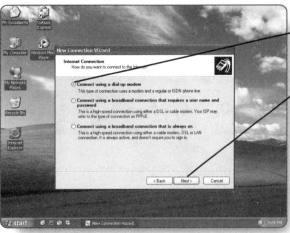

3. **Click** on the **connection type** you use. The option will be selected.

4. **Click** on **Next**. The screen you see next depends on the option you select. For this exercise, we'll set up a dial-up connection.

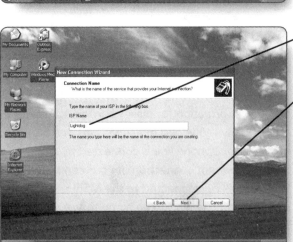

5. **Enter** a **name** for your ISP. Doing so will help you identify the connection.

6. **Click** on **Next**. The Phone Number to Dial screen will appear.

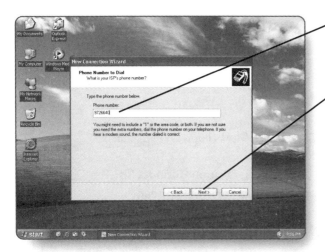

7. Enter the **access number** for your ISP. Enter numbers only; no special characters are necessary.

8. Click on **Next**. The Internet Account Information screen will appear.

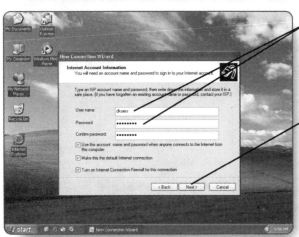

9. Enter your **user name and password** as required by your ISP. The password and password confirmation will appear as dots on the screen.

10. Click on **Next**. A confirmation screen will appear.

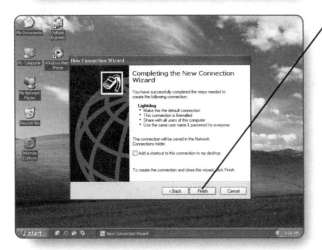

11. Click on **Finish**. The New Connection Wizard will close and Windows will save your connection information.

NOTE

Your ISP may give you additional instructions for working with their connections. Follow the instructions given by your ISP.

Dialing Your Connection

After you create a dial-up connection, Windows places a new Connect To item on the Start menu to help you quickly dial into your ISP.

1. **Click** on **Start**. The Start menu will appear.

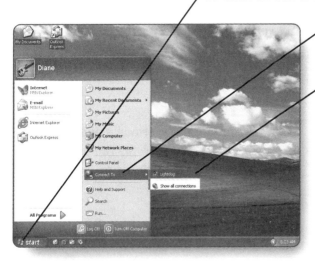

2. **Click** on **Connect To**. The Connect to submenu will appear.

3. **Click** on your **connection name**. The Connect dialog box will open.

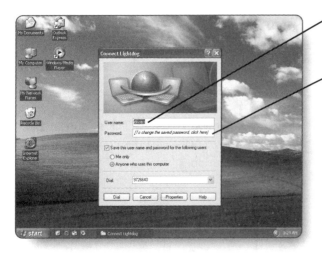

4. **Verify** the **user name**. Type a different one if necessary.

5. **Click** in the **password box**. A blinking insertion point will appear.

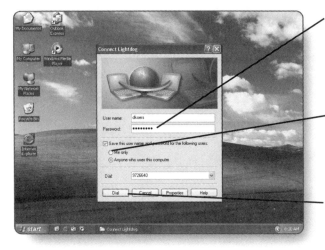

6. Type your **password**. A series of dots will appear.

7. Click on **Dial**. You will probably hear some strange noises coming from your computer. That's OK. It's your computer talking to your ISP's computer.

Starting Your Web Browser

Now that your connection is established, you'll need to use a program to view the HTML document that have been created for the Web. These programs, called *Web browsers*, were briefly mentioned earlier in "Signing Up for a New Internet Account." There are a number of good Web browsers available and two of them, Internet Explorer and Microsoft Explorer, come with Windows XP. Another popular Web browser is called Netscape Navigator.

1. Double-click on the **icon** for your Web browser.

If you are not already connected to the Internet, you may be prompted to connect. Usually, cable modem, DSL, and other types of permanent connections will not prompt you for information.

2. Enter your **password** if it's not already in the password box. A series of dots will appear as you type.

3. Click on **Connect**. The connection to your ISP will open.

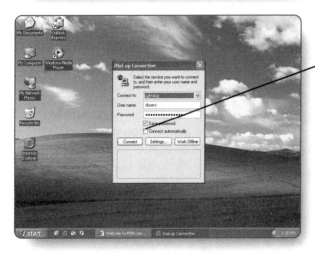

TIP

To bypass the Dial-Up connection box in the future, click on Connect automatically.

The Web browser will launch and a Web page will appear. You'll learn about exploring Web pages in Chapter 22, "Surfing with Internet Explorer."

22

Surfing with Internet Explorer

The Internet is a collection of millions of computers around the world: Learning opportunities and hours of fun are at your fingertips. But how do you get to these computers? Internet Explorer enables you to gain access to the vast stores of information on these computers while protecting your children and others from undesirable material. In this chapter, you'll learn how to:

- Browse the Web with Internet Explorer
- Set and use Favorites
- Review your Web usage history
- Set parental controls

Browsing the Web with Internet Explorer

Screens that you access on the Internet are called *Web pages* or *home pages*. You call the starting point of a series of connected Web pages a *home page*. Web pages have *addresses*. A typical Web address starts with http://www. Then you need to specify an exact address, such as microsoft.com or whitehouse.gov. Therefore, a completed Web address might look something like http://www.microsoft.com or http://www.whitehouse.gov.

Starting Internet Explorer

Access Internet Explorer from the desktop or from the Quick Launch bar.

1. Double-click on **Internet Explorer**. If you connect to the Internet through a modem and you are not currently connected, a Dial-up Connection dialog box will open.

NOTE

If you have a permanent connection such as cable modem, DSL, or T1, you won't see the Connect To box.

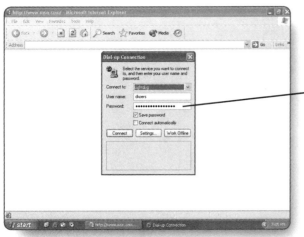

2. Type your **password**, if it's not already entered in the Password text box. A series of dots will appear.

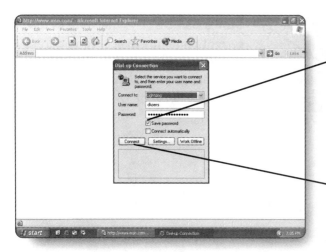

TIP
Leave the Save Password box checked if you want Internet Explorer to remember your password. Uncheck the box if you want to enter it yourself each time.

3. Click on **Connect**. Your ISP will establish a connection, and the Internet Explorer home page will display.

A *home page* is the first page a browser looks at when you launch your Web browser. The terms *start page* and *home page* are sometimes interchangeable.

Exploring the Internet Explorer Window

When you first launch Internet Explorer, the MSN Web page opens. Web pages change frequently, so your page may look different from the one displayed here.

• **Toolbar**. The Internet Explorer window has a toolbar with buttons to help you navigate the Web. If you don't have a toolbar showing, click on View, Toolbars, and then Standard Buttons.

• **Address bar**. Displays the address of the currently displayed Web page. Typing a different address in the address bar will cause Internet Explorer to display a new Web page.

- **Status bar**. Displays the state of the current page, the exact Web address of a hyperlink, and other information about Internet Explorer such as Working Offline or Security Properties.

Following Hyperlinks

One of the easiest ways to use the Internet is to click on a *hyperlink* on your start page. Doing so whisks you away to some other page, which in turn contains its own hyperlinks that you can click on. Moving around the Internet this way is called *surfing*. When you position your mouse on underlined text or pictures and the mouse turns into a hand, you are pointing to a hyperlink. You click a hyperlink to go to a Web page referenced by the hyperlink.

When you point to a hyperlink, its Web address appears at the bottom of the Internet Explorer window.

1. Point to a **hyperlink**. The mouse pointer will become a hand.

2. Click on the **hyperlink**. The Web page represented by that hyperlink will load.

Moving Backward and Forward

After clicking on a hyperlink, you may want to return to the preceding Web page you were viewing.

1. **Click** on the **Back button**. The previously viewed Web page will redisplay.

2. **Click** on the **Forward button**. Internet Explorer will reload the page you viewed prior to pushing the Back button.

TIP

Occasionally a page won't load correctly and you can't read the text or view graphics. Click on the Refresh button to try loading the same page again.

Returning to Your Home Page

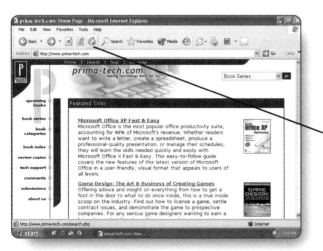

The Internet Explorer window includes a button to quickly return you to your home page. By default, Windows XP will load the http://www.msn.com as the home page.

1. **Click** on the **Home button**. Your home page will redisplay.

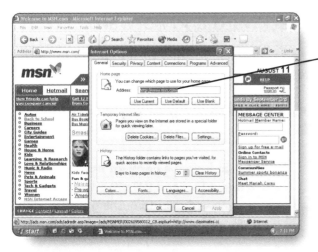

TIP

You can change which page is your home page. Click on Tools, Internet Options and enter your preferred home page in the address box on the general tab.

Entering a Specific Web Address

Web addresses are displayed almost everywhere you look these days. You can easily visit a Web address by typing its specific address.

1. Double-click in the **Address text box**. The current address will be highlighted.

2. Type the specific **Web address.** The address will appear in the Address list box.

3. Press the **Enter key**. Internet Explorer will display the specified Web page.

Playing Favorites

If you have a special poem that you like to read often, you might place a bookmark at the location of that poem. You'll find that Internet Explorer Favorites are like bookmarks to your favorite Web sites.

Adding Favorites

NOTE

Favorites aren't limited to Web pages. You can make any document or folder on your computer a Favorite.

Favorites are a convenient way to organize the Web sites that you visit frequently.

1. Go to the **page** you want to add to your list of favorite sites. The page will appear in the Internet Explorer window.

2. Click on **Favorites**. The Favorites menu will appear.

3. Click on **Add to Favorites**. The Add Favorite dialog box will open.

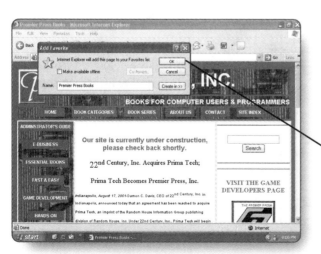

TIP

Optionally, click in the Name box and type a new name for the favorite.

4. Click on **OK**. Internet Explorer will add the Web address to your list of favorites.

TIP

To add a Favorite really quickly, display the Web page and press Ctrl+D.

Accessing Your Favorite Sites

Now, to get to one of your favorite sites, you don't have to remember the Web address or even type it. You can access your favorite site with a simple click of the mouse.

1. Click on **Favorites**. The Favorites list will appear.

2. Click the **page** you want to open. Internet Explorer will open the specified Web page.

TIP

Optionally, click on the Favorites button and make a selection from the Favorites window. Click on the Favorites button again to close the Favorites window.

Searching for Information Online

A variety of sites on the Internet are devoted to searching for other sites. Such sites are called *search engines*. Search engines are free to use. One popular search engine (and there are many) is the Microsoft Network service (MSN).

1. Click on the **Home button**. The MSN.COM page will display.

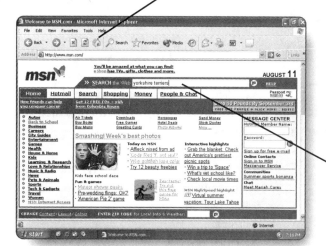

2. Click in the **Search the Web text box**. A blinking insertion point will appear.

3. Type the **search term(s)** in the text box. You can type a single word, several words, or a question.

4. Click on **Go** or **press** the **Enter key**. A list of results will appear.

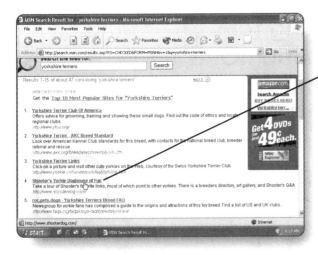

Each result will display a description and the Web page location.

5. Click on the **hyperlink** for a page that interests you. That page will load.

Viewing Your Surfing History

Want to revisit a page you previously found, but can't remember where it was? Use the History pane to review a list of recently viewed Web sites.

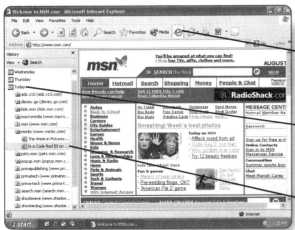

1. Click on the **History button**. The History pane will open on the left side of the screen.

2. Click on a **time frame**. Hyperlinks to all sites viewed within the selected time frame will be listed.

3. Click on a **hyperlink**. The Web page will appear.

4. Click on the **History button**. The History pane will close.

Setting Content Restrictions

You'll find the Web filled with information. Just about any topic you want to research can be found on the Web. However, you might want to monitor the information you, your children, or others can access. With the Content Advisor, you can screen out objectionable or offensive content by using the voluntary, industry-standard ratings defined independently by the Platform for Internet Content Selection (PICS) committee. You must be logged on as an administrator to set or modify content restrictions.

1. **Click** on the **Tools menu**. The Tools menu will appear.

2. **Click** on **Internet Options**. The Internet Options dialog box will appear.

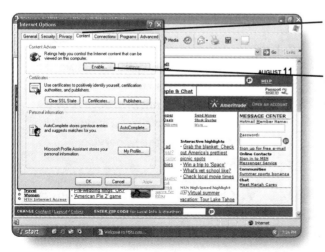

3. **Click** on the **Content tab**. The Content tab will appear in front.

4. **Click** on **Enable**. The Content Advisor dialog box will open.

Here you can control the level of language, nudity, sex, and violence of the Web pages displayed. Each category has a five-level rating beginning with zero (the strictest rating) and extending to four (the most lenient rating).

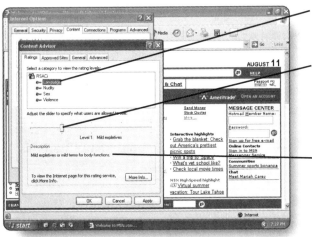

5. Click on the **category** you want to change. A Rating slide bar will appear.

6. Slide the **rating bar** to the desired level.

NOTE

A description of each rating displays under the Rating slide bar.

7. Repeat steps 5 and **6** for each category you want to restrict.

8. Click on the **General tab**. The General tab will appear in front.

The General tab has additional options from which you can select.

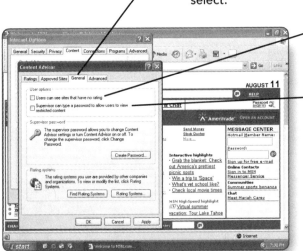

- **Users can see sites that have no rating**. This enables access to an un-rated site.

- **Supervisor can type a password to allow users to view restricted content**. This enables access to a restricted Web site for anyone who has access to the supervisor password.

9. Click any desired **User options check boxes**. A check mark appears in the box next to a selected item.

Tell the Content Advisor if you have specific Web sites you want to allow or disallow.

10. Click on the **Approved Sites tab**. The Approved Sites tab appears in front.

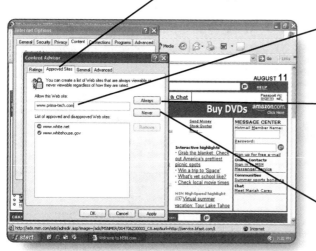

11. Type the **Web address** you want to allow or disallow. The address appears in the Allow this Web site text box.

12a. Click on **Always**. Internet Explorer adds the Web site to the list of approved and disapproved Web sites.

OR

12b. Click on **Never**. Internet Explorer adds the Web site to the list of approved and disapproved Web sites.

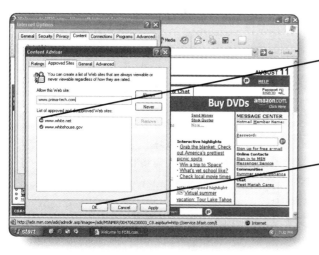

TIP

Internet Explorer indicates allowed Web sites with a green check mark, whereas disallowed Web sites are indicated with a red minus sign.

13. Click on **OK**. The Create Supervisor Password box appears.

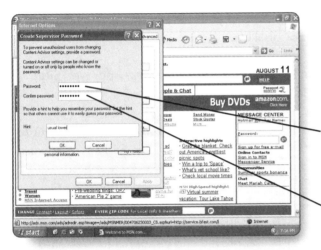

When you enable the Content Advisor, you must assign a supervisor password to prevent others from changing the settings. Only someone who knows the password can modify the settings.

14. **Type** a **password** in the Password text box. A series of dots will appear in the text box.

15. **Type** the same **password** in the Confirm password text box. A series of dots will appear in the text box.

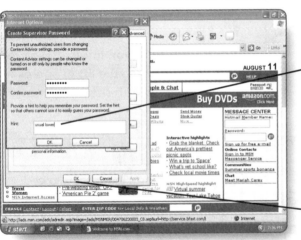

TIP

Optionally, in the Hint text box enter a piece of information that will help jog your memory should you forget the supervisor password. Do *not* enter the password in the Hint box.

16. **Click** on **OK**. A Content Advisor dialog box appears.

17. **Click** on **OK**. The Content Advisor confirmation box will close.

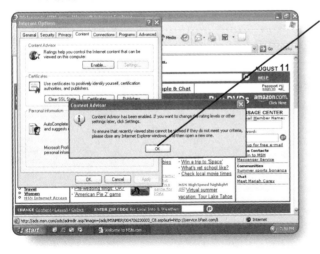

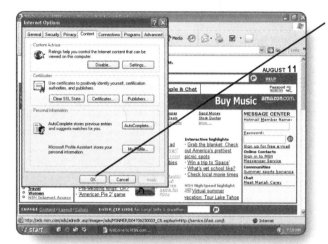

18. Click on **OK**. The Internet Properties dialog box closes.

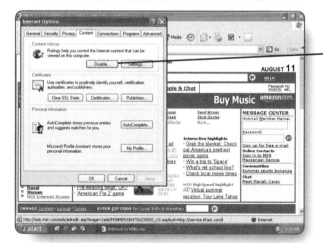

NOTE

Don't lose your supervisor password! If you want to disable ratings restrictions, return to the Content tab of the Internet Properties dialog box, click on Disable, enter the supervisor password, and then click on OK.

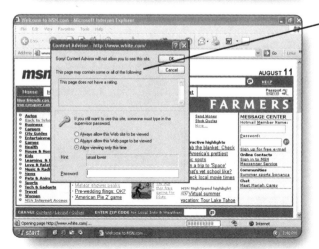

If you try to access a blocked site, the Content Advisor appears advising the site is blocked. You can view the requested site only after providing the supervisor password.

23

Working with Outlook Express

For many people, the capability to send and receive e-mail is one of the most important features of a computer. What is e-mail? Well, e-mail is defined as the exchange of text messages and computer files over a communications network, such as the Internet or an intra-company network. You'll find that Outlook Express is a full-featured e-mail and news-reading client that comes with Windows. In this chapter, you'll learn how to:

- Create e-mail accounts
- Create and send e-mail
- Attach a file to an e-mail
- Receive and manage e-mail

Starting Outlook Express

To send or receive e-mail or to access newsgroups, your computer must have a modem that is connected to a telephone line, and you must have access to some type of online service.

Windows provides a couple of different ways you can start the Outlook Express program.

- **Double-click** on the **Outlook Express icon** on the desktop.

- **Click** on the **Outlook Express icon** on the Quick Launch toolbar.

1. Double-click on **either** of the **Outlook Express icons**. The Outlook Express program will start.

Setting Up an E-mail Account

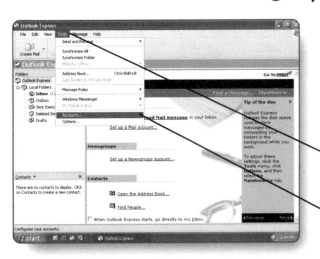

Before you can send or receive e-mail, you must first set up a mail account. Outlook Express uses the Internet Connection Wizard to quickly lead you through the process of setting up a new or additional e-mail account.

1. Click on **Tools**. The Tools menu will appear.

2. Click on **Accounts**. The Internet Accounts dialog box will open.

3. Click on **Add**. The Add menu will appear.

4. Click on **Mail**. The Internet Connection Wizard will open to assist you through the e-mail account setup process.

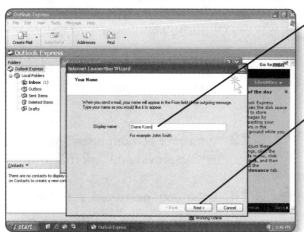

5. Type your **name** as you would like others to see it when they receive e-mail from you. Your name will appear in the Display Name: text box.

6. Click on **Next**. The Internet E-mail Address screen will appear.

In this chapter, I'm assuming you have already established an Internet connection.

NOTE

See Chapter 21, "Connecting to the Internet," for help with creating an Internet connection.

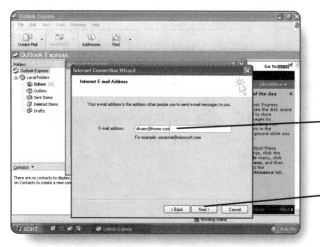

7. Type your **e-mail address**. The address will appear in the E-mail Address: text box.

8. Click on **Next**. The E-mail Server Names screen will appear.

It gets a little trickier here. When you get to this screen, contact your ISP and ask for the information. They'll be happy to provide it.

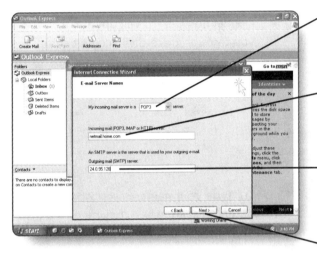

9. **Click** on the correct type of **mail server** (POP3 or IMAP). Your selection will appear in the list box.

10. **Type** the **incoming mail server name**. The text you type will appear in the Incoming Mail Server: text box.

11. **Type** the **outgoing mail server name**. The text you type will appear in the Outgoing Mail Server: text box.

12. **Click** on **Next**. The Internet Mail Logon screen will appear.

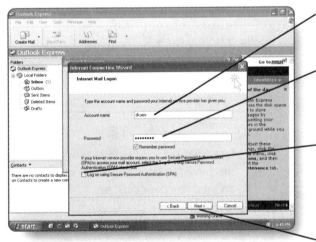

13. **Type** your **account name**. Again, your ISP can provide this information.

14. **Enter** your **password**. A series of dots will appear in the Password text box.

15. If required by your ISP, **click** on the **Log On Using Secure Password Authentication (SPA)** box. (Most ISPs do not require this feature.)

16. **Click** on **Next**. The Congratulations screen will appear.

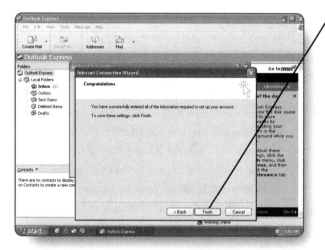

17. **Click** on **Finish**. The Internet Connection Wizard will close and the Internet Accounts dialog box will reappear.

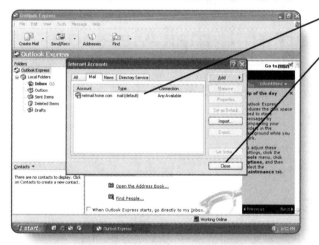

Your e-mail connection is displayed.

18. **Click** on **Close**. The Internet Accounts dialog box will close.

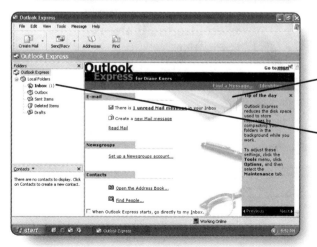

Outlook Express lists several folders in the local folder list.

The **Outlook Express Start page** will appear on the right side.

The **Inbox folder** is the next folder under the Local Folders folder. When you are connected to your ISP, Outlook Express places any incoming mail in the Inbox folder.

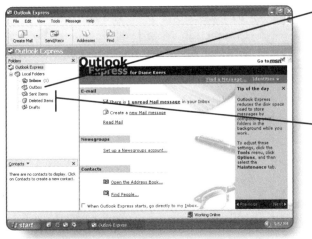

When you create e-mail messages, you have the option to send them immediately or send them at a later time. The **Outbox folder** indicates any messages waiting to be sent.

Other folders created with Outlook Express include a **Sent Items** folder to keep copies of any e-mail you send, a **Deleted Items** folder to throw away e-mail, and a **Drafts folder** in which to keep unfinished messages.

Creating an E-mail Message

If you want to communicate with someone quickly, send him or her an e-mail message. In Outlook Express, you can read, create, and send your e-mail messages.

1. Click on **Create Mail**. The New Message dialog box will open.

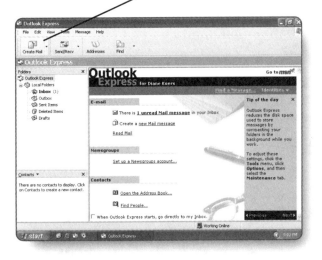

TIP

If you can't see your toolbar, click on View and choose Toolbar then select Standard Buttons or Formatting Bar.

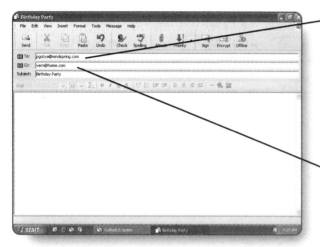

2. Type the **e-mail address** of the person to which you want to send the message. The name will appear in the To: line.

3. Press the **Tab key**. The insertion point will move to the Cc: line.

4. Type an **e-mail address** of anyone to whom you want to send a carbon copy (Cc:) of the message. The e-mail address will appear in the Cc: box.

NOTE

If you have more than one person to list on any of the address lines, separate the e-mail name of each recipient by a semicolon. For example, typing jsmith@abc.com; kjones@123.net;swilson@home.com would send the message to jsmith, kjones, and swilson.

---

5. Press the **Tab key**. The insertion point will move to the Subject: line.

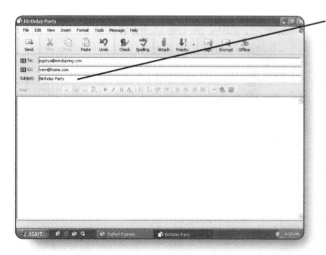

6. Type a **subject** for the message. The text will appear in the Subject: line.

An e-mail message doesn't require a Subject: line, but for the sake of clarity I recommend you enter one. If you try to send a message without a subject, Outlook Express asks if you're sure you want to do so.

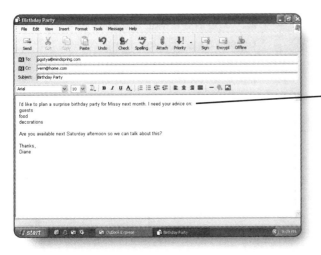

7. Press the **Tab key**. The insertion point will move to the body of the message.

8. Type your **message** in the body of the message box. The typed text will appear in the lower half of the window.

Formatting an E-mail Message

You can dress up your e-mail messages. Instead of plain text, you can insert bullets, images, and horizontal lines. Add color and style with different fonts and sizes or add a graphic background. You'll format text in Outlook Express almost the same way you would format text in WordPad or other word-processing programs.

1. Click and drag across the **text** you want to modify. The text will be highlighted.

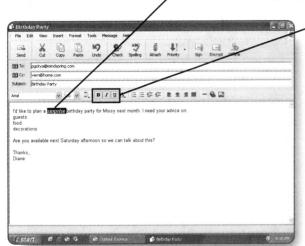

2. Click on the **Bold, Italic,** or **Underline buttons**. The text will appear bolded, italicized, and/or underlined.

> **TIP**
>
> If you don't see the toolbar with the Bold, Italic, or Underline button, click on Format and choose Rich Text.

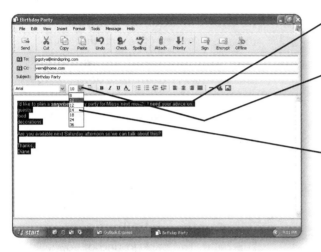

3. Select the **text** you want to modify. The text will be highlighted.

4. Click on the **down arrow** next to the font size. A selection of font sizes will appear.

5. Click on the **font size** you want to use. The selected text will change to the new font selection.

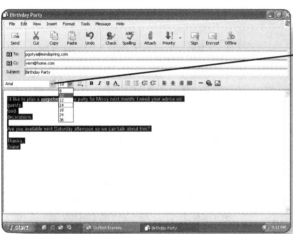

TIP

Similarly, click on the Font name down arrow to select a different font for the selected text.

You can add bullet points or numbering to lists in your e-mail messages.

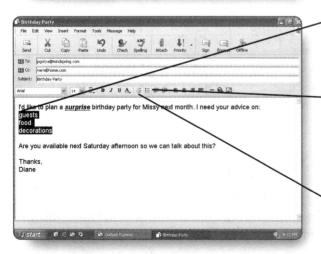

6. Click and **drag** across the text to which you want to apply bullets or numbers. The text will be selected.

7a. Click on **Bullet**. Outlook Express will place a bullet in front of the selected items.

OR

7b. Click on **Numbering**. Outlook Express will place a number in front of the selected items.

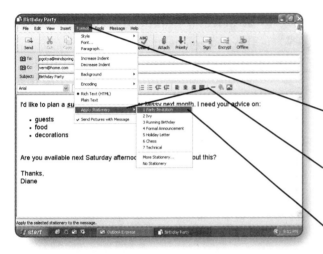

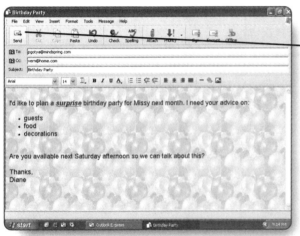

Next, add a background to your message. You can use one that comes supplied with Outlook Express, or you can apply your own .jpeg or .gif image.

8. Click on **Format**. The Format menu will appear.

9. Click on **Apply Stationery**. The Apply Stationery submenu will appear.

10. Click on a **selection** from the submenu. The background of your message will change to your selection.

11. Click on the **Send button**. Outlook will immediately send the message to the recipients and place a copy of the message in the Sent Items folder.

TIP

If you don't want to send the message immediately, click on File and then choose Send Later.

Attaching Files to E-mail

You might want to include a spreadsheet or other document with an e-mail message. Outlook Express can send files of any type—pictures, documents, spreadsheets, or any text or binary files.

To open the attached document, the recipient must have a program that supports the file format you are sending. For example, if you send an Excel file, the recipient must either have Excel on his or her system, or a spreadsheet application that can read Excel files.

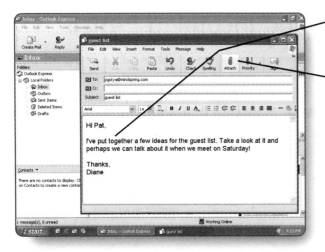

1. **Create** the **e-mail message**. The message will appear on your screen.

2. **Click** the **Attach button**. The Insert Attachment dialog box will open.

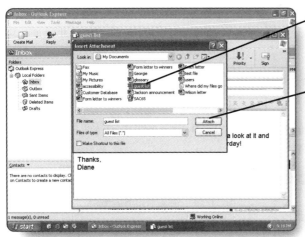

3. **Locate** and **click** on the **file** you want to attach to the message. The file name will be highlighted.

4. **Click** on **Attach**. The Insert Attachment dialog box will close.

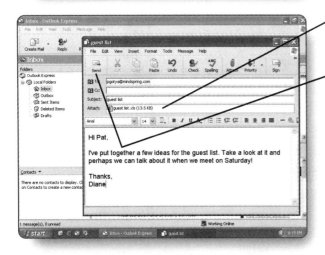

Outlook Express displays an icon representing the attached file.

5. **Click** on **Send**. Outlook Express will send the file along with the message.

Retrieving Incoming E-mail

Outlook Express tells you when you have new messages by putting the number of new messages in parentheses (and in boldface) next to the Inbox. If you are online, Outlook Express checks for new messages at specified intervals. A light tone notifies you when you receive a new message.

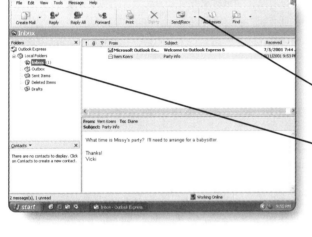

1. **Click** on **Send/Receive**. Outlook Express will check for new messages.

2. **Click** on the **Inbox**. A list of new messages will appear on the right side of the screen.

3. **Click** on a **message** to read. The message will appear in the preview pane.

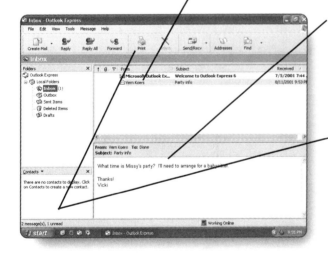

4. **Read** the **message** in the Preview pane. Use the scroll bar to see more of the message.

TIP

You can print any message by clicking the Print button.

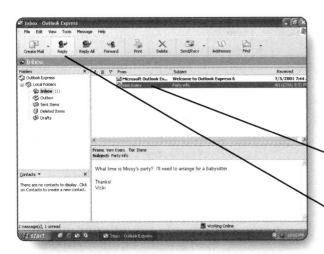

Replying to a Message

Now that you've read the message, you might want to reply to the sender. Outlook Express enables you to answer a message.

1. Click on the **message** to which you want to reply. The message is selected.

2. Click the **Reply button**. A mail message window will appear with the sender's e-mail address and subject already entered.

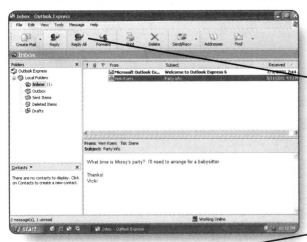

TIP

If the original message was sent to more than one person, you can click on Reply All instead of Reply. Outlook Express sends your reply to each person who received the original message.

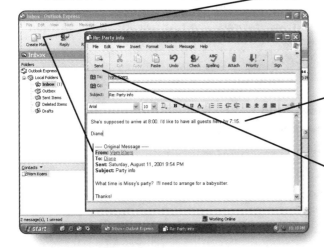

The original message is displayed in the body of the new e-mail message. The original message will have a line in front of it, denoting it as part of the original message.

3. Type the **reply** in the message body. The text will appear in the bottom half of the window.

4. Click on the **Send button**. If you are already online, Outlook Express will send the reply immediately and place a copy of the reply in the Sent Items folder.

Forwarding a Message

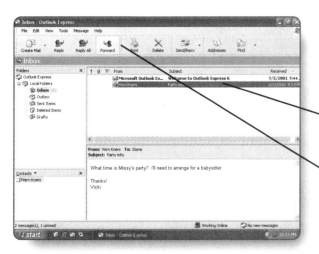

You can send a received message on to another person by forwarding it. You can even add your own message along with it.

1. **Click** on the **message** you want to forward. The message is highlighted.

2. **Click** on the **Forward button**. A new mail message window will open and the To: line will be blank. The Subject: line contains the same subject as the mail you received, and the original message is placed in the body of the new e-mail message.

3. **Type** the **recipient's e-mail address** in the To: line.

4. **Click** in the **body** of the e-mail message. The insertion point will flash in the bottom half of the window.

5. **Type** the **message** you want to send in addition to the original message, if desired. The text will appear in addition to the original message.

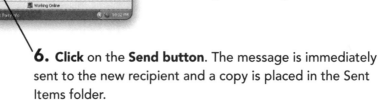

6. **Click** on the **Send button**. The message is immediately sent to the new recipient and a copy is placed in the Sent Items folder.

Receiving E-mail with Attachments

You've seen how to attach a file to a message you send, and you've seen how to receive e-mail, but what if someone sends you an e-mail message with an attachment? What should you do with the file you receive?

CAUTION

If you don't know who sent the file, *don't open it*! Frequently, computer viruses are transmitted through attached files. This doesn't mean you should never open an attached file; just be sure you know where it came from and keep your anti-virus software up-to-date.

A paper clip indicates that the e-mail has an attachment.

1. Double-click on the **e-mail message**. A window displaying the message will open.

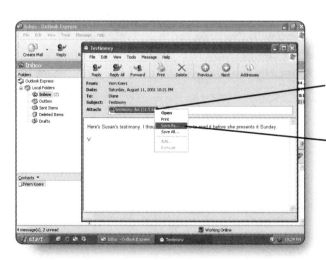

You can open, print, or save the attached file.

2. Right-click the **e-mail attachment**. A shortcut menu will appear.

3. Click on **Save As**. The Save As dialog box will open.

NOTE

To open the received document, you must have a program that supports the file format you are receiving. For example, if you receive an Excel file, you must either have Excel on your system, or a spreadsheet application that can read Excel files.

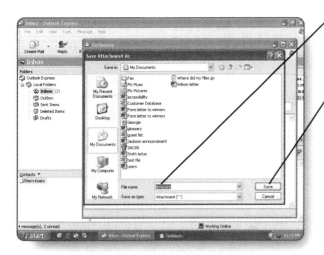

4. Enter a **name** for the file and **choose** a **location**. The information will appear in the Save As dialog box.

5. Click on **Save**. Windows will save the file in the location you specified.

You can now close, reply, delete, forward, or file the e-mail as usual. If you reply to the message, the attachment is not included in the reply. If you forward the message, the attachment *is* included.

Managing E-mail

Outlook Express stores incoming messages in the Inbox until you do something with them. As more and more e-mail arrives, the Inbox can get very full. You'll want to organize your e-mail, especially the ones you want to keep for future reference.

Creating an E-mail Folder

Create new folders to organize your mail.

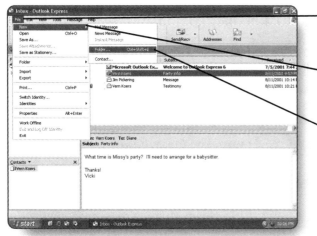

1. **Click** on **File**. The File menu will appear.

2. **Click** on **New**. The New submenu will appear.

3. **Click** on **Folder**. The Create Folder dialog box will open.

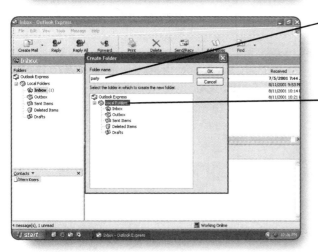

4. **Type** a **name** for the new folder. The name will appear in the Folder name: text box.

5. **Click** on the **folder** in which you want to place the new folder. The selected folder is highlighted.

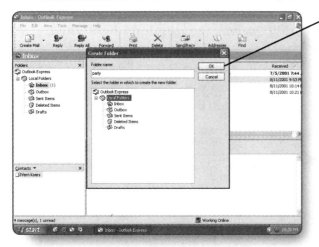

6. **Click** on **OK**. Outlook Express will create a new folder.

Moving an E-mail Message

You can move any e-mail from the Inbox to any existing folder. Move e-mail in the same manner as you move files in the Windows Explorer.

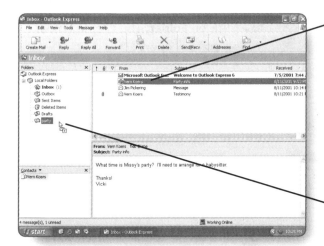

1. Click on the **message** you want to move. The message will be selected.

> **TIP**
> To select multiple messages, hold down the Ctrl key while clicking on additional messages.

2. Click and **drag** the **message** to the new folder. The message will disappear from the current folder and appear in the new folder.

Deleting an E-mail Message

Outlook Express stores deleted messages in a Deleted Items folder.

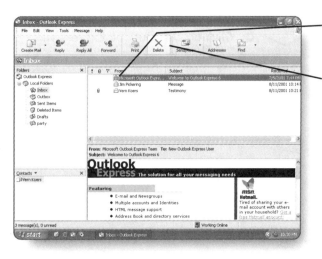

1. Click on the **message** you want to delete. The message is highlighted.

2. Click the **Delete button**. Outlook Express will move the message to the Deleted Items folder.

TIP

If you want to "undelete" a mail message, click on the Deleted Items folder and drag the message to a different folder.

You'll want to periodically empty the Deleted Items folder.

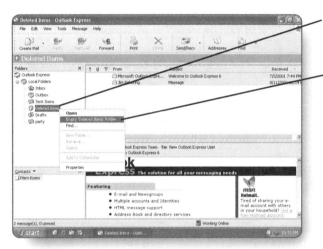

3. Right-click on the **Deleted Items folder**. A shortcut menu will appear.

4. Click on **Empty Deleted Items Folder**. A confirmation message will appear.

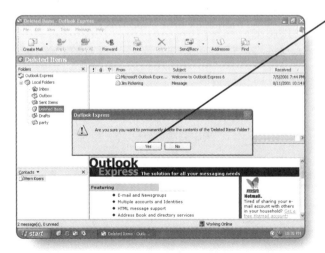

5. Click on **Yes**. Outlook Express will empty the folder.

E-mailing a File from Windows

Earlier in this chapter you learned how to attach a file to an e-mail message. Windows also includes a quick way to send a file without launching Outlook Express first.

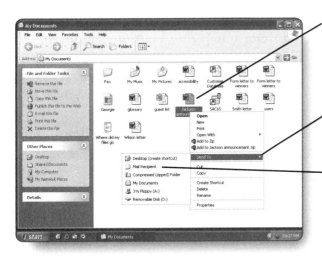

1. **Locate and right-click** on the **file** you want to send. A shortcut menu will appear. Use the Windows Explorer or open the folder that contains the file.

2. **Click** on **Send to**. A Send to submenu will appear.

3. **Click** on **Mail Recipient**. An e-mail window will open with the file attached.

TIP

Optionally, click on a file name, then click on E-mail this file.

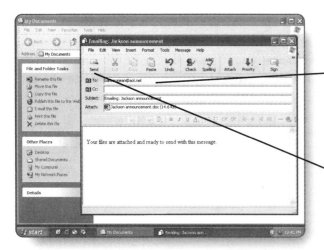

Windows automatically adds a subject with the name of the attached file.

5. **Enter** the **recipient information** and (optionally) change the subject information or add additional information to the message body.

6. **Click** on **Send**. Windows will send the message via Outlook Express.

Minding Your E-Manners

I'd just like to add a final note about e-mail. In this chapter, you've seen how to send and receive e-mail, the fastest growing method of communication today. Here are a couple of tips to keep in mind when working with e-mail.

- **Reply promptly**. If someone has sent you a message, they are most likely anxiously awaiting your reply. Good manners suggest you reply the same day you receive the message, even if it's a brief "I'll get back to you" answer.

- **Be brief**. Less is more. Most e-mail readers find mails that messages are longer than one screen long too bothersome to read.

- **Make it easy to read**. Don't type in ALL CAPS (that's shouting), don't type in all small caps (that's hard to read) and make sure your spelling is correct before you send a message. (Hint: Outlook Express has a spell check feature available in the message window: Click on Tools, Spelling).

- **Don't forward chain letters, petitions and rumors.** There is a lot of misinformation on the Net and very few e-mail readers like these types of e-mails. Resist forwarding them unless you know for sure they are accurate and important. Here's a couple of Web addresses you can go to check and see if a claim is true or if it's a hoax.

  http://www.symantec.com/avcenter/hoax.html
  http://urbanlegends.about.com

24

Using the Windows Address Book

Windows and Outlook Express join forces to provide an address book that you can use to maintain a variety of information about business and personal contacts. You can use the Address Book to send e-mail to a contact or to print a phone list. In this chapter, you'll learn how to:

- Add, edit, or delete an Address Book entry
- Send e-mail from the Address Book
- Sort Address Book entries
- Print a phone list

Managing Address Book Contacts

You can access the Address Book through Outlook Express or through the Start menu.

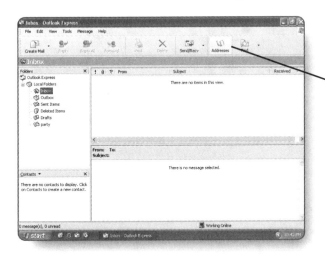

1. Open Outlook Express. The Outlook Express window will open.

2. Click on **Addresses**. The Address Book window will open.

TIP

Optionally, click on Start, All Programs, Accessories, and choose Address Book.

Adding Contacts

It is easy to add entries to the Address Book. As you add contacts, the Address Book lists them in alphabetical order by first name. You'll discover later in this chapter how to sort the entries in a different order.

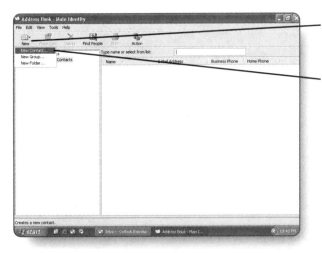

1. Click on the **New button**. A drop-down list will appear.

2. Click on **New Contact**. The Properties dialog box will open.

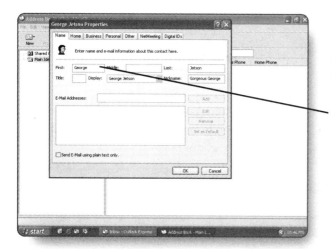

The Name tab will appear first. This is where the Address Book stores the contact name and e-mail addresses. All information is optional.

3. Type the contact's **first name**. The name will appear in the First: text box.

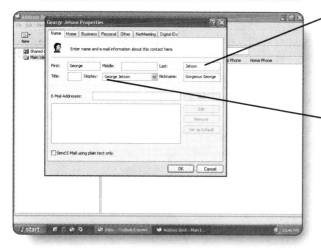

4. Enter any additional **name information** in the appropriate text box. Remember that all information is optional.

As you enter the name, Address Book automatically fills in the Display: box. The display name is the one to appear in the title bar. If desired, you can change the display name.

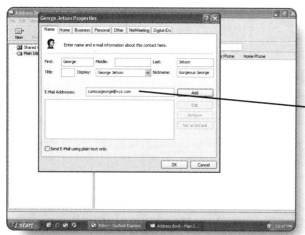

5. Click in the **E-Mail Addresses: text box**. The blinking insertion point will appear in the E-Mail Addresses: text box.

6. Type the contact's **e-mail address**.

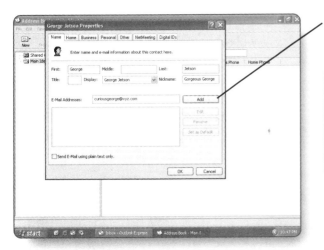

7. Click on **Add**. The e-mail address will be added.

TIP

Repeat Steps 5 through 7 to add as many e-mail addresses as you want for this contact.

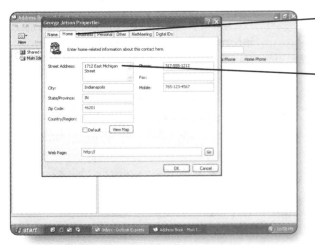

8. Click on the **Home tab**. The Home tab will move to the front.

9. Enter any available **home address information** for the contact. The information you type will appear in each field. Press the Tab key to move from field to field. All Home information is optional.

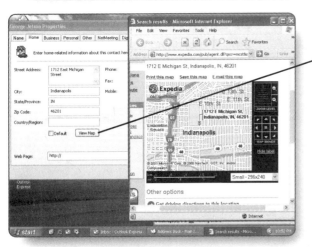

TIP

If you click on the View Map button, your Web browser will launch and direct you to the expedia.com Web site. See a map of the street address you entered!

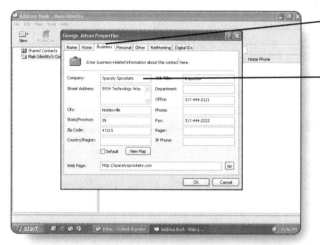

10. **Click** on the **Business tab**. The Business tab will move to the front.

11. **Enter** any available **business information** for the contact. The information you type will appear in each field. Press the Tab key to move from field to field. All business information is optional.

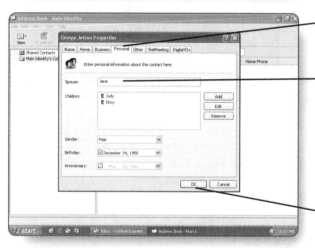

12. **Click** on the **Personal tab**. The Personal tab will move to the front.

13. **Enter** any available **personal information** for the contact. The information you type will appear in each field. Press the Tab key to move from field to field. All personal information is optional.

14. **Click** on **OK**. The Properties dialog box will close.

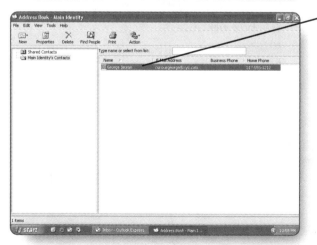

A portion of the contact information will appear in the Address Book. Click on any contact to select it.

TIP

Pause the mouse over a selected contact to see the entire contact information.

Editing Contacts

Only the display name, e-mail address, and two phone numbers appear in the Address Book. You'll need to open the record to edit or view the entire contact information.

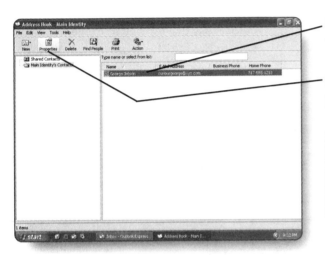

1. **Click** on the **entry** you want to edit. The entry is highlighted.

2. **Click** on the **Properties button**. The Properties dialog box will open.

TIP

Optionally, double-click an entry to open the Properties dialog box.

3. **Click** on the **tab for the information** you want to edit. The selected contact information will appear.

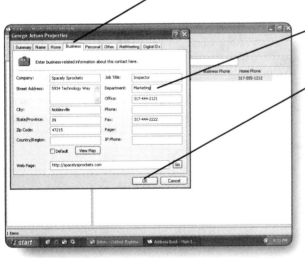

4. **Change or add** any desired **information**.

5. **Click** on **OK**. The Properties dialog box will close.

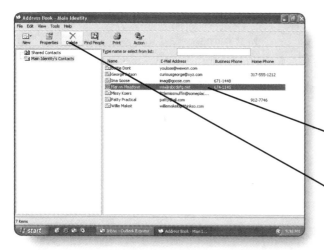

Deleting Contacts

If you no longer want a contact listed in your Address Book, you can easily delete it.

1. Click on the **contact name** you want to delete. The name is highlighted.

2. Click on the **Delete button**. A confirmation box will appear.

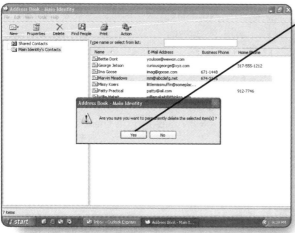

3. Click on **Yes**. The contact and all its information will be deleted. Be careful: You cannot undo the delete action.

Sorting Address Book Contacts

By default, the Address Book lists your contacts by first name. However, you can sort them by last name, e-mail address, business phone number, or home phone number.

1. Click on **View**. The View menu will appear.

2. Click on **Sort By**. The Sort By submenu will appear.

3. Click the **method** by which you want to sort. Depending on your selection, you may have additional choices.

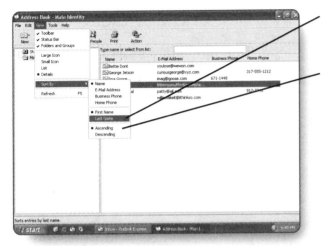

If you select by name, you can choose first name or last name.

You can sort in ascending or descending order.

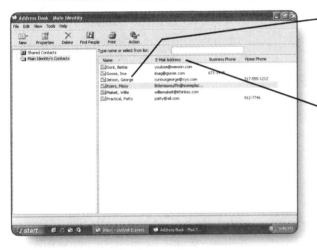

The Address Book sorts by the method you selected.

TIP
You can optionally sort the Address Book by clicking on the displayed headings.

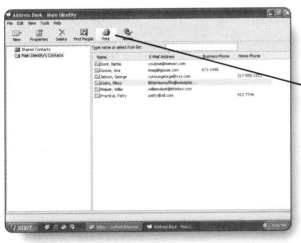

Printing a Phone List

You can print the contact information in any of three formats: Memo Style, Business Card Style, and Phone List Style.

1. Click on the **Print button**. The Print dialog box will open.

You can print your entire contact list, or only the currently selected record—the one highlighted before you clicked on the Print button.

2. Click on a **print range**. The option is selected.

You can print the Address Book in any of the following three different print styles:

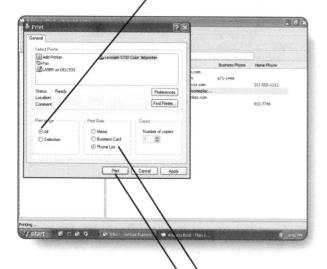

- **Memo**. Prints all available information from the Name, Home, and Business tabs.

- **Business Card**. Prints names, address, phone numbers, and e-mails in a format similar to a traditional business card.

- **Phone List**. Prints an alphabetical list of names and phone numbers. Names are grouped together by alpha letter. For example, all the A's print, then all the B's, and so forth.

3. Click on a **print style**. The style will be highlighted.

4. Click on **Print**. The Address Book contacts will print.

Closing the Address Book

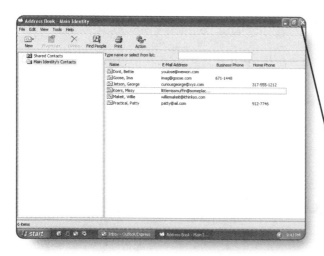

Address Book automatically saves information as you enter it. When you're finished with the Address Book, close it like you would any other Windows application.

1. Click on the **Close button**. The Address Book window will close. If you opened the Address Book from Outlook Express, the Outlook Express window will remain open.

Sending E-mail to a Contact

In Chapter 23, "Working with Outlook Express," you learned how to send e-mail with Outlook Express. The Address Book makes sending e-mail even easier. You don't have to memorize—or even type—the sometimes complicated e-mail address of the person to whom you're sending mail.

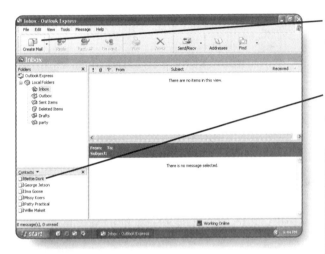

1. From the Outlook Express window, **click** the **Create Mail button**. The New Message window will appear.

Notice the Contacts window listing your Address Book entries.

TIP

Optionally, right-click on a contact name and choose Send E-mail. Outlook Express will open a new e-mail window with the recipient information already selected.

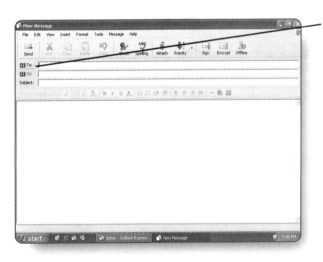

2. Click the **To: button**. The Select Recipients window will appear with a list of your contacts from the Address Book.

3. Click the e-mail **recipient name**. The contact name is highlighted.

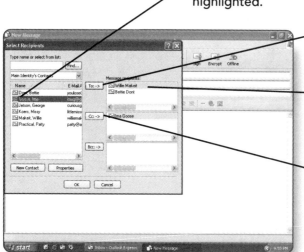

4. Click the **To: arrow**. The contact is added to the Message recipients list.

5. Repeat Steps 3 and 4 for each e-mail recipient. The selected names appear in the Message recipients list.

Click a **name**, then the **Cc:** or **Bcc: button** to send other recipients a carbon copy or blind carbon copy of the e-mail.

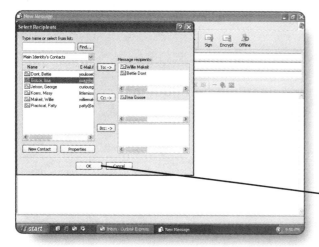

TIP

Click on a name from the To:, Cc:, or Bcc: box then press the delete key to remove it from the current message recipient list. This does not delete the person from the address book.

6. Click on **OK**. The names (not the e-mail addresses) appear in the e-mail To, Cc, or Bcc lines.

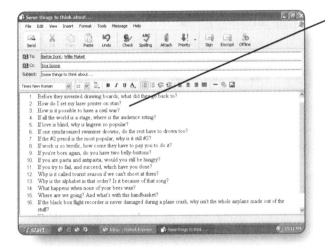

7. Enter the **subject and body** of the e-mail as you learned in Chapter 23. The e-mail is ready to send.

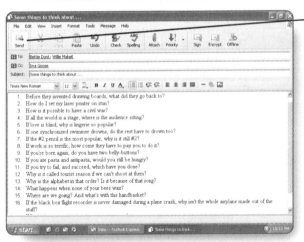

8. Click on **Send**. Outlook Express will send the e-mail message.

25

Using Windows Messenger

In Chapter 23 you learned how to send e-mail using Outlook Express. Now discover how our fast-paced world becomes a little faster! Included with Windows XP is an instant messaging application called Windows Messenger. With an instant messaging program, you can communicate with your friends and family in real time. In this chapter you'll learn how to:

- Sign up for a Windows Passport
- Log on to Windows Messenger
- Engage in an instant message conversation
- Change fonts and add emoticons to messages
- Send files to others
- Modify your status and settings

Starting Windows Messenger

Windows Messenger can be launched from the Start menu or from the System Tray/Notification Area

1. **Click** on **Start**. The Start menu will appear,

2. **Click** on **All Programs**. The All Programs menu will appear.

3. **Click** on **Windows Messenger**. The Windows Messenger window will open.

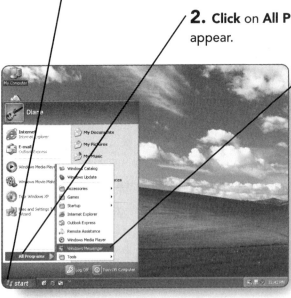

> ### TIP
>
> Optionally, double-click on the Messenger icon in the System/Notification area. (It's the icon of two people together.)

Signing up for a Passport

The first time you start Messenger, you'll be guided through signing up for a Microsoft Passport.

Passport is an online service that makes it possible for you to use your e-mail address and a single password to securely sign in to any Passport-participating Web site or service. A Passport is required for Windows Messenger.

> ### TIP
>
> A *Kids Passport*, for children under 12, is available from http:// kids.passport.com. With a Kids Passport, you can control what information they share.

1. Click on **Click here to sign-in**. The .NET Passport Wizard will launch.

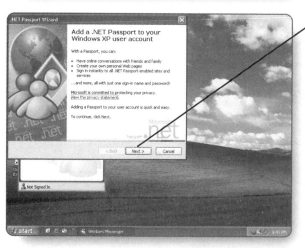

2. Click on **Next**. The .NET Password Wizard will prompt you for your e-mail information.

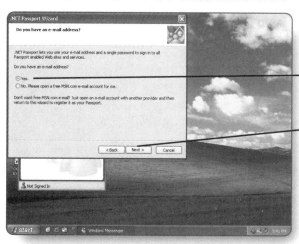

You can use your existing e-mail address with the Passport.

3. Click on **Yes**. The option will be selected.

4. Click on **Next**. The e-mail address screen will appear.

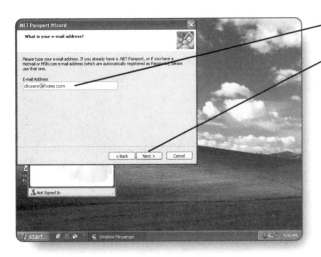

5. **Enter** your **e-mail address**.

6. **Click** on **Next**. The password box will appear.

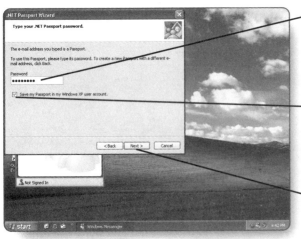

7. **Enter** your **Password**. A series of dots will appear as you type.

TIP

Optionally, click on Save my Passport in my Windows XP user account.

---

8. **Click** on **Next**. The final .NET Passport Wizard screen will appear.

9. **Click** on **Finish**. The Windows Messenger box will display.

Signing On to Messenger

Once you've established your Passport information, Windows Messenger will know you by your e-mail ID.

1. Click on **Click here to sign in as (your name/e-mail account)**. Your personal Messenger window will open.

Adding Contacts

In order to communicate with others, you need to add them to your contact list. The people you wish to chat or communicate with must also use Windows Messenger and have a .NET Passport.

1. Click on the **Add button**. The Add a Contact Wizard will open.

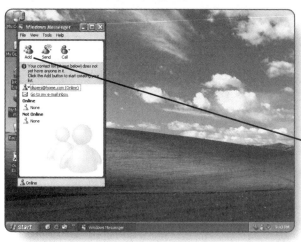

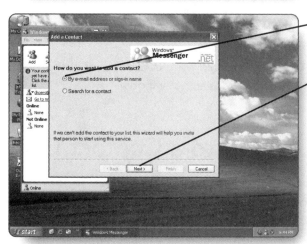

2. Click on **By e-mail address or sign-in name**. The option will be selected.

3. Click on **Next**. The next screen will appear.

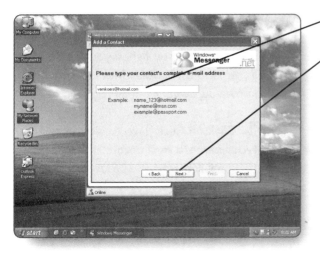

4. **Enter** the **contact's e-mail address**.

5. **Click** on **Next**. A notification screen will appear.

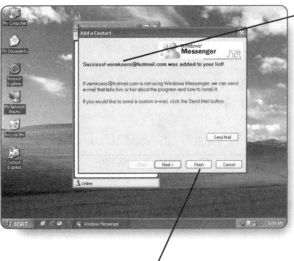

If the contact also has a .NET Passport, the screen will advise you that the contact has been added to your list. If the contact does not have a .NET Passport, you'll be advised that the contact could not be added to your list.

TIP

If the contact does not have Windows Messenger you can send them an e-mail inviting them to sign up for the free Windows Messenger service.

---

6. **Click** on **Finish**. The added contact will appear at the bottom of the Windows Messenger window.

Being Added to a Contact List

Other members can add you to their contact list. You have the option of allowing or blocking them from seeing when you are online and contacting you.

Windows Messenger will display an indication box when others have added you to their contact list.

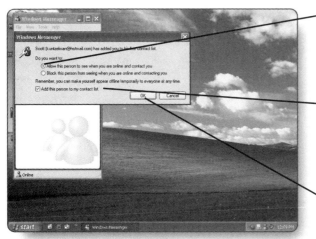

1. Click on an **option**. The option will be selected.

> **TIP**
>
> Optionally, click on Add this person to my contact list to automatically include them on your list.

2. Click on **OK**. The message box will close.

Sending Instant Messages

When the person you wish to contact is signed on to Windows Messenger, his or her name will move up from the Not Online area to the Online area. That way, you'll always know who's available to chat with!

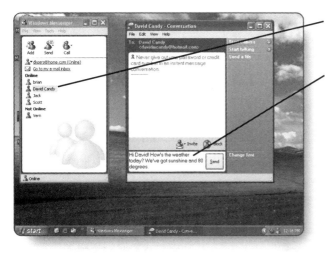

1. Double-click on the **contact's name**. A conversation window will open.

2. Type your **message**. The text will appear in the message box.

3. Click on **Send** or **press Enter**.

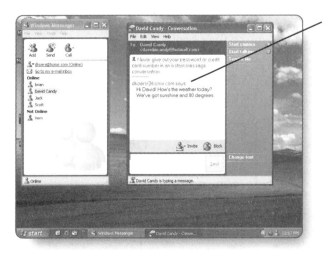

The message text will appear in the conversation area.

The recipient will also see the message text and can respond.

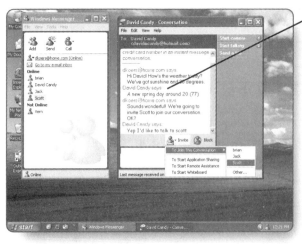

The message window displays the response text and the name of the person who responded.

Inviting Others to Join a Conversation

With Windows Messenger you can invite others to join your conversation.

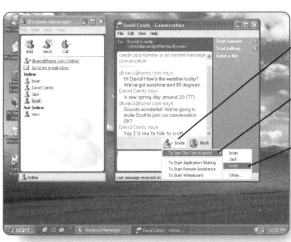

1. Click on **Invite**. The invite menu will appear.

2. Click on **To Join This Conversation**. A list of online contacts will appear.

3. Click on a **name**. The other person will be contacted, and the message window will indicate the other person has joined in the conversations.

Changing the Message Font

Sometimes, especially when several people are involved in a conversation, it gets difficult to see who is saying what. You can customize your font setting for the conversation to make your comments different from the others.

1. Click on **Change Font**. The Change My Message Font dialog box will open.

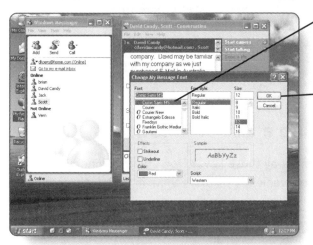

2. Click on a font **name, style, size, effect, or color**. A sample will appear in the Sample box.

3. Click on **OK**. The Change My Message Font dialog box will close and your text will appear in the new font.

Adding Emoticons

Windows Messenger allows you to create a number of different emoticons, ranging from smiley faces to musical notes to birthday cakes. *Emoticons* are small icons that allow you to express your feelings or emotions. (Emot-icons—get it?)

Typing Emoticons

Emoticons are created by typing a specific series of keystrokes (usually two or three characters).

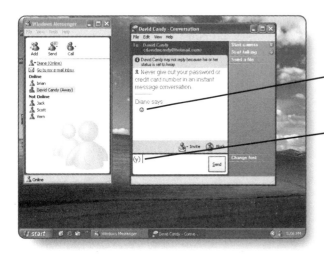

1. **Type** a **colon and a closing parenthesis**.

2. **Press Enter**. A smiley face will appear in your message text.

3. **Type** an **open parenthesis, the letter Y** (capitalized or lower-cased) and then **a closing parenthesis**.

4. **Press Enter**. A thumbs-up sign will appear in your message text.

Displaying a List of Emoticons

Can't remember all those keys? Don't worry, Windows Messenger conveniently displays them in their Help section.

1. **Click** on **Help**. The Help menu will appear.

2. **Click** on **Help Topics**. The Windows Messenger help window will open.

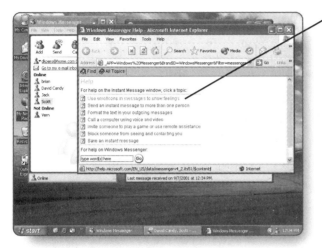

3. **Click** on **Use emoticons in messages to show feelings**. A list of available emoticons and their keystrokes will appear.

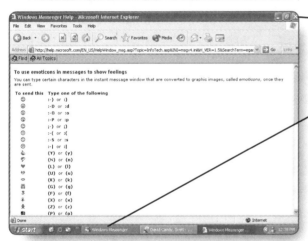

4a. **Click** on the **Close button**. The Help window will close.

OR

4b. **Click** on the **Windows Messenger button** on the taskbar. The Help window will remain open, but move to the background.

Sending a File

Windows Messenger also allows you to send your message contact a file.

1. **Click** on **File**. The File menu will open.

2. **Click** on **Send a File to**. A list of conversation participants will appear.

3. **Click** on the **contact** you want to send the file. The Send a File to dialog box will open.

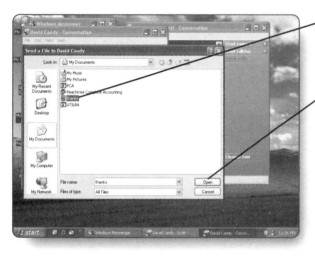

4. Locate and click on the **file name** you want to send. The file name will be highlighted.

5. Click on **Open**. Windows Messenger will send the recipient a message that you are trying to send a file.

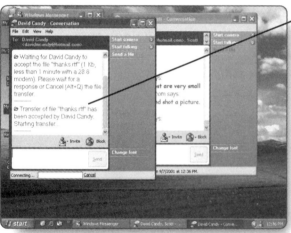

When the recipient has indicated that he or she will accept the file, the file will be transferred.

Answering an Invitation

When others see you are online, they can send you an instant message. The Windows Messenger icon on the system tray/notification area will display a pop-up window indicating who is calling and their initial message.

1. Click on the **message box**. A conversation window will open.

You can then continue your conversation as you learned earlier in this chapter.

Changing Your Status

Even though you're online, you may not want to be bothered by others, or perhaps you're going to be unavailable for a while but don't want to sign off. You can change your status, letting others know your availability.

1. Click on the **down arrow** next to your name. A list of status options will appear.

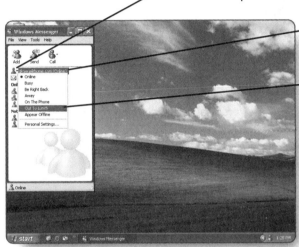

2. Click on an **option**. Others will see the status you selected.

3. When you return or are ready to be seen by others, **repeat step 1 and choose Online**. Your status will change to Online.

NOTE

If you attempt to contact someone who is unavailable, the conversation window will open, but Windows Messenger warns you that the recipient may not respond.

Modifying Your Personal Settings

Windows Messenger lets you modify personal settings such as your contact name, file locations, and sound preferences.

1. **Click** on **Tools**. The Tools menu will appear.

2. **Click** on **Options**. The Options dialog box will open.

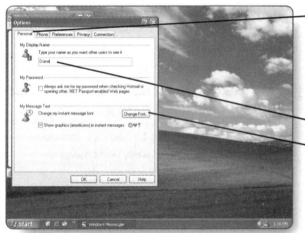

3. **Click** on the **Personal tab**. The Personal tab will move to the front.

A couple of items you might want to modify include:

- Your display name
- Your default instant message font

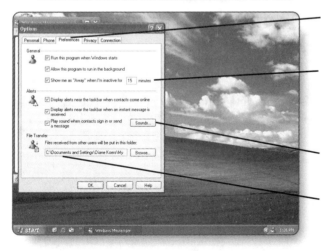

4. **Click** on the **Preferences tab**. The Preferences tab will move to the front.

- Windows Messenger can automatically change your status to "Away" if your computer is sitting idle.
- Click on Sounds to select from a variety of notification sounds.
- You can modify the location where received files are stored.

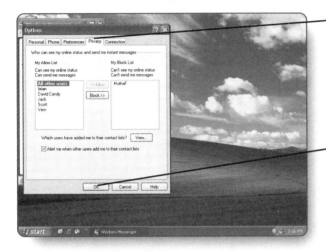

5. **Click** on the **Privacy tab**. The Privacy tab will move to the front.

On the Privacy tab, you can move your contacts status back and forth from Allowed to Blocked.

6. **Click** on **OK**. The options dialog box will close.

Checking E-mail

Windows Messenger contains a link to Outlook Express. You can quickly launch Outlook Express or your default e-mail client and check your e-mail.

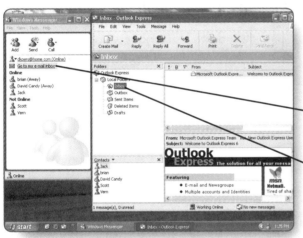

1. **Click** on **Go to my e-mail inbox**. Your e-mail application will open.

2. **Click** on the **Inbox and review** your **messages**. (You learned how to work with Outlook Express in Chapter 23.)

Signing Out

When you are finished with Windows Messenger, you should sign out.

1. **Click** on **File**. The File menu will appear.

2. **Click** on **Sign out**. The sign-in box will reappear.

If you just close the Messenger Window without signing out, you will remain online and be notified of incoming messages.

3. Click on the **Close button**. The Windows Messenger window will close.

Part VI Review Questions

1. Why might you want to map a network drive? *See "Mapping a Network Drive" in Chapter 20*

2. What does a typical Web address begin with? *See "Browsing the Web with Internet Explorer" in Chapter 22*

3. What does it mean when you point your mouse to underlined text and the mouse pointer turns into a hand? *See "Following Hyperlinks" in Chapter 22.*

4. What types of sites are devoted to searching for other sites? *See "Searching for Information Online" in Chapter 22*

5. What is e-mail? *See "E-mailing with Outlook Express" in Chapter 23*

6. What do you use to separate multiple names on an e-mail message? *See "Creating an E-mail Message" in Chapter 23*

7. How can you add a background to an e-mail message? *See "Formatting an E-mail Message" in Chapter 23*

8. What type of information can be stored in the Address Book? *See "Adding Contacts" in Chapter 24*

9. What is Passport? *See "Signing up for Passport" in Chapter 25*

10. What are Emoticons? *See "Adding Emoticons" in Chapter 25*

A

Upgrading to Windows XP

If you go out today and buy a new computer, most likely it will have Windows XP pre-installed on it. But if you're upgrading from an earlier version of Microsoft Windows, you'll be pleasantly surprised with the ease of upgrading to Windows XP.

During an upgrade, the Setup Wizard replaces existing Windows files but preserves your existing settings and applications. Be aware that some applications might not be compatible with Windows XP Home Edition and therefore might not function properly after an upgrade. You can upgrade to Windows XP Home Edition from Windows 98 (all versions) or Windows Millennium Edition. If you are using Windows 3.1 or Windows 95 you must install from the full version instead of the upgrade version. In this appendix you'll learn how to:

- Install the Windows XP upgrade
- Register and activate Windows XP

Understanding the Upgrade Process

Setup is a simple process with Windows and requires very little interaction between you and the computer. During the Setup process, Windows recognizes your current configuration on the PC and retains those settings.

Windows easily detects your hardware and existing software and it has a built-in setup recovery system. If the setup process should fail in the middle (which rarely happens), the process remembers where it left off and begins at that step. This feature saves time because you won't have to redo the successful installation steps.

System Requirements

To install Windows XP, your PC must meet the following requirements:

- 233 megahertz (MHz) Pentium or higher microprocessor
- 128 megabytes (MB) recommended (64 MB of RAM minimum)
- 1.5 GB of free space on your hard disk
- VGA monitor
- Keyboard
- Mouse or compatible pointing device
- CD-ROM or DVD drive

Installing the Windows XP Upgrade

Installation of the Windows upgrade requires five basic parts, all of which are run almost automatically by the Setup program.

1. **Insert** the **Windows XP CD-ROM**. The Welcome to Microsoft Windows XP screen will appear.

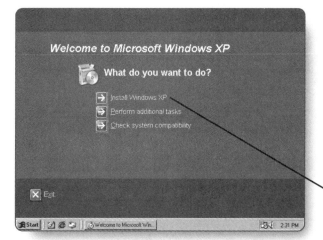

TIP

If the Welcome to Microsoft Windows XP screen doesn't appear automatically, click on Start, Run and enter D:\Setup (replacing D: with the drive letter of your CD-ROM drive). Press Enter.

---

2. **Click** on **Install Windows XP**. The Windows XP Setup Wizard will launch.

3. **Click** on **Next**. The License Agreement will appear.

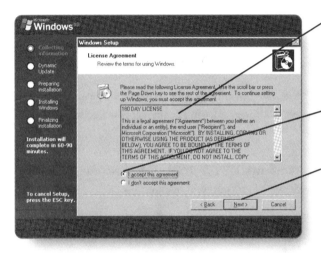

The Microsoft licensing agreement is displayed. You can read through the agreement. Press the Page Down key to see more of it.

4. Click "I accept the Agreement." The option will be selected.

5. Click on **Next**. The Product Key screen will appear.

The Product Keycode that Setup asks for pertains to your license to use Windows XP. This code could be located in one of two places. First, look on the CD-ROM case. Second, look on the certificate of authenticity included with the paperwork that came with your Windows upgrade.

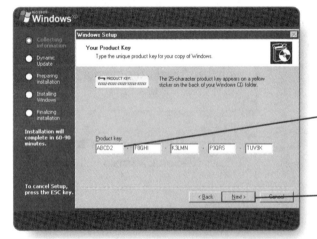

6. Enter the **Product Key code**. The letters and numbers you type appear in the text box.

7. Click on **Next**. The Upgrade Report screen will appear.

Windows XP is a major change from previous versions, therefore some applications or hardware may not work as expected. Windows can create a report of possible problems.

8. Click on an **option**. The option will be selected.

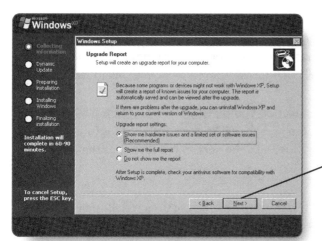

NOTE
Only antivirus programs written for the Windows XP will run correctly. Contact your antivirus software vendor for updates.

9. Click on **Next**. The Get Updated Setup Files screen will appear.

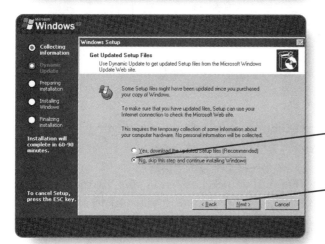

It's possible that Microsoft has created setup files newer than the ones on your CD. If you had an Internet connection established, Windows Setup can check for those updated files.

10. Click on an **option**. The option will be selected.

11. Click on **Next**. The installation process will begin.

Be patient—this part might take a little while. Read the screens for information about Windows XP new features and enhancements.

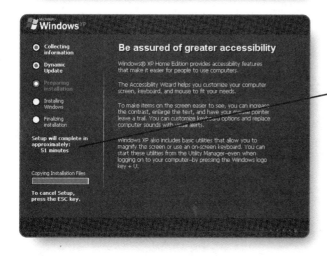

On the left side of the screen, a progress indicator keeps you up-to-date on the status of the upgrade.

At several different points, the Setup Wizard will restart your machine. It does so automatically, so you don't need to do anything.

NOTE

If the computer stops responding for a long time, turn it off and then back on.

Setup detects the hardware on your machine and your current configuration and matches it with Windows. It is also looking for the various software programs you have installed on your machine and configures them to work with Windows.

After the installation completes, you may see a dialog box about making a screen adjustment. If the changes are OK, click on OK, otherwise the screen will return to the original settings.

A Welcome to Windows & Music screen will appear to help complete the setup process.

12. **Click** on **Next**. An Activation screen will appear. You have 30 days to activate your copy of Windows.

13. **Make** an **activation selection**. The option will be selected.

NOTE

If you do not activate the product within 30 days, you will be unable to proceed past the Activation screen until you complete the procedure.

See the next section for instructions on Activating and registering your copy of Windows.

14. **Click** on **Next**. If you clicked Yes in step 13, the Ready to register with MS screen will appear. If you clicked No in step 13, the Let's Get on the Internet screen will appear.

You now have an option to sign up with MSN Internet Access. You'll learn about setting up Internet Access in Chapter 21, "Connecting to the Internet."

15. **Click on Do not setup an Internet connection at this time**. The option will be selected.

16. **Click** on **Next**. The "Who will use this computer" screen will appear.

You must setup at least one user name. User names are discussed in Chapter 13, "Tinkering with the Control Panel."

17. **Click** on **Next**. The Thank you screen will appear.

18. **Click** on **Finish**. Windows will start up and display user log on screen.

Activating and Registering Windows

Microsoft has implemented a security program called Program Activation. Basically, it means you have to let Microsoft know that you're using the product and register it with them. No one else can use your copy of Microsoft Windows XP Home Edition and it will only work on the computer on which you're activating it. If you have other computers, you must purchase separate copies of Windows XP Home Edition.

You have 30 days to activate and register your copy of Windows XP. As the time approaches, a reminder will appear on your screen.

1. **Click** on the **reminder message**. The Let's Activate Windows screen will appear.

You can activate over the Internet if you have an Internet connection or you can activate over the telephone.

2. **Click** on one of these **options**:

- Yes, lets activate Windows over the Internet now (if you have a connection established)

- Yes, I want to telephone a customer service representative to activate Windows

> **NOTE**
>
> For the rest of this exercise, we'll review the Internet activation steps.

3. Click on **Next**. The Register with MS? screen will appear.

4. Click on **Yes**, I want to register and activate Windows at the same time.

5. Click on **Next**. The Collecting Registration Data screen will appear.

6. Enter your **name, address and other information**, pressing the Tab key to move from screen to screen. The asterisk (*) beside a field indicates it is required info.

7. Click on **Next**. Microsoft will be contacted.

> **NOTE**
>
> You may be prompted to connect to your Internet Service Provider.

After the registration process is complete, a Thank you screen will appear.

8. Click on **OK**. The activation and registration process will be complete.

Index

Symbols

- subfolder indicator, 116
+ subfolder indicator, 116

A

Accessibility Options dialog box, 198-199
Accessibility Wizard, 195-199
accessing. *See* starting
accounts
    e-mail, setting up, 304-308
    Internet
        dialing up, 284-285
        security, 285
        setting up, 282-283
        signing up, 279-281
        Web browsers, 285-286
    users
        creating, 172-173
        deleting, 177-178
        icons, 176-177
        naming, 173-174
        passwords, 175-176
Accounts command (Tools menu), 304
Add a Contact Wizard, 341-342
Add Network Place Wizard, 265-269
Add or Remove Programs Properties dialog box, 166
Add Printer Wizard, 204-208, 211-213
Add to Favorites command (Favorites menu), 293
Add to Favorites dialog box, 293
Additional Drivers dialog box, 210
Address Book
    closing, 333
    contacts
        adding, 326-329
        business cards, 332-333
        deleting, 331
        editing, 330
        e-mailing, 334-336
        phone lists, 332,-333
        printing, 332-333
        sorting, 331-332
        street addresses, 328
    opening, 326
    searching, 141-143
alignment, text, 74-75
All Programs command (Start menu), 8, 18, 190
Alt key
    Alt+Tab keyboard shorcut, 19
    commands, 27-28
    troubleshooting, 37
anti-virus programs, 10
applications. *See* programs
Apply Stationery command (Format menu), 312
Arrange Icons by command (View menu), 127
arrow keys (dialog boxes), 31
Ask for Assistance (Help), 49-60
Attach button, 313
Attachment dialog box, 313
attachments, 312-313, 317-318

audio
    Narrator, 192-193
    SoundSentry, 195-199
    Windows Media Player, 100
        buttons, 97
        CDs, 94-96
        icon, 6
        radio, 98-100
        skins, 100-102
        volume, 102-103
        customizing, 180-182
Audio CD dialog box, 94-96
automatic Windows updates, 247-248

B

background
    color, 82-83
    desktop, 182-183
backing up
    files, 229-233
    hard drive, 229-233
    installing backup program, 226-228
    restoring, 233-236
    settings, 229-233
Backspace key, 68-69
Backup or Restore Wizard, 229-236
Backup Progress dialog box, 233
borders, windows, 20
Browe For Folder dialog box, 119-120
Browse for Folder dialog box, 266-267
browsers, 285-286
browsing networks
    computers, 263
    workgroups, 264-265
bullets
    deleting, 76
    e-mail messages, 311
    text, 75-76
Bullets button, 75-76
business cards (Address Book), 332-333
buttons. See also icons
    Attach, 313
    Bullets, 75-76
    calculator, 60-61

    Cancel, 30
    clicking, 5
    Close, 20
    Close (X), 5
    ellipses, 9
    Favorites, 294
    Forward, 316
    History, 296
    Home, 291
    Maximize, 20-24
    Minimize, 20, 23
    mouse, 163
    OK, 29
    option, 30
    Print, 34
    Print Preview, 33
    Reply, 315
    Send, 313
    Start, 7-8
    Taskbar, 7
    ToolTips, 7
    View Map, 328
    Windows Media Player, 97

C

cable modems, 262
calculator
    buttons, 60-61
    clicking, 61-62
    Clipboard, 62-63
    copying, 62-63
    keyboard, 61-62
    scientific, 63-64
    starting, 60
Cancel button, 30
cards (network), 262
CD-ROM drives, 111
    playing CDs, 94-95
        buttons, 97
        playlists, 96
        visualizations, 95-96
    volume, 102-103
    sharing, 276
Change Icon dialog box, 163-164

Change My Message Font dialog box, 346
check boxes, 29
Check Disk dialog box, 238-240
check marks
    active indicators, 123
    commands, 27
circles, drawing, 81-82
clicking
    buttons, 5
    calculator, 61-62
    commands, 26-27
    customizing, 163
    folders, 127-128
    icons, 5
    scroll bars, 21-22
    text, 70-71
    title bar, 24
Clipboard, 62-63
clock. *See* time
Close button (X), 6
closing
    Address Book, 333
    documents, 35
    programs, 35
color
    desktop, 182-183
    e-mail messages, 312
    Paint tools, 79-83
        drawing, 80
        troubleshooting, 81
    resolution, 186-188
    windows, 185-186
commands
    check marks, 27
    clicking, 26-27
    Edit menu
        Copy, 63
        Copy To Folder, 119
        Cut, 72
        Move To Folder, 119
        Paste, 72
        Select All, 71
        Undo, 81
    ellipses, 9, 27

Favorites menu, Add to Favorites, 293
File menu
    Delete, 130
    New, 120-121
    Open, 36, 269-270
    Print, 34
    Print Preview, 33
    Restore, 133
    Save, 32, 269-270
    Sign out, 351-352
Format menu
    Apply Stationery, 312
    Font, 73
Insert menu, Date and Time, 69-70
keyboard shortcuts, 27-28, 36-37
overview, 36-37
Start menu
    All Programs, 8, 18, 190
    Connect to, 284-285
    Control Panel, 9
    Help and Support, 9, 47, 244
    Log Off, 12-14
    My Documents, 9
    My Network Places, 9
    Run, 9
    Search, 136
    Turn Off Computer, 14
Tools menu
    Accounts, 304
    Folder Options, 128
    Internet Options, 297
    Options, 350
View menu
    Arrange Icons by, 127
    display options, 126
    Scientific, 64
    Sort By, 331
    Standard, 64
    Toolbars, 123, 308
computers, networks
adding, 265-269
browsing, 263
sharing, 275-276
workgroups, 264-265

configuring
  faxing, 220-221
  Internet connection, 278-279
Confirm File Delete dialog box, 130-132, 162
Connect dialog box, 284-286
Connect to command (Start menu), 284-286
connecting, networks, 262
contacts
  Address Book
    adding, 326-329
    business cards, 332-333
    deleting, 331
    editing, 330
    e-mailing, 334-336
    phone lists, 332-333
    printing, 332-333
    sorting, 331-332
    street addresses, 328
  Windows Messenger, 341-342
    contact lists, 342-343
Content Advisor dialog box, 297-301
Control Panel
  adding programs, 169-171
  viewing, 160
Control Panel command (Start menu), 9
copies, e-mail messages, 309
Copy command (Edit menu), 63
Copy to Folder command (Edit menu), 119
copying
  calculator, 62-63
  files, 118-120
  folders, 118-120
crashes, troubleshooting, 38-39
Create Folder dialog box, 318-319
Ctrl key
  Ctrl+D (favorites shortcut), 294
  troubleshooting, 37
customizing. See also properties
  audio, 180-182
  desktop, 148-149
    background, 182-183
    colors, 182-183
  mouse, 162
    buttons, 163

  clicking, 163
  pointers, 163-164
  speed, 163
  viewing, 165-166
printers, 208-209
resolution, 186-188
screen savers, 183-185
window color, 185-186
Cut command (Edit menu), 72
cutting text, 72

D

Date and Time command (Insert menu), 69-70
Date and Time dialog box, 69-70
Date and Time Properties dialog box, 160-162
dates
  documents, 69-70
  editing, 160-162
  files, searching, 138-140
default printers, 213-214
defragmenting, 250-252
Delete command (File menu), 130
Delete key, 68-69
deleting
  bullets, 76
  contacts, 331
  e-mail messages, 320-321
  files, 130-132
    hard drive, 252-253
    permanently, 134
    recovering, 132-133
  folders, 130-132
    permanently, 134
    recovering, 132-133
  icons, 152
  print jobs, 216-217
  programs, 168-169
  shortcuts, 132
  text, 68-69
  user accounts, 177-178
desktop
  background, 182-183
  color, 182-183

folders, 149-150
icons
 changing, 153-154
 deleting, 152
 moving, 151-152
 naming, 154-155
overview, 4-11
programs, 18
properties, 148-149
shortcuts
 creating, 150-151, 154
 deleting, 132
 printers, 214-215
Desktop Items dialog box, 148-149
Details view, 126
dialing up Internet accounts, 284-286
dialog boxes. *See also* programs
Accessibility Options, 198-199
Add or Remove Programs Properties, 166
Add to Favorites, 293
Additional Drivers, 210
arrow keys, 31
Attachment, 313
Audio CD, 94-95
Backup Progress, 233
Browse for Folder, 119-120, 266-267
Cancel button, 30
Change Icon, 153-154
Change My Message Font, 345
check boxes, 29
Check Disk, 238-240
Close button, 20
Confirm File Delete, 130-132, 152
Connect, 284-285
Content Advisor, 297-301
Create Folder, 318-319
Date and Time, 69-70
Date and Time Properties, 160-162
Desktop Items, 148-149
Dial-up Connection, 288-289
Disconnect Network Drive, 274-275
Disk Cleanup, 252-253
Display Properties, 148-149, 182-183, 187-188
drop-down lists, 29

ellipses, 9
Enter key, 31
Esc key, 31
Find People, 142-143
Folder Options, 128
Font, 73
Internet Accounts, 304-308
Internet Options, 297
list boxes, 29
Log Off, 12-14
Magnifier Settings, 191
Maximize button, 20
Microsoft Magnifier, 190
Microsoft Narrator, 192-193
Minimize button, 20
Mouse Properties, 162-163
MSN Gaming Zone, 88-91
New Message, 308-310
OK button, 29
Open, 36, 269-270
option buttons, 30
Options, 350
Print, 34
Printers and Faxes, 204-208
Printing Preferences, 208-209
Properties, 153-154
Restore Process, 236
Run, 9
Save, 269-270
Save As, 32, 317-318
Screen Saver Properties, 183-185
Send a File to, 347-348
Sharing and Security, 275-276
Shortcut, 214-215
Sounds and Audio Devices Properties, 180-182
space bar, 31
Tab key, 31
Taskbar and Start Menu Properties, 157-158
text boxes, 30
Turn Off Computer, 14
Typing Mode, 194-195
Windows Components Wizard, 169-171
Dial-up Connection dialog box, 288-289

Disconnect Network Drive dialog box, 274-276
Disk Cleanup dialog box, 262-263
Disk Defragmenter, 260-262
disk drives. *See* drives
Display Properties dialog box, 148-149, 182-183, 187-188
displaying. *See* viewing
documents. *See also* files; text
    closing, 35
    creating, 31, 67
    date and time, 69-70
    editing, 68-69
    embedding media, 104-106
    faxing, 219
    naming, 32
    opening, 35-36
    printing, 33-34
    saving, 32-33
    word wrap, 67
dragging. *See also* moving, 123
    e-mail messages, 320
    objects (Paint tools), 83-84
    Recycle Bin, 132
    scroll bars, 21-22
    toolbars, 124
    windows
        moving, 25
        sizing, 24
drawing. *See* Paint tools
drives
    CD-ROM, 111
    floppy, 111
    hard, 111
        backing up, 229-233
        defragmenting, 250-252
        deleting files, 252-253
        restoring, 240-244
        troubleshooting, 238-240
    My Computer, 110-111
    network, 111
        disconnecting, 274-275
        mapping, 270-273
        opening files, 269-270
        saving files, 269-270
    sharing, 275-276

    viewing contents, 112-113
    Zip, 111
drop-down lists, 29
DSL networks, 262

E

Edit menu commands
    Copy, 63
    Copy To Folder, 119
    Cut, 72
    Move To Folder, 119
    Paste, 72
    Select All, 71
    Undo, 81
editing
    bullets, 76
    contacts, 330
    dates, 160-162
    documents, 68-69
    icons, 153-154
    time, 160-162
ellipses, 9, 27
e-mail
    accounts, setting up, 304-308
    Address Book
        adding contacts, 326-329
        business cards, 332-333
        closing, 333
        deleting contacts, 331
        editing contacts, 330
        e-mailing contacts, 334-336
        opening, 326
        phone lists, 332-333
        printing, 332-333
        sorting contacts, 331-332
        street addresses, 328
    addresses, searching, 142-143
    contacts, 334-336
    folders, creating, 318-319
    Inbox, 307
    messages
        attachments, 312-313, 317-318
        copies, 309
        creating, 308-310

deleting, 320-321
ettiquette, 323-324
formatting, 310-312
forwarding, 316
from Windows, 322-323
moving, 320
multiple recipients, 309
printing, 314
replying, 315
retrieving, 314
subjects, 309
Outbox, 308
start page, 307
troubleshooting rumors, 324
Windows Messenger, 351
embedding media in documents, 104-106
emoticons, 345-347
emptying Recycle Bin, 134
Enter key (dialog boxes), 31
Esc key (dialog boxes), 31
ettiquette, e-mail messages, 323-324
Expedia Web site, 328
Explorer
Internet. *See* Internet Explorer
Windows. *See* Windows Explorer

F

favorites
Internet Explorer, 293-294
keyboard shorcuts, 294
Favorites button, 294
Favorites menu command, Add to Favorites, 293
Fax Configuration Wizard, 220-221
faxing
configuring, 220-221
documents, 219
installing, 218
sending, 221-224
File menu commands
Delete, 130
New, 120-121
Open, 36, 269-270
Print, 34
Print Preview, 33

Restore, 133
Save, 32, 269-270
Sign out, 351-352
filename extensions, viewing, 127-128
files. *See also* documents; text
attaching to e-mail messages, 312-313
backing up, 229-233
copying, 118-120
deleting, 130-132
hard drive, 252-253
permanently, 134
recovering, 132-133
moving, 118-120
naming, 121-122
opening
networks, 269-270
troubleshooting, 122
restoring, 233-236
saving, 269-270
searching, 136-138
by dates, 138-140
selecting, 117-118
sending (Windows Messenger), 347-348
sharing, 276
viewing filename extensions, 127-128
Windows Explorer
display options, 125-126
sorting, 127
Find People dialog box, 142-143
floppy drive, 111
Folder Options command (Tools menu), 128
Folder Options dialog box, 128
folders
+ and - signs, 116
clicking, 127-128
copying, 118-120
creating, 120-121, 149-150
deleting, 130-132
permanently, 134
recovering, 132-133
e-mail
creating, 318-319
levels, 116
moving, 118-120

folders *(continued)*
    naming, 121-122
    searching, 136-138
    selecting, 117-118
    sharing, 276
    shortcuts, 150-151, 154
    viewing, 112-113
    Windows Explorer options, 127-128
Font command (Format menu), 73
Font dialog box, 73
fonts
    e-mail messages, 311
    text, 73-74
    toolbar, 74
    Windows Messenger, 345
Format menu commands
    Apply Stationery, 312
    Font, 73
formatting
    e-mail messages, 310-312
    text, 73-76
Forward button, 316
forwarding e-mail messages, 316

G

games
    Internet Hearts, 88-91
    saving, 88
    Spider Solitaire, 86-88
    starting, 86

H

hard drives, 111
    backing up, 229-233
        defragmenting, 250-252
    deleting files, 252-253
    restoring, 240-244
    sharing, 276
    troubleshooting, 238-240
Help. *See also* troubleshooting
    Help and Support Center
        accessing, 47
        Ask for Assistance, 49-50

        index, 53-54
        Microsoft online assistance, 50-53
        overview, 48
        searching, 55
        topics, 48-49
    updates
        automatic, 247-248
        manual, 244-247
    Windows XP Tour, 46-47
Help and Support Center
    accessing, 47
    Ask for Assistance, 49-50
    index, 53-54
    Microsoft online assistance, 50-53
    overview, 48
    searching, 55
    topics, 48-49
Help and Support command (Start menu), 9, 47,
    244
hibernation, 16
hiding. *See* viewing
history, surfing, 296
History button, 296
Home button, 291
home page
    defined, 289
    Internet Explorer, 289-292
hubs, 262
hyperlinks, 290

I

icons. *See also* buttons
    clicking, 5
    desktop
        changing, 153-154
        deleting, 152
        moving, 151-152
        naming, 154-155
        printers, 214-215
    Internet Explorer, 6
    My Documents, 6
    My Network Places, 6
    Outlook Express, 6
    Quick Launch toolbar, 10

Recycle Bin, 6
System/Notification tray, 10-11
user accounts, 176-177
Windows Media Player, 6
Icons view, 126
Inbox
Outlook Express, 307
retrieving messages, 314
index (Help), 63-64
Insert menu command, Date and Time, 69-70
inserting text, 68
installing
faxing, 218
printers, 204-208
programs, 166-167
Windows backup program, 226-228
Internet. *See also* Web
accounts
dialing up, 284-285
security, 285
setting up, 282-283
signing up, 279-281
Web browsers, 285-286
configuring connection, 278-279
searching, 295-296
Internet Accounts dialog box, 304-308
Internet Connection Wizard, 304-308
Internet Explorer
Content Advisor, 297-301
favorites, 293-294
home page, 289-292
hyperlinks, 290
launching, 288-289
navigating, 290-292
surfing, 290
history, 296
Web addresses, 292
Internet Explorer icon, 6
Internet Hearts, 88-91
Internet Options command (Tools menu), 297
Internet Options dialog box, 297
invitations (Windows Messenger)
answering, 348
sending, 344

ISP accounts
dialing up, 284-285
security, 285
setting up, 282-283
signing up, 279-281
Web browsers, 285-286

K

keyboard
Backspace key, 68-69
calculator, 61-62
Delete key, 68-69
On-Screen Keyboard, 193-195
keyboard shortcuts
Alt+Tab, 19
commands, 27-28, 36-37
cutting and pasting, 72
favorites, 294
locked up programs, 38-39
troubleshooting, 37
Windows key, 8, 13
Kids Passport Web site, 338

L

landscape printing, 208-209
laptops, power, 10
launching
Internet Explorer, 288-289
Outlook Express, 304
programs from toolbar, 10
Windows Messenger, 338
linking Web sites, 123
list boxes, 29
List view, 126
lists, bullets, 75-76
loading Windows, 4
locked up programs, 38-39
locked up system, 16
locking
Taskbar, 155-158
toolbars, 124
Log Off command (Start menu), 12-14
Log Off Windows dialog box, 12-14

logging off, 12-14
logging on, 12-14
 troubleshooting, 273
 Welcome screen, 4
 Windows Messenger, 341

M

Magnifier, 190-191
Magnifier Settings dialog box, 191
maintenance
 Disk Cleanup, 252-253
 Disk Defragmenter, 250-252
managing users, 172
manual Windows updates, 244-247
Map Network Drive Wizard, 270-273
mapping
 contacts, 328
 network drives, 270-273
  disconnecting, 274-275
Maximize button, 20, 23-24
media, embedding in documents, 104-106
media player. *See* Windows Media Player
menus. *See* commands
messages
 e-mail. *See* e-mail
 Windows Messenger
  answering invitations, 348
  emoticons, 345-347
  fonts, 345
  sending, 343-344
  sending files, 347-348
Microsoft Magnifier dialog box, 190
Microsoft Narrator dialog box, 192-193
Microsoft online assistance (Help), 60-63
Microsoft Web site, 190
Minimize button, 20, 23
minus sign (-) subfolder indicator, 116
monitor. *See* desktop
mouse, customizing, 162
 buttons, 163
 clicking, 163
 pointers, 163-164
 speed, 163

 viewing, 165-166
Mouse Properties dialog box, 162-163
Move to Folder command (Edit menu), 119
moving. *See also* dragging
 e-mail messages, 320
 files, 118-120
 folders, 118-120
 icons, 151-152
 Taskbar, 156
 toolbars, 123-124
MSN Gaming Zone dialog box, 88-91
multimedia. *See* Windows Media Player
music. *See* Windows Media Player
My Computer drives, 110-111
My Documents command (Start menu), 9
My Documents icon, 6
My Network Places, 262
 adding computers, 265-269
 browsing
  computers, 263
  workgroups, 264-265
My Network Places command (Start menu), 9
My Network Places icon, 6

N

names, searching, 142-143
naming
 documents, 32
 files, 121-122
 folders, 121-122
 icons, 154-155
 user accounts, 173-174
Narrator, 192-193
navigating Internet Explorer, 290-292
.NET Passport Wizard, 338-340
Netscape Navigator Web site, 286
networks
 browsing
  computers, 263
  workgroups, 264-265
 cable modems, 262
 cards, 262

computers
    adding, 265-269
    sharing, 275-276
connecting, 262
drives, 111
    disconnecting, 274-275
    mapping, 270-273
DSL, 262
files
    opening, 269-270
    saving, 269-270
hubs, 262
My Network Places, 262
printers, 211-213
printing, 209-213
New command (File menu), 120-121
New Connection Wizard, 278-279
New Message dialog box, 308-310

O

objects, dragging, 83-84
OK button, 29
online. *See* Internet; Web
On-Screen Keyboard, 193-196
Open command (File menu), 36, 269-270
Open dialog box, 36, 269-270
opening
    Address Book, 326
    documents, 35-36
    attachments, 317-318
    files
        networks, 269-270
        troubleshooting, 122
    programs, 18-19
    windows, 5
option buttons, 30
Options command (Tools menu), 360
Options dialog box, 360
Outbox (Outlook Express), 308
Outlook Express
    Address Book
        adding contacts, 326-329
        business cards, 332-333

        closing, 333
        deleting contacts, 331
        editing contacts, 330
        e-mailing contacts, 334-336
        opening, 326
        phone lists, 332-333
        printing, 332-333
        sorting contacts, 331-332
        street addresses, 328
    e-mail
        attachments, 312-313, 317-318
        copies, 309
        creating folers, 318-319
        creating messages, 308-310
        deleting messages, 320-321
        ettiquette, 323-324
        formatting messages, 310-312
        forwarding, 316
        from Windows, 322-323
        moving messages, 320
        multiple recipients, 309
        printing, 314
        replying, 315
        retrieving, 314
        setting up accounts, 304-308
        subjects, 309
    icon, 6
    Inbox, 307
    launching, 304
    Outbox, 308
    start page, 307

P

Paint
    starting, 78
    tools, 78-79
        color, 82-83
        dragging objects, 83-84
        drawing, 80
        selecting, 81
        selecting objects, 83-84
        shapes, 81-82
        troubleshooting, 81

Passports (Windows Messenger), 338-340
passwords
    Internet accounts, 285
    logging on, 4
    security, 285
    user accounts, 175-176
Paste command (Edit menu), 72
pasting text, 72
pausing, print jobs, 216-217
performance
    Disk Cleanup, 252-253
    Disk Defragmenter, 250-252
phone lists (Address Book), 332-333
Pick a Help topic (Help), 49
PICS (Platform for Internet Content Selection), 297
Platform for Internet Content Selection (PICS), 297
playing
    CDs, 94-95
        buttons, 97
        playlists, 96
        visualizations, 95-96
    Internet Hearts, 88-91
    radio, 98-100
    Spider Solitaire, 86-88
    volume, 102-103
    Windows Media Player
        buttons, 97
        CDs, 94-96
        icon, 6
        radio, 98-100
        skins, 100-102
        volume, 102-103
playlists (CD), 96
plus sign (+) subfolder indicator, 116
pointers (mouse), 163-164
power, laptops, 10
Print button, 34
Print command (File menu), 34
Print dialog box, 34
print jobs
    deleting, 216-217
    pausing, 216-217
    viewing, 215-216

Print Preview button, 33
Print Preview command (File menu), 33
printers
    customizing, 208-209
    default, 213-214
    desktop shortcuts, 214-215
    installing, 204-208
    networks, 211-213
    sharing, 209-211, 276
    users, 209-211
Printers and Faxes dialog box, 204-208
printing
    contacts, 332-333
    documents, 33-34
        e-mail messages, 314
    landscape, 208-209
    networks, 209-213
    print jobs
        deleting, 216-217
        pausing, 216-217
        viewing, 215-216
    System/Notification tray, 10
    troubleshooting, 207
Printing Preferences dialog box, 208-209
Printing Troubleshooter, 207
Program Compatibility Wizard, 39-43
program events, audio, 180-182
programs. *See also* dialog boxes
    Accessibility Wizard, 195-199
    Add a Contact Wizard, 341-342
    Add Network Place Wizard, 265-269
    Add Printer Wizard, 204-213
    adding to Control Panel, 169-171
    Backup or Restore Wizard, 229-236
        backup, installing, 226-228
    closing, 35
        Content Advisor, 297- 301
    deleting, 168-169
        Disk Cleanup, 252-253
    Disk Defragmenter, 250-252
    Fax Configuration Wizard, 220, 221
    installing, 166-167
    Internet Connection Wizard, 304-308
    launching, 10
    Magnifier, 190-191

Map Network Drive Wizard, 270-273
My Network Places, 262
    adding computers, 265-269
    browsing computers, 263
    browsing workgroups, 264-265
Narrator, 192-193
.NET Passport Wizard, 338-340
New Connection Wizard, 278-279
On-Screen Keyboard, 193-195
opening, 18
Paint, 78-79
    color, 82-83
    dragging objects, 83-84
    drawing, 80
    selecting, 81
    selecting objects, 83-84
    shapes, 81-82
    troubleshooting, 81
Printing Troubleshooter, 207
running status, 10
Scheduled Task Wizard, 254-257
scheduling running, 254-257
Send Fax Wizard, 221-224
SoundSentry, 195-199
switching, 19
troubleshooting
    locked up, 38-39
    Program Compatibility Wizard, 39-43
Windows Backup Utility Installation Wizard,
    226-228
properties. *See also* customizing
date and time, 160-162
desktop, 148-149
Properties dialog box, 163-164

Q

Quick Launch bar, 10, 157-158

R

radio
    playing, 98-100
    volume, 102-103
radio buttons, 30

recipients, multiple, 309
Recycle Bin
    deleting folders, 130-132
    emptying, 134
    icon, 6
    recovering folders, 132-133
removing. *See* deleting
Reply button, 316
replying
    e-mail messages, 315
    Windows Messenger invitations, 348
resizing. *See* sizing
resolution, 186-188
restarting, 15-16
Restore command (File menu), 133
Restore Process dialog box, 236
restoring
    files, 233-236
    system, 240-244
right-clicking, 27
Run command (Start menu), 9
Run dialog box, 9

S

Save As dialog box, 32, 317-318
Save command (File menu), 32, 269-270
Save dialog box, 269-270
saving
    attachments, 317-318
    documents, 32-33
    files, 269-270
    games, 88
Scheduled Task Wizard, 264-267
scheduling running programs, 254-257
scientific calculator, 63-64
Scientific command (View menu), 64
Screen Saver Properties dialog box, 183-186
screens. *See also* desktop
    resolution, 186-188
    screen savers, 183-185
scroll bars
    clicking, 21-22
    dragging, 21-22
    windows, 20

Search command (Start menu), 136
search engines, 295-296
searching
    Address Book, 141-143
    files, 136-138
        by dates, 138-140
    folders, 136-138
    Help, 66
    online, 295-296
security
    anti-virus programs, 10
    Content Advisor, 297-301
    e-mail attachments, 317
    Internet accounts, 285
    Sharing and Security dialog box, 275-276
    System/Notification tray, 10
Select All command (Edit menu), 71
selecting
    files, 117-118
    folders, 117-118
    objects, 83-84
    Paint tools, 81
    text, 70-71, 74
    Windows Media Player skins, 100-102
Send a File to dialog box, 347-348
Send button, 313
Send Fax Wizard, 221-224
sending
    e-mail messages
        forwarding, 316
        replies, 315
    faxing, 221-224
    Windows Messenger
        emoticons, 345-347
        files, 347-348
        invites, 344
        messages, 343-344
        replies, 348
setting up
    e-mail accounts, 304-308
    Internet accounts, 282-283
settings
    backing up, 229-233
    Windows Messenger, 349-351
shapes (Paint tools), 81-82

sharing printers, 209-211
Sharing and Security dialog box, 275-276
Shortcut dialog box, 214-216
shortcut menus, 27
shortcuts
    creating, 150-151, 154
    deleting, 132
    dialog box navigation, 31
    keyboard
        Alt+Tab, 19
        commands, 27-28, 36-37
        cutting and pasting, 72
        favorites, 294
        locked up programs, 38-39
        troubleshooting, 37
        Windows key, 8, 13
    printers, 214-215
shutdown, 14
    hibernation, 15
    restarting, 15-16
    troubleshooting, 16
Sign out command (File menu), 361-362
signing in (Windows Messenger), 341
signing out (Windows Messenger), 351-352
signing up for Internet accounts, 279-281
sites
    Expedia, 328
    Kids Passport, 338
    Microsoft, 190
    Netscape Navigator, 285
    surfing history, 296
    Symantec, 324
    Urban Legends, 324
sizing
    Taskbar, 156
    title bar, 24
    windows, 20-24
skins (Windows Media Player), 100-102
Sort By command (View menu), 331
sorting
    contacts, 331-332
    files, 127
Sounds and Audio Devices Properties dialog
    box, 180-182
SoundSentry, 195-199

space bar, 31
speed, mouse, 163
Spider Solitaire, 86-88
squares, drawing, 81-82
Standard command (View menu), 64
Start button, 7-8
Start menu commands
    All Programs, 8, 18, 190
    Connect to, 284-285
    Control Panel, 9
    Help and Support, 9, 47, 244
    Log Off, 12-14
    My Documents, 9
    My Network Places, 9
    Run, 9
    Search, 136
    Turn Off Computer, 14
start page
    defined, 289
    Outlook Express, 307
starting
    calculator, 60
    games, 86
    Paint, 78
    WordPad, 66
status
    running programs, 10
    Windows Messenger, 349
street addresses (contacts), 328
subjects, e-mail messages, 309
support
    Help, 49-60
    Microsoft online, 60-63
surfing, 290
    Content Advisor, 297-301
    history, 296
switching programs, 19
Symantec Web site, 324
system
    maintenance
        Disk Cleanup, 252-253
        Disk Defragmenter, 250-252
    scheduling tasks, 254-257
    troubleshooting
        crashes, 38-39

restoring, 240-244
System/Notification tray, 10

T

Tab key
    Alt+Tab keyboard shorcut, 19
    dialog boxes, 31
Task panes, 113-114
Taskbar
    buttons, 7
    locking, 155-158
    moving, 156
    Quick Launch toolbar, 10
    sizing, 156
    Start button, 7-8
    System/Notification tray, 10
    viewing, 157-158
Taskbar and Start Menu Properties dialog box,
    167-168
tasks, scheduling, 254-257
text. See also documents
    alignment, 74-75
    bullets, 75-76
    clicking, 70-71
    cutting, 72
    deleting, 68-69
    e-mail messages, 310-312
    fonts, 73-74
        toolbar, 74
        Windows Messenger, 345
    formatting, 73-76
    inserting, 68
    pasting, 72
    selecting, 70-71, 74
    word wrap, 67
text boxes, 30
Thumbnails view, 126
Tiles view, 126
time
    documents, 69-70
    editing, 160-162
    scheduling programs, 254-257
    screen savers, 183-185
    System/Notification tray, 10

title bars
clicking, 24
sizing windows, 24
windows, 20
toolbars
dragging, 124
fonts, 74
launching programs, 10
locking, 124
Quick Launch, 10
windows, 20
Windows Explorer
moving, 123-124
viewing, 123
Toolbars command (View menu), 123, 308
tools. *See* programs
Tools menu commands
Accounts, 304
Folder Options, 128
Internet Options, 297
Options, 350
ToolTips, 7
topics (Help), 48-49
troubleshooting. *See also* Help
e-mail rumors, 324
hard drive, 238-240
keyboard shortcuts, 37
laptop power, 10
logon, 273
opening files, 122
Paint tools, 81
performance
Disk Cleanup, 252-253
Disk Defragmenter, 250-252
printing, 207
programs
locked up, 38-39
missing, 169
Program Compatibility Wizard, 39-43
system
restore, 240-244
locked up, 16
Turn Off Computer command (Start menu), 14

Turn Off Computer dialog box, 14
Typing Mode dialog box, 194-196

U

Undo command (Edit menu), 81
uninstalling. *See* deleting
unlocking
Taskbar, 155-158
toolbars, 124
updates
System/Notification tray, 10
Windows
automatic, 247-248
manual, 244-247
Urban Legends Web site, 324
URLs, 292
users
accounts
creating, 172-173
deleting, 177-178
icons, 176-177
naming, 173-174
passwords, 175-176
changing quickly, 13
managing, 172
printers, 209-211
supervising content, 297-301
user names, 4, 12-14

V

View Map button, 328
View menu commands
Arrange Icons by, 127
display options, 126
Scientific, 64
Sort By, 331
Standard, 64
Toolbars, 123, 308
viewing
contacts' street addresses, 328
Content Advisor, 297-301
Control Panel, 160

drive contents, 112-113
files
   display options, 125-126
   filename extensions, 127-128
folders, 112-113
Magnifier, 190-191
mouse, 165-166
Narrator, 192-193
On-Screen Keyboard, 193-195
print jobs, 215-216
Quick Launch bar, 157-158
SoundSentry, 195-199
surfing history, 296
System/Notification tray icons, 11
Task panes, 113-114
Taskbar, 157-158
toolbars, 123
Windows Explorer, 114-115
visualizations (CD), 95-96
volume
audio, 102-103
System/Notification tray, 10

W

Web. *See also* Internet
browsers, 285-286
Content Advisor, 297-301
games, 88-91
Internet Explorer
   addresses, 292
   favorites, 293-294
   home page, 289-292
   hyperlinks, 290
   launching, 288-289
   navigating, 290-292
   surfing, 290
   surfing history, 296
online Microsoft assistance, 60-63
radio. *See* Windows Media Player
sites
   Expedia, 328
   Kids Passport, 338
   linking, 123
   Microsoft, 190

Netscape Navigator, 285
surfing history, 296
Symantec, 324
Urban Legends, 324
Windows Messenger online status, 349
Welcome screen, 4
windows
borders, 20
Close button, 20
color, 185-186
desktop. *See* desktop
dragging, 25
Maximize button, 20
Minimize button, 20
opening, 5
scroll bars, 20
sizing, 20-24
title bars, 20
toolbars, 20
viewing Task panes, 113-114
Windows
adding components, 169-171
   e-mail messages, 322-323
installing backup program, 226-228
loading, 4
restarting, 15-16
shutdown, 14
   hibernation, 15
   troubleshooting, 16
updates
   automatic, 247-248
   manual, 244-247
Windows Backup Utility Installation Wizard,
226-228
Windows Components Wizard dialog box,
169-171
Windows Explorer
files
   copying, 118-120
   display options, 125-126
   moving, 118-120
   naming, 121-122
   selecting, 117-118
   sorting, 127

Windows Explorer *(continued)*
  folders
    + and - signs, 116
    copying, 118-120
    creating, 121
    levels, 116
    moving, 118-120
    naming, 121-122
    options, 127-128
    selecting, 117-118
  toolbars
    moving, 123-124
    viewing, 123
  viewing, 114-115
Windows key, 8, 13
Windows Media Player
  buttons, 97
  CDs, 94-95
    playlists, 96
    visualizations, 95-96
  icon, 6
  radio, 98-100
  skins, 100-102
  volume, 102-103
Windows Messenger
  adding contacts, 341-342
  answering invitations, 348
  contact lists, 342-343
  e-mail, 351
  emoticons, 345-347
  fonts, 345
  invites, 344
  Kids Passports, 338
  launching, 338
  online status, 349
  Passports, 338-340
  sending files, 347-348
  sending messages, 343-344
  settings, 349-351
  signing in, 341
  signing out, 351-352
Windows Task Manager, 38-39
Windows XP Tour, 46-47
wizards. *See* programs
word wrap, 67
WordPad
  date and time, 69-70
  documents
    creating, 67
    date and time, 69-70
    editing, 68-69
  starting, 66
  text
    alignment, 74-75
    bullets, 75-76
    cutting, 72
    fonts, 73-74
    formatting, 73-76
    pasting, 72
    selecting, 70-71
  word wrap, 67
workgroups
  adding computers, 265-269
  browsing, 264-265

X

X (Close button), 6

Z

Zip drives, 111, 276